STEPHEN E. AMBROSE is the author of numerous
books of history, including the *Sunday Times* number
one bestseller *Band of Brothers* and other international
bestsellers such as *Citizen Soldiers* and *D-Day,* as well
as multi-volume biographies of Dwight D. Eisenhower
and Richard Nixon. He is founder of the Eisenhower
Center, president of the National D-Day Museum in
New Orleans, and recipient in 1998 of a National
Humanities Award. He lives in Bay St. Louis,
Mississippi, and Helena, Montana.

Also by Stephen E. Ambrose

Band of Brothers

D-Day

Citizen Soldiers

Pegasus Bridge

The Victors

Nothing Like It In The World

Comrades

POCKET BOOKS

NEW YORK   LONDON   TORONTO   SYDNEY   SINGAPORE

STEPHEN E. AMBROSE

WILD BLUE

741 SQUADRON – ON A WING AND A PRAYER OVER OCCUPIED EUROPE

First published in Great Britain by Simon & Schuster UK Ltd, 2001
This edition published by Pocket Books, 2002
An imprint of Simon & Schuster UK Ltd
A CBS COMPANY

The right of Stephen E. Ambrose to be identified as author of this work
has been asserted in accordance with sections 77 and 78 of the
Copyright, Designs and Patents Act, 1988.

12

Simon & Schuster UK Ltd
Africa House
64–78 Kingsway
London WC2B 6AH

www.simonsays.co.uk

Simon & Schuster Australia
Sydney

A CIP catalogue record for this book is available from the British
Library

ISBN-13: 978-07434-5062-1

Printed and bound in Great Britain by
Cox & Wyman Ltd, Reading, Berkshire

For Eleanor

ACKNOWLEDGMENTS

THE AUTHOR AND HIS ASSISTANT would like to thank all those who helped us with this book.

Horace W. Lanford, former commanding officer of the 741st Bomb Squadron, deserves special mention because he allowed us to use a copy of his self-published history of the 741st, which contains a wealth of information. He also provided us with many contacts to veterans. We owe a great deal to Mr. Lanford.

We would also like to thank Francis J. Lashinsky and Gus Wendt of the 455th Bomb Group Association. Without their assistance and the assistance of other members of the board, we would not have been able to tell this tale. We gained a great deal of information from the association's newsletter, *The Cerignola Connection.*

We also owe thanks to George and Michele Welsh and their staff at the International B-24 Liberator Club. The Welshes have been preserving the history and celebrating the accomplishments of the B-24 and the World War II Army Air Forces for many years. Their enthusiasm for their topic and willingness to share their knowledge with all and sundry is an inspiration. The International B-24 Liberator Club publishes a journal, *The Briefing.* The club's address is 15817 Bernardo Center Drive, Suite 102, Box 124, San Diego, CA 92127, b24club@pacbell.net.

Almost all the photographs for this book come from the private collections of veterans or their families. We would like to thank the following veterans for sharing their photographs with us and the world: Alex Boggio, Russell Clark, Harold Cook, Carroll W. Cooper, C. E. Ben Franklin, Jim Gordon, John Greenman, Kenneth Higgins, Joseph Maloney, William McAfee, J. S. McCullough, Dan McGeary, George McGovern, Leo Mercer, Anthony J. Picardi, Richard D. Rogers, John Skelton, Darrell Snook, Jim VanNostrand, Gus Wendt, and Matija Zganjnar.

We would like to thank the following for their help in locating photographs and/or oral histories: the Airmen Memorial Museum and its curator, Sean Muskimins; Miles Todd of the San Diego Air and Space Museum; Ben Franklin of the Fifteenth Air Force Association; Tom Gerzel of the March Field Museum Foundation; Air Force historian Fred Johnsen; and Rob Hoskins of the 461st Bomb Group Association.

Thanks also to Charles Watry, an Air Force career man, who flew everything from transports in World War II to Mach 2 jet fighters in Vietnam. Colonel Watry provided us with invaluable technical advice for the book, whether it dealt with training procedures, plane instrumentation, navigation, armament, and all of the other details that accompany a subject of this scope and complexity.

We offer our thanks to Judy Edelhoff, an American on Ambassador George S. McGovern's staff at the United Nations in Italy. She helped us in many ways, most especially by organizing a trip to Cerignola for the ambassador and us. With her help, we met and interviewed Italians who remembered the airmen of the Fifteenth Air Force. She also introduced us to the mayor of Cerignola, Dr. Francesco Musto, and his assistant, Luigi Pelligrino.

We would like to thank Messrs. Musto and Pelligrino, who arranged for us to visit the old air bases, and for their help in connecting us with members of the community who remember the Americans. We would like to thank the following Italians for allowing us to interview them about their experiences: Michele Barcole, Mario Carpocefala, Gionanna Pistachio Colucci, and Francesco Musto.

The following associations made meaningful contributions and have our thanks:

741st Squadron Association

376th Bomb Group Association

450th Bomb Group Association

455th Bomb Group, the Vulgar Vultures

456th Bomb Group Association

461st Bomb Group Association

449th Bomb Group Association

483rd Bomb Group Association

2nd Air Division Association

Fifteenth Air Force Association

ACKNOWLEDGMENTS

We would like to thank the following veterans and their family members for donating memoirs, collections of letters, diaries, and photographs for our research. We also appreciate those who allowed us to record their memories as an oral history. This book could not have been done without their assistance.

Kenneth Apple
Art Applin
Ken Applin
Alfred Asch
H. Homer and Louise
  G. Aschmann
Cecil Grant Ash
Dick Ashbury
William Ashlock
Charles R. Ayers
Albert J. Bakun
Clyde G. Ball
Robert K. Barmore
William V. Barnes
Robert E. Basala
Donald Bauer
Stuart A. Bemis
Andy J. Benedict
Sheldon B. Benscoter
Gene V. Benson
Alfred Berger
Casimir E. Bialas
Charles B. Black
Bill Blocker
Maurice M. Bloom, Jr.
Alex Boggio
Kenneth P. Bondy
Linda Boyd
Walter E. Brady
Douglas Brown

Stuart C. Brown
Marie H. Bruce
Helen M. Bruce-Ireland
  (daughter)
Sterling Bryant
Stanley Buck
Ormond Buffington
Leon O. Burke
Henry Burkle
Jay Calkins
Clifton Callahan
Roger Caple
Robert S. Capps
John Carey
Linda Carry
John W. Carson
Guy Robert "Bob"
  Champney
Terri Champney
  (daughter of Bob)
F. C. "Hap" Chandler
William Chapin
Morris Clark
L. P. Clemens
J. Walton Colvin
Harold E. Cook
Carroll W. Cooper
Howard Robert Cooper
John Copeland
Anthony Corsello

Lensworth Cottrell, Jr.
James E. Counsilman
Marjorie S. Counsilman
  (wife)
Mary J. Crawford
  (widow of Benjamin)
Bill Crim
Richard Laurens Critz
Bruce H. Cumming
George M. Curio
Paul Daugherty
Robert A. Davis
Kevin Day
Robert W. Day
George Defenbaugh
Robert DeGroat
Paul H. Ditchett
Joseph Dolinsky
John R. Dominey
Rene DuFour
Robert F. Emick
Richard J. Ennis
William Feder, Sr.
Russ Felzer
Paul L. Fergot
Donald A. Fischer
Thomas K. Follis
J. B. Foote
Donald C. Foster
Walter Fox

Robert Frank
C. E. Ben Franklin
Kenneth Fuller
Roland Geiger
Tom Gerzel
Lamar H. Good
Alvin Goodman
Jim A. Gordon
Carl Graziano
John W. Greenman
Robert E. Greenquist
Walter Greenwell
C. Philip Gressani
William O. Gustafson
Paul Hallman, Sr.
William F. Hallstead III
Rob Hammer
Norman M. Hardy
Bill Haskins
C. Haynes
Herbert Hengst
George C. Henry
Louis Herman
Ruth J. Herrmann
Burton E. Hewett
C. Harvey Hewit
Kenneth Higgins
Royce M. Hilliard
Raymond M. Hook
Jules Horowitz
Chet Hosac
Francis Hosimer
Eugene Hudson

Henry Hutchings III
Ted A. Hutton
Howard Jackson
William F. Johns
Art Johnson
John Jolissaint
Betty (James) Karle
　(daughter)
Frank Kautzmann
Donald P. Kay
Mr. and Mrs. Roger E.
　Kelley
Lloyd C. Kestner
Erling Kindem
Doug Kirchen
Monika Kokalj Kocevar
Fred Konkel
Gene Koscinski
Paul Kuhns, Jr.
Robert Lamborn
Horace W. Lanford
Robert Lankford
John LaRivee
　(son of Leo M.)
Gene Larson
Francis Lashinsky
Willard S. Layne, Jr.
Ronald Lee
　(son of Emerson)
John L. Lenburg
Wilbur W. Leupold
Jack A. Levin
Edward Lincoln, Jr.

Robert A. Long
Del Lyman
William Tom Magee
Joseph L. Maloney
John W. Marsching
J. K. Mattison
Donald J. Fitz-Maurice
Wilbur W. "Bill" Mayhew
William McAfee
Herbert F. McCollom, Jr.
Thomas P. McConnell
Ed McConnon
J. S. McCullough
Dan McGeary
George S. McGovern
R. N. McLean, Jr.
Walker McNutt
Victor McWilliams
Betty Lee Meadville
　(widow of Joe W.)
Jim Merritt, Jr.
James B. Miller
Sean Miskimins
Clarence Mitchell, Jr.
Robert W. Mitchell
Suzanne Mongomery
Victor Murray
Robert E. Newberg
Peter Newman
Russell B. Newton, Jr.
R. L. O'Connor
David T. Oliveri
Dick Olson

Robert R. Ott
Alex Palmer
Henry Paris
Roland Pepin
Anthony J. Picardi
Claude L. Porter
David Proud
Francis W. Purdy
Thomas A. Ramey
Robert Reichard
Glenn E. Rendahl
Harley W. Rhodehamel
Charles W. Richards
C. E. "Ed" Riggs
Essie Roberts
Woody Russel Roberts
Raymond Roemer
Richard D. Rogers
John Rollins
Albert Romero
Louise Rorer
  (daughter of
  L. Frank "Mickey")
Charles Rosenberg
Hal A. Ross
Sgarro Ruggiero
Leslie Running
Robert B. Russell
Al Saldarini
Bill Sauerwein
Donald W. Saunders
E. Frank Schermerhorn
Sam Scheider
William Schnyer

Bob Schuetz
Jerome Schwartzman
Richard Seabridge
Lewis F. Setzer
Morris Shane
Alan B. Shaw
E. D. Shaw, Jr.
Thomas Sheehan
D. William Shepherd
Robert Shinnick
Walter Shostack
Joseph W. Shuster
Louis Siembor
John E. Skelton
John M. Smidl
Irving Smirnoff
James H. Smith
John G. Smith
Edward Soderstrom
Samuel Speakman
Charles E. Stark
Dwight G. Stauffer
Samuel Stein
Donald E. Stern
C. E. Stevens
James S. Stewart
Joan Stinton
Mike Stohlman, Jr.
Owen Sullivan
Roy Swafford
Adrain Swain
Robert M. Tank
David E. Tavel
Paul Taylor

L. B. Teator
David Thayer, Jr.
Samual R. Thompson
Robert F. Thorne
Wilson Tuten
Donald H. Vance
Dr. Raymond VanDerVeer
Jim VanNostrand
James W. Walker
Edgar A. Walsh
Linda L. Walter
John T. Ward
Winston C. Watson
Gus Wendt
Don West
H. A. Wilkes
Charles B. Wills
Fred B. Wilmot
Daniel E. Wilson
Timothy Wilson
Robert E. Winter
William Wittman
Mrs. Theresa Wittman
  McLauhlin
David W. Wolf
Lazarus Wolk
Robert L. Woods, Jr.
Henry Wooten
Tom Wright
Benedict Yedlin
Julie Zimmerman
Walter T. Zumpe

CONTENTS

I HAVE BEEN A FRIEND and supporter of George McGovern's for nearly three decades. I knew something about his career in the Army Air Forces, which I always felt he could have used to more effect in his 1972 presidential campaign. Politics aside, I had long been an admirer of what he had done in his B-24 bomber. He seemed to me to be a good representative of his generation, a man who had risked all not for his own benefit but to help bring about victory.

In the summer of 1999, McGovern, his wife, Eleanor, my son Hugh, and I were together for dinner. In the course of the conversation, McGovern said he had done some interviews recently with reporter Michael Takiff, who was interested in doing a book on McGovern's World War II career. I said that was a fine idea and told McGovern to tell Takiff that he should open with the story of the bomb McGovern's B-24 dropped on a farmhouse in Austria, and the sequel.

McGovern replied that he wished I were writing the book and asked if I would do it. I hesitated, not out of any lack of interest but because Takiff had already begun his work. McGovern urged me to talk to Takiff to see if he would yield to my being the writer and if he would provide me with copies of his interviews with him. I did and Takiff agreed. So I told McGovern and my editor, Alice Mayhew, that I would do it. Alice liked the idea—she is McGovern's editor as well as mine—but said that it should be a book not only about McGovern but also about the men with whom he served. As always—or at least almost always—she was right.

I have long wanted to study and write about the American airmen of World War II. Previously I had written books about the high command in the European war, then turned to the men on the front line—a British airborne company (*Pegasus Bridge*) and an American Company of the 101st Airborne, E Company, 506th Parachute Infantry Regiment (*Band of Brothers*). In a book entitled *D-Day* and a follow-up called *Citizen Soldiers*, I had studied the role of junior officers and enlisted men fighting on the ground. In the course of preparing those books I had interviewed many of the men doing the actual fighting. What I wanted to do next after a book on the first transcontinental railroad was a book on the American airmen, not those at the top of the command structure but the men who flew the bombers. How did they do it? That was my question. McGovern and his crew and his squadron, the 741st of the 455th Bomb Group of the Fifteenth Air Force, seemed a good way to try to answer at least part of the question. My resolve was strengthened because of my respect for George McGovern and his men; my curiosity about how a son of South Dakota became, at age twenty-two, a bomber pilot; my interest in how American designers and workers and the industrial plants created the world's greatest air force; my wanting to learn about the strategic air campaign and how it was planned and carried out; and my desire to tell readers the story of how the leading opponent of the Vietnam War was, in World War II, a distinguished bomber pilot. So I went to work.

I did a lot of reading, of both books and memoirs. I am in the deepest debt to all those who have written about the air war, or their own experiences, including but not limited to all those cited in the notes and bibliography. Most of all I need to thank and acknowledge my gratitude to Michael Sherry, author of *The Rise of American Air Power*, Wesley Frank Craven and James Lea Cate, editors of the seven-volume official history, *The Army Air Forces in World War II*, and Colonel Horace Lanford, USAF, who did a four-volume mimeograph work entitled "741st Bomb Squadron History." I also deeply indebted to my college fraternity brother and lifelong friend Jim Burt, an Air

Force pilot after graduation, who read the manuscript and saved me from many errors. Hugh and I did a lot of interviews, with McGovern and his surviving crew, with the pilots and men of the 741st Squadron and the 455th Bomb Group and others, each listed in the Acknowledgments. We are grateful to all of them.

On October 9, 2000, Hugh and I rode in a B-24 and a B-17. We got to sit in the co-pilot's seat and fly the airplanes. It was an extraordinary experience. We thank the Collings Foundation (Box 248, Stow, Massachusetts 01775), who made it possible. The foundation flies the two bombers to airports around the country so that everyone, especially children, can experience the thrill of examining and flying in a World War II airplane.

The B-24 is the only one still flying. The foundation paid $1.3 million and required thousands of hours of volunteer labor to restore and reconstruct this vintage plane—called *Dragon and His Tail,* with appropriate artwork on the nose. Thousands come to see, and a few get to ride, in the B-24 and the B-17. They can climb from fore to aft inside the planes, into the nose and tail gunner turrets. They can sit at the bombsight, or at the radioman's position. They can move forward or aft on the catwalk, see the bombs in their rack, or the oxygen tanks and everything else. On the B-24 the waist windows are open. In flight, wind streams flow through the planes to the tail. Although Hugh and I went up only a couple of thousand feet, on a lovely October day in central Pennsylvania, from Williamsport to Harrisburg, it was cold. The flights in the big craft were bumpy, noisy—and a perfect delight.

Hugh and I got to fly thanks to the children of the Makos family—some still in high school, others getting started on their college educations—who have created the magazine *Ghost Wings,* which is written and published by them. It is devoted to airplanes of the past and the men and their planes of World War II, the Korean War, the Vietnam War, the Cold War. Educating our children about how their freedoms came about is a sacred cause to me, so naturally I was drawn to the magazine. Now my debt to *Ghost Wings* includes what the family did to make our trip to Williamsport so special.

Flying the B-24 and the B-17 from the co-pilot's seat, even in smooth weather—little wind, few clouds—made Hugh and me realize how cumbersome the bombers are, how long it takes for them to respond to the controls, how difficult they are to turn. But the flying brought smiles to our faces and joy to our hearts, smiles as big as all outdoors and joy as deep as the ocean. It was an experience with machines that could be compared only to being at the controls of a locomotive going up the Sierra Nevada. And it increased beyond measurement our respect for and admiration of the pilots and crews who flew those planes on combat missions that lasted six, eight, or ten hours. We encountered no flak. There were no enemy fighters shooting at us. We don't know how the airmen did it—but we appreciate what they did even more than before.

My uncle, Ty Ambrose, was a twenty-one-year-old co-pilot on a B-26 in the Eighth Air Force. In June 1944, he married Sabra Jean Starr, his girlfriend at Illinois State Normal University. Then he went overseas. On September 16, 1944, returning from a mission over the Continent, his plane crashed on landing in England and blew up. His body was never recovered.

My wife, Moira, who helped as she always does, in the research and in being the first to read or listen to a chapter, commented that what struck her most was how young the airmen were. Georges Clemenceau put it best. In a 1944 letter to Tex McCrary, author of *First of the Many*, Bernard Baruch quotes Clemenceau, who wrote, "They were kittens in play but tigers in battle."

THE B-24 WAS BUILT LIKE A 1930s MACK TRUCK, except that it had an aluminum skin that could be cut with a knife. It could carry a heavy load far and fast but it had no refinements. Steering the four-engine airplane was difficult and exhausting, as there was no power except the pilot's muscles. It had no windshield wipers, so the pilot had to stick his head out the side window to see during a rain. Breathing was possible only by wearing an oxygen mask—cold and clammy, smelling of rubber and sweat—above 10,000 feet in altitude. There was no heat, despite temperatures that at 20,000 feet and higher got as low as 40 or even 50 degrees below zero. The wind blew through the airplane like fury, especially from the waist gunners' windows and whenever the bomb bay doors were open. The oxygen mask often froze to the wearer's face. If the men at the waist touched their machine guns with bare hands, the skin froze to the metal.

There were no bathrooms. To urinate there were two small relief tubes, one forward and one aft, which were almost impossible to use without spilling because of the heavy layers of clothing the men wore. Plus which the tubes were often clogged with frozen urine. Defecating could be done only in a receptacle lined with a wax paper bag. A man had to be desperate to use it because of the difficulty of removing enough clothing and exposing bare skin to the arctic cold. The bags were dropped out of the waist windows or through the open bomb bay doors. There were no kitchen facilities, no way to warm up food or coffee, but anyway there was no food unless a crew member had packed in a C ration or a sandwich. With no pressurization, pockets of gas in a man's intestinal tract could swell like balloons and cause him to double over in pain.

There was no aisle to walk down, only the eight-inch-wide catwalk running beside the bombs and over the bomb bay doors used to move forward and aft. It had to be done with care, as the aluminum doors, which rolled up into the fuselage instead of opening outward on a hinge, had only a 100-pound capacity, so if a man slipped he would break through. The seats were not padded, could not be reclined,[1] and were cramped into so small a space that a man had almost no chance to stretch and none whatsoever to relax. Absolutely nothing was done to make it comfortable for the pilot, the co-pilot, or the other eight men in the crew, even though most flights lasted for eight hours, sometimes ten or more, seldom less than six. The plane existed and was flown for one purpose only, to carry 500 or 1,000 pound bombs and drop them accurately over enemy targets.

It was called a Liberator. That was a perhaps unusual name for a plane designed to drop high explosives on the enemy well behind the front lines, but it was nevertheless the perfect name. Consolidated Aircraft Corporation first made it, with the initial flight in 1939. When a few went over to England in 1940, the British Air Ministry wanted to know what it was called. Reuben Fleet of Consolidated answered, "Liberator." He added, "We chose the name Liberator because this airplane can carry destruction to the heart of the Hun, and thus help you and us to liberate those millions temporarily finding themselves under Hitler's yoke."

Consolidated, along with the Ford Motor Company, Douglas Aircraft Company, and North American Aviation—together called the Liberator Production Pool—made more than 18,300 Liberators, about 5,000 more than the total number of B-17s.* The Liberator was not operational before World War II and was not operational after the war (nearly every B-24 was cut up into pieces of scrap in 1945 and 1946, or left to rot on Pacific islands). The number of people involved in making it, in servicing it, and in flying the B-24 outnumbered those involved with any other airplane, in any country, in any time. There were more B-24s than any other American airplane ever built.2

It would be an exaggeration to say that the B-24 won the war for the Allies. But don't ask how they could have won the war without it.

The Army Air Forces needed thousands of pilots, and tens of thousands of crew members, to fly the B-24s. It needed to gather them and train them and supply them and service the planes from a country in which only a relatively small number of men knew anything at all about how to fly even a single-engine airplane, or fix it. From whence came such men?

---

* The United States utilized primarily five bombers during the war. The B-17 was a four-engine bomber that could carry three tons of bombs a distance of 2,000 miles at a cruising speed of 187 miles per hour. Top speed was 287 miles per hour. It had a single tail and a tail wheel. It was armed with thirteen .50 caliber machine guns.

The B-24 was a four-engine bomber with twin tails and a nose wheel. It could attain a speed of 303 miles per hour; cruising speed was 200 miles per hour. It had ten .50 caliber machine guns and could carry 8,800 pounds of bombs.

The B-25 was a twin-engine, twin-tail medium bomber with tricycle landing gear. It was the bomber used on the famous Doolittle raid on Tokyo. It could carry 3,000 pounds of bombs. It had six machine guns, and some models carried a 75 mm cannon in the nose. Its top speed was 275 miles per hour.

The B-26 was a twin-engine, single-tail bomber and had a top speed of 317 miles per hour. It had a dozen machine guns and could carry 5,000 pounds of bombs.

The B-29, which came into action in 1944, was the largest combat aircraft of the war. It had eight .50 caliber machine guns in remotely controlled turrets and a 20 mm cannon in a manned tail turret. It could carry 10 tons of bombs. It was pressurized and could fly in excess of 30,000 feet at a top speed of 365 miles per hour. Its maximum range was 5,830 miles.

CAST OF CHARACTERS

<u>McGovern's Crew</u>

George McGovern, pilot

Ralph "Bill" Rounds, co-pilot

Kenneth Higgins, radioman

Carroll Wilson "C. W." Cooper, navigator

Isador Irving Seigal, tail gunner

William "Tex" Ashlock, waist gunner

Robert O'Connell, nose gunner

Mike Valko, flight engineer

William McAfee, ball turret gunner

Sam Adams, navigator and bombardier

Marion Colvert, navigator

John B. Mills, tail gunner

<u>Others</u>

Art Applin, a B-24 tail gunner

Robert "Ken" Barmore, a B-24 co-pilot

Walter Malone Baskin, a B-24 pilot

Henry Burkle, in command of ground crews in Cerignola

Robert S. Capps, a B-24 pilot

Kenneth A. Cool, first commander of the 455th Bomb Group

Donald R. Currier, a B-24 navigator

David R. Davis, designer of the Davis wing for the B-24

Vincent Fagan, a B-24 pilot

Richard Farrington, a B-24 pilot

Howard Goodner, a B-24 radioman

Robert Hammer, a B-24 radioman

Francis Hosimer, a B-24 pilot

Art Johnson, a B-24 waist gunner

Donald P. Kay, a B-24 bombardier

Horace W. Lanford, first commander of the 741st Squadron

Francesco Musto, a Cerignola resident who worked for the Americans

Charles Painter, a B-24 pilot

Roland Pepin, a B-24 navigator

Guyon Phillips, a B-24 pilot

Anthony Picardi, a B-24 crew member

Joe Quintal, athletic director in Mitchell, South Dakota

Norman Ray, from Custer, South Dakota, who persuaded McGovern to take Civilian Pilot Training, then became his instructor on the B-24 before becoming a B-29 pilot

Glenn Rendahl, a B-24 pilot

Harold Schuknecht, 741st Squadron flight surgeon

Walter Shostack, a B-24 pilot

John G. Smith, a B-24 pilot

William L. Snowden, Cool's replacement as commander of the 455th Bomb Group

Ed Soderstrom, a B-24 pilot

Howard Surbeck, a B-24 pilot with whom McGovern served as co-pilot for his first five missions

Mel TenHaken, a B-24 radioman

Charles Watry, a C-47 pilot

CHAPTER ONE

Where They Came From

THE PILOTS AND CREWS OF THE B-24s came from every state and territory in America. They were young, fit, eager. They were sons of workers, doctors, lawyers, farmers, businessmen, educators. A few were married, most were not. Some had an excellent education, including college, where they majored in history, literature, physics, engineering, chemistry, and more. Others were barely, if at all, out of high school.

They were all volunteers. The U.S. Army Air Corps—after 1942 the Army Air Forces—did not force anyone to fly. They made the choice. Most of them were between the ages of two and ten in 1927, when Charles Lindbergh flew the *Spirit of St. Louis* from Long Island to Paris. For many boys, this was the first outside-the-family event to influence them. It fired their imagination. Like Lindbergh, they too wanted to fly.

In their teenage years, they drove Model T Fords, or perhaps Model A's—if they drove at all. Many of them were farm boys. They plowed behind mules or horses. They relieved themselves in outdoor privies. They walked to school, one, two, or sometimes more miles. Most of them, including the city kids, were poor. If they were lucky enough to have jobs they earned a dollar a day, sometimes less. If they were younger sons, they wore hand-me-down clothes. In the summertime, many of them went barefoot. They seldom traveled. Many had never been out of their home counties. Even most of the more fortunate had never been out of their home states or regions. Of those who were best off, only a handful had ever been out of the country. Almost none of them had ever been up in an airplane. A surprising number had never even seen a plane. But they all wanted to fly.

There were inducements beyond the adventure of the thing. Glamour. Extra pay. The right to wear wings. Quick promotions. You got to pick your service—no sleeping in a Navy bunk in a heaving ship or in a foxhole with someone shooting at you. They knew they would have to serve, indeed most of them wanted to serve. Their patriotism was beyond question. They wanted to be a part of smashing Hitler, Tojo, Mussolini, and their thugs. But they wanted to choose how they did it. Overwhelmingly they wanted to fly.

They wanted to get off the ground, be like a bird, see the country from up high, travel faster than anyone could do while attached to the earth. More than electric lights, more than steam engines, more than telephones, more than automobiles, more even than the printing press, the airplane separated past from future. It had freed mankind from the earth and opened the skies.

They were astonishingly young. Many joined the Army Air Forces as teens. Some never got to be twenty years old before the war ended. Anyone over twenty-five was considered to be, and was called, an "old man." In the twenty-first century, adults would hardly give such youngsters the key to the family car, but in the first half of the 1940s the adults sent them out to play a critical role in saving the world.

Most wanted to be fighter pilots, but only a relatively few attained that goal. Many became pilots or co-pilots on two- or four-engine bombers. The majority became crew members, serving as gunners or radiomen or bombardiers or flight engineers or navigators. Never mind. They wanted to fly and they did.

This is mainly the story of one airplane and the men who flew it. It draws on other experiences of other men and other planes in the U.S. Army Air Forces, but basically it is about a B-24 bomber named the

Dakota Queen, its crew and squadron pilot George McGovern, and the 741st of the 455th Bomb Group. They were neither typical—how could they be in an air force that numbered thousands of bombers and tens of thousands of crew members?—nor unique.

On July 19, 1922, in the Wesleyan Methodist parsonage in Avon, South Dakota, George Stanley McGovern was born. He had an older sister, Olive, and later a younger sister, Mildred, and then a younger brother, Larry. George's grandfather, born in Ireland, had served in the Civil War on the Union side and then was a coal miner. George's father, Joseph, born in 1868, had been a professional baseball player in the St. Louis Cardinals' organization but because of his Methodist religion he was disturbed by the amount of drinking and gambling and wild women associated with his team. He gave it up when he heard a "call to preach" and went to a Methodist seminary in Houghton, New York. Upon graduation he volunteered to go out to the Dakotas. There he used his handyman skills to build churches—some of which still stand—where he preached. His first wife died, leaving him childless. When he was fifty years old he married Frances McLean, a twenty-eight-year-old who was a soloist in his church and had a beautiful voice.

In 1927, when George was five years old, the family was living in Canada. When Lindbergh made his flight, as he recalled it, "the news just saturated all the conversation, newspapers, the radios. I remember that flight as though it was yesterday. Pictures of Lindbergh with his helmet and goggles were on the front pages. I just thought he was the most glamorous creature on God's earth. I grew up thinking Lindbergh was our greatest American."[1]

In 1928 the McGoverns moved to Mitchell, in eastern South Dakota, a town of some 12,000 residents, where Joseph continued in the ministry. In all his life, George never heard his mother call his father by his first name (he did hear her say "dear," once at least). There were few displays of affection, even though they were devoted to each other and their children. There was no extra money and precious little of it at that—Joseph never got as much as $100 a month in salary from the church. He did get a sack of potatoes from a farmer in his congregation, or a bushel of apples, or a crate of eggs, or some beef or pork. He supplemented his income by buying old houses, fixing them up, and then selling them, and he managed to buy a home in Mitchell on the corner of Fifth and Sanborn, where George grew up.

George was a "preacher's kid," but unlike some others in that category he had no wild streak. He was an average student whose one fling was going to the movies, which were forbidden to good Wesleyan Methodists, but he went anyway. He went pheasant hunting too, as most South Dakota boys did. It was his father's passion and his father taught him how to shoot a shotgun, a 16-gauge single-barrel. While hunting he saw dust storms turn the sky black. He saw hordes of grasshoppers eating the crops and even chewing their way through hoe handles. In town he saw banks and stores close their doors in bankruptcy. Once, while hunting with his father, he saw a farmer named Art Kendall sitting on the steps of his back porch, tears streaming down his face. Kendall explained to McGovern's father that he had just received a check from the stockyards for that year's production of pigs. The check did not cover the cost of trucking the pigs to market. By the time McGovern entered high school, nearly one farmer in five had lost his land to foreclosure.[2]

In high school, Joe Quintal was the athletic director of four elementary schools, the junior and senior high schools, and coached the school's football, basketball, and track teams. He also taught the gymnastic classes at the elementary schools. An excellent athlete, he had been the quarterback for the University of South Dakota. McGovern describes him as a "very articulate, intelligent man. I both admired him and feared him."

One of the exercises Quintal had his seventh-grade gym classes do was to dive headfirst over a leather sawhorse and do a somersault. "You had to run at full speed," McGovern remembered, "dive over, tuck your head, hit the mat and roll." McGovern couldn't bring himself to do it. He would run up to the sawhorse "and I knew I'd break my neck if I went over the top." So when he got to the sawhorse he balked. Not once, not twice, but a number of times.

Quintal blew his whistle. "Mac, come here," he shouted. "What's the matter with you?"

"Well, Mr. Quintal, I just can't do that."

"What do you mean, you can't do it? Have you seen these other boys going over that horse? You've got a pair of legs, a pair of arms, don't you have the same equipment they do?" McGovern said again that he just couldn't do it.

"You want me to tell you why?" McGovern said he would like to know.

"Well," Quintal said, "you're a physical coward—that's why."

The entire class, some sixty or so students, was watching. "I was just mortified to tears," McGovern recalled. But he still couldn't do it. Quintal "really made me feel that I was a coward. That haunted me." When he entered high school, he was determined to do something in athletics. A fast runner, he joined the track team, where he set no records but did make a respectable showing. Still he would get flashbacks to the sawhorse incident.[3]

In 1940, after graduation, McGovern entered Dakota Wesleyan College (enrollment: 500), just down the street from his family home. The war was on in Europe and China. To get prepared, the U.S. government had inaugurated a program called Civilian Pilot Training. The idea was to augment the nation's reserve of pilots with at least some introductory training of new civilian students. There was an opportunity to start a CPT program at Mitchell Field, just outside town. McGovern's fellow student and friend, Norman Ray from Custer, South Dakota, was desperate to fly. They were in the same freshman class. Ray was so poor that when he showed up at Wesleyan he had an old pair of ratty tennis shoes, blue jeans, and a couple of T-shirts. One day McGovern told him he ought to ask a girl for a date. Ray replied, "George, I can't afford to date."

"Well, if you go down to the College Inn all you need is ten cents," McGovern pointed out.

"Well, I haven't got ten cents."

He certainly had the desire to fly. The requirement was to have ten students enrolled before the course—which included ground school instruction as well as flight training and carried college credit—could begin. The CPT would supply the airplane and pay the instructor. So Ray went around talking to all his friends. He persuaded nine of his fellow students, including one woman and the eighteen-year-old McGovern, to sign up.

McGovern had never before been up in a plane but he agreed to be one of the students because he felt, "If I can fly an airplane that will show Joe Quintal that it isn't heights that I'm worried about, that I'm not too cowardly to fly a plane." He had to pass a physical, discovering in the process that he had good depth perception—and he found out later from other physicals that he would score almost off the charts on depth perception.

The plane was a single-engine Aeronca, built in Middletown, Ohio, with a front and rear cockpit. The instructor, Cliff Ferguson, a big, bulky, heavyset man, sat in front. There were two sets of controls, and they were connected so Ferguson could overwhelm the student and take control if he needed to. On McGovern's first flight, when Ferguson opened the throttle for takeoff, "I was scared to death—terrified." He thought, What the hell have I gotten myself into? I just can't do this. It was a typical South Dakota day, with lots of wind. The wings were fluttering and the plane was bouncing. Ferguson nevertheless told McGovern that he was in control. Toward the end of the lesson, he told McGovern, "You're doing okay."

McGovern continued the course, though "I was even more terrified in subsequent lessons when he demonstrated spins and stalls." Still, "Big Cliff would give me a little signal that I was doing okay, and nothing made me happier." After eight hours of instruction, Ferguson told McGovern that he had good coordination and was making good landings. Taking off and landing were two of the hardest things for a student to learn, but McGovern knew how far the plane was off the ground, when to level off, how to land the plane on its two front wheels, then gradually set the tail down onto the rear wheel. So Ferguson told him, "You're ready to solo." It went well. McGovern circled over Mitchell, gazing down at the water tower, the Corn Palace, and the Wesleyan campus, then over Lake Mitchell. When he landed he had a sense of exhilaration and a determination that if America entered the war and his time to serve came, it would be in the Army Air Corps.[4]

In the fall of 1941 McGovern, then a sophomore with his flying classes completed, saw B-24 bombers for the first time. He watched them going overhead—they were based in Omaha, Nebraska—on practice missions. The pilots used the Mitchell Airport runway as an auxiliary landing field. He saw no fighter airplanes, nor any B-17s. Occasionally McGovern would see one or two B-24s land. They were big and cumbersome but impressive. He never got aboard one. He never thought, Someday I'm going to fly one of those birds. But he noticed and did think, Those pilots are really something.

The B-24s and the pilots that McGovern saw were brand-new. The United States in 1940 and 1941 had only minuscule armed forces. The Navy was the best off, but its fleet was badly outnumbered and outgunned by the Japanese, not to mention the British. The U.S. Army at the beginning of World War II had fewer than 200,000 men (26,000 of them in the Army Air Corps), which meant it ranked sixteenth in the world, right behind Romania. The Army was pitifully smaller than the millions of men in the Japanese, German, and Italian armies. By June 1941, the U.S. Army Air Corps had been built up to 1,257 combat planes, nearly all of them inferior to the Japanese Zero, which outnumbered them anyway, and to the German *Luftwaffe's* fighter fleet, which was four times larger than the American fleet and growing rapidly.

When the war began in Europe in September 1939, the Depression continued to grip America. The unemployment rate was 25 percent. Those with jobs were earning only a little more than $100 a month. There was no unemployment insurance, no welfare paid for by the government, no antibiotics. Most diseases were life-threatening. Transportation was by automobile, bus, or train, slow and crude. Nearly all roads were two lanes. Few people traveled. What money they had went to feeding, clothing, and housing themselves.

In technology, America was far behind the Germans and Japanese, especially in airplanes. Commercial air travel was for a privileged few wealthy people and not reliable at that. The new twin-engine Douglas DC-3 was the most advanced plane. It carried twenty-one passengers. It took twenty-four hours to fly from New York City to Los Angeles, but only when weather permitted, and even then the DC-3 had to make three refueling stops along the way. It could make 155 miles per hour and had a range of 900 miles, at best. The passenger cabin was not pressurized. There was no oxygen available for passengers. It cruised at 10,000 feet, with a maximum of 15,000, which meant it flew in the clouds much of the time. There was no radar and what little electronic navigation aids were available were poor. They consisted of low-frequency radio beams that the pilots could follow, but they were almost useless in bad weather, as the radio signals were jammed by static from radio waves emitted by thunderstorms. There were light beacons on the waves that the pilots could use as navigation aids, but they too were useless in bad weather.

By late 1941, there were only a few civilian pilots or crew members. Of those who later served in the Fifteenth Air Force, an estimated 85 percent had no prior military experience, nor had they ever been in an airplane.[5] McGovern was lucky, but he had been off the ground only eight times and that had been in a single-engine plane with no armament. Those who served in the Fifteenth Air Force came from all forty-eight states and the territories of Hawaii, Alaska, and Puerto Rico, and had different backgrounds and experiences.

Ralph C. "Bill" Rounds was born in 1924 in Wichita, Kansas. His father owned a lumber business and was a wealthy man. Rounds was handsome and enthusiastic, especially for girls and airplanes. He was a wisecracking prankster, the image of a devil-may-care flyboy. His desire was to be a fighter pilot. His life experiences, his attitude, and his personality were completely different from McGovern's.[6]

Kenneth Higgins was born in 1925 in Dallas, Texas. In 1941 he was a junior at Highland Park High School. He would give anything to learn to fly.

Robert Hammer, born in 1923, one of five children, was a North Dakota boy. His father was a trapper and hunter. In the harsh wintertime, Hammer recalled seeing muskrat pelts hanging to dry from wires stretched from wall to wall in nearly every room in his family house. Death was ever present. As a seven-year-old, he saw his two-year-old sister die of pneumonia. When he was in fifth grade, his mother died in childbirth, as did the baby. Another sister died in 1938, of strep throat.

Hammer made what money he could, when he could. In the summer, he would walk seven miles to the local nine-hole golf course. School was a mile away; he would walk in the morning, return home for lunch, walk back to school, then home, so the seven miles wasn't much. He would caddy, at 25 cents per round. In high school, he got a job at the Dakota Hide and Fur firm, packing wool, stretching jackrabbit hides, loading rabbit meat for shipment to mink farms. He was paid 25 cents per hour, which was somewhat better than he got working in the harvest fields from sunup to sundown, hauling bundles, field pitching, and shocking, at $1.50 per day. When he was fifteen years old he had lied about his age to get into the Citizens Military Training Camp, which he attended for three summers, learning how to march and a bit about being an infantryman.

Hammer had never been out of North Dakota, but by the time of his high school graduation, in 1940, he was eager to see the world and wanted to join the Navy to do so. But he was only seventeen and his father refused to sign the papers. How about the Coast Guard? No. The Army? No. "So I finally decided I would have to be content with seeing North Dakota."[7]

Roland Pepin was born on July 4, 1924, and was three years old when Lindbergh made his flight. Pepin's father bought him a pedal-type airplane toy "and a little Lindy flying suit complete with leather helmet and goggles." From then on, he built and drew airplanes. He was determined to join the Army Air Corps as soon as he was old enough.[8]

William V. Barnes and his twin brother, Robert N. Barnes, were seventeen years old in 1941, attending a small military school in Texas. Naturally they were in the ROTC, where they learned the rudiments of being soldiers.[9]

Walter Shostack, born in 1919 in Constantinople, was the son of a pilot in the czar's air force in World War I. Both his grandfathers had been generals in the czar's army. His father was shot down on the Turkish front. He survived and, to escape the revolution, went to Turkey. In 1923, together with his family, he emigrated to the United States. Walter grew up in New York City. At first he and his parents spoke no English. They fed themselves and found shelter by selling his grandmother's jewelry. His father went to work making airplanes. When he was old enough, so did Walter, who moved to Detroit for his job. There he met a Hungarian girl, whose father, Stephen Balogh, had emigrated to America shortly after World War I began to avoid conscription in the Hungarian army. He married and in 1920 had a daughter, whom he named Aranka Gizela, Hungarian for Gold

Grace. Walter met her on a blind date arranged by his friend, Stephen Balogh, Jr. Both young men graduated from the Manhattan School of Aviation Trade and got jobs at Wright Field, in Dayton, Ohio. Before entering the service, Shostack married Gold Grace.[10]

Eugene Hudson was born in 1922 in Los Angeles. His father was a Lutheran minister in Beverly Hills, right on the edge of Hollywood. Hudson graduated from Fairfax High School in 1940 and entered Los Angeles City College. His brother had joined the Air Corps in 1938, which fired his imagination after listening to his brother's stories. Hudson worked the midnight shift at Douglas Aircraft while going to college. He was a riveter working on the XB-19, an experimental bomber. Speaking for himself as well as his friends, Hudson remarked, "We all had a flair for adventure."[11]

———

Carroll Wilson Cooper was unusual in the Army Air Forces. He was older than most and had been in the military before the war. Born on May 10, 1917, in McCaulley, Texas, he was the fifth child of Sam and Fannie Cooper (one of his older brothers had died as a youth). His father was a stout Baptist so he named his fifth child after a Baptist leader, Carroll, and he was a staunch Democrat, so he gave his son as a middle name Wilson, after Woodrow Wilson. As a boy, Cooper discovered that his first name was commonly a girl's name, so he went by "C. W. Cooper." Although his father had a dry goods store and the first car in town, C.W. suffered the misery of going to the two-hole privy, or outhouse, in the middle of the night, until he got a porcelain pot—usually called a "thunder jug"—that was kept under his bed. In the daytime he put it outside in the sun to sanitize it and air it out. When his folks got an indoor bathroom, C.W. thought it a good improvement, especially since his mother no longer gave him his Saturday night bath in a galvanized wash tub in the kitchen. "We took a bath every Saturday night whether we needed it or not."

His meals were filling but frugal. He drank "blue john," milk mixed with water. His noon meal was often red beans, but sometimes his mother would fix lima beans as the main, and often only, course. The evening meal was usually corn bread and blue john. When he went to Tonkawa Boy Scout camp, near Buffalo Gap, for two weeks, he gained ten pounds thanks to the food. He also grew tomatoes, not so much to eat as to sell at 5 cents a pound.

Church functions were his social life. Sometimes these were all-day singing, but they included a picnic prepared by the ladies. The tables under the arbor would groan under the weight of fried chicken, chocolate cakes, apple and lemon meringue pies, iced tea, and much more. It was dusk before it was time to leave. C.W. remembers his father cranking the Model T Ford to get it started. As C.W. was left-handed, he made a vow that when he grew up he would become rich enough to buy a car that cranked left-handed. He never got that done, although he did start driving a car when he was thirteen years old.

While working on the wheat harvest, he was awestruck by the big threshers and the steam tractor. "It was a sight to see," he recalled, "with chaff and wheat going every which direction and the huffing and puffing machines creeping along on their iron-cleated wheels." He was a teenage boy when he saw his first airplane. It had crashed on the roof of a house next to the pasture it had been trying to use as a landing field. C.W. made a sextant out of cigar box wood, and used the same material to build planes that he put on a string and flew using a fishing pole.

The Cooper family took two vacations. One was to Lampasas, Texas. By starting at sunrise and driving until dark, they made the 300-mile trip in two days. C.W. and his parents slept beside the road. Once his father followed some dim car tracks through a pasture until the track ran out; he turned around, finally found a farmhouse, and asked where the road was located. The other trip, to Chicago, was much longer, in the family's first Model A Ford. The people in Chicago pointed at C.W.'s overalls and his bare feet and laughed. For him, the big thrills were riding on the elevated train, a visit to the

Marshall Field Museum, and another to the top of the Wrigley Tower.

After all that traveling, C.W. decided he wanted to see the world, and there was no way better to do that than as a naval officer. So in his junior year in high school he began to improve his grades to reach his goal, and went to work for Charles L. South, who was running for Congress. If he made it, South could appoint C.W. to Annapolis. C.W. delivered circulars for South and did odd jobs. In school that fall he tried out for the football team, figuring that would improve his chances for an appointment, but as he weighed only 117 pounds that didn't work. So he joined the track team, without any great success. When he graduated from high school, Congressman South had already given out his Annapolis appointment. At his father's suggestion, C.W. went to junior college to take a year of engineering. There he was in ROTC and found that the military life was for him. He gained honors for being in the best-drilled squad and platoon and was in the Honorary Corps of Cadets. That summer South gave him his appointment to Annapolis, but by then C.W. was two weeks too old to be accepted. But his grades were good enough to earn him a scholarship to Texas A&M.

More ROTC, more drilling, lots of studying. Together with four others, Cooper bought a used Model T for $40. After a year or so the partners decided to sell it back, but it died about a block from the dealer. He gave them $25 for it anyway. Cooper smoked Bull Durham, which cost 5 cents a bag, except on Saturdays when he would treat himself to a 20-cent pack of Lucky Strikes. A&M was a military school. When Cooper graduated in 1941, he got his degree in civil engineering one day and his commission as a second lieutenant in the infantry of the U.S. Army the next.

His first posting was as assistant provost marshal at Camp Bowie. Then it was off to the Fort Benning Infantry School, called Fort Benning's School for Boys by the young officers. The training in that summer of 1941 was haphazard at best. When the class was completed, Cooper was asked to give his choice of three places to go,

Camp Roberts in California, Fort Dix in New Jersey, or Camp Wolters in Texas. Camp Wolters was only 100 miles from his home. He had been in the Army long enough to know how things worked, so he put down Roberts as his first choice, Dix as his second, and Wolters as his third. Sure enough, exactly as he hoped, he was assigned to Camp Wolters.

There he was assigned to train a platoon in a heavy weapons company. The men were mainly hill boys from Kentucky and Tennessee. Some of them, according to Cooper, "were not too sharp." But in the fall of 1941 he could feel America getting closer to entering the war and he was sure they would be sent into combat, so he got the platoon together and said, "Look fellas, this is going to be hell on you. You're going to hate me before this is over because I'm going to work you as hard as I can to get you ready for combat because I don't want your blood on my hands." On December 1, the thirteen-week training period was over and a couple of days later the platoon was ordered to the Pacific. "I fought back the tears as I shook their hands as they went to the troop train to go."

That fall, Cooper was promoted to first lieutenant. As a reward, he got additional duty as morale officer for the battalion, responsible for court-martial cases as well as morale. In his first month in the job, he had sixteen courts-martial. He thought, Something has to be done about this. I don't want to spend all my time on these cases, especially as they were mainly fistfights, drunks, and AWOLs. The cause, he decided, was that the enlisted men had nothing to do on their off hours. He decided to use the battalion officers and enlisted men's fund, with about $3,000 in it, to do something about that.

One of the new privates had been the leader of the Hardin Simmons Cowboy Band. Cooper called him in and asked if he would organize a band. "Would I?" the private responded. "You bet! This is great!" He started to recruit players. One private had played accordion in a nightclub in California. Cooper spent $8 to get his instrument shipped to him at Camp Wolters. There was a carpenter in the battalion; Cooper bought the wood and he put together music stands. Cooper found an artist who designed a battalion crest and painted it on the stands. He bought sheet music for the band.

At that time there was a play on Broadway called *Life Begins at 40*. The bandleader found some men who thought they could sing and put on a play he called *Life Begins at 5:30*. The regimental commander came to opening night. He sat in the front row with his staff and the other high-ranking officers beside him. The play featured dancing and singing "girls." One two three kick, one two three kick, and so on. The girls wore sarongs and their GI shoes with their hairy legs bare. They wore new white mops for hair and had a black missing tooth painted on. For bras, they used halves of grapefruits, big ones, tied around their chests. They were doing their one-two-three-kick routine when, as per plan, one of the bra strings broke and the grapefruit dropped into the commander's lap. Corny though it was, it sent the audience into peals of laughter.

Cooper found a just-graduated West Pointer who had been middleweight boxing champion at the Point. He set him to putting together a boxing team. Cooper found a quarterback from Oklahoma and a big guy, a coal miner, from Indiana "who could catch any pass that was thrown to him." They became the nucleus for the football team. Cooper used the fund to buy equipment. He also bought a new pool table and put the carpenter to work making writing tables so the men could write home to their parents.

Court-martial cases dropped to zero. Cooper had $300 left in the fund. In late November, the battalion commander called him in and said, "Lieutenant, we need a public address system for the training here. It's a lot of red tape to get one through the normal channels. Use that $300 in the fund to buy a PA system for us to use in training. You can justify it by saying that you need it for the entertainment of the enlisted men."

"Sir, I can't do that," Cooper replied. "The men need athletic equipment, new music for the orchestra, and more. I just can't do it."

"Lieutenant," the commander shot back, "I don't believe you're hearing me. I want you to buy a PA system." Cooper again refused, popped him a salute, did an about-face, and got out of there. A couple of days later he got orders to go to the 2nd Filipino Infantry. That was how things were done, at least much of the time, in the prewar U.S. Army.[12]

Every American born before 1936 remembered exactly where he or she was when they heard the news that the Japanese had attacked the U.S. fleet at Pearl Harbor.

George McGovern was in his second year at Dakota Wesleyan. It was a liberal arts school that emphasized philosophy, history, English literature, foreign languages, and the arts. He was taking a required course in music appreciation taught by Robert Brown from Oberlin College. Brown was a violinist. He assigned his students to listen every Sunday to the New York Philharmonic Orchestra's radio concert on NBC and write a critique. Nineteen-year-old McGovern was listening and writing notes, saying he thought the violins should be a bit more prominent—"Strictly BS," he recalled, but "I don't know how Brown thought a bunch of college sophomores were going to critique the New York Philharmonic"—when the program was interrupted with the news flash that Pearl Harbor had been bombed. "I have to confess I'd never heard of Pearl Harbor, didn't even know where it was." But he could tell from his father's reaction and the way he turned the radio up that it was a serious matter. That afternoon he decided that he would have to be involved in the war.

The following day, at school, "everyone was talking about it." The instructors had maps to show the students where Pearl Harbor was and what it meant. McGovern knew that his decision was correct, that "there was no logical alternative to this than for all of us to get involved." Some of the Dakota Wesleyan students already were in the service. Norman Ray, who had persuaded McGovern to take the

Civilian Pilot Training course the previous year, was already in the Army Air Corps, and another student, John Nowling, a star on the college's football team, had been killed in a training accident. McGovern talked to the others who had been in the course and to a couple of faculty members, and made up his mind. Along with ten fellow students, he decided to drive to Omaha to enlist in either the Army Air Corps or naval aviation.

They borrowed the president's car and the dean's car—"In a little school you can do things like that," he recalled, and indeed the students called many of the faculty by their first names—to drive down to Omaha. Their only question was, the Army or the Navy? They debated all the way to Omaha. Being from South Dakota, they were all land lovers and had an instinct that it was better to be landing and taking off from the ground than from the water. Still, there was a sentiment that the enemy couldn't bomb you as easily on an aircraft carrier as at an air base. But shortly after they had parked the cars and began looking for the recruiting stations, one of the young men said he had heard that if you joined the Army Air Corps you would receive a free meal ticket for the cafeteria next door. On the basis of that unsubstantiated rumor, all ten joined the Army Air Corps. The rumor turned out to be true, and they got a lunch worth about 75 cents. "It wasn't bad," McGovern commented. "Roast beef, gravy, and mashed potatoes."

They were not sworn in, but they did sign a statement that it was their intention to be in the Army Air Corps and agreed to report when called. The statement made them exempt from the draft. The Army did not have the airfields and training planes or instructors to take them in as yet, but they were Air Corps property. They returned to Mitchell and school, thinking they would be called up in two or three months.

On December 7, 1941, Bill Barnes and his twin brother, Robert, were on parade with their ROTC unit for parents day. The news from Pearl Harbor was broadcast over the loudspeakers. "We have vivid memories of the moment," Barnes said.[13] As soon as they were eighteen they signed up for the Army Air Corps, but were not called into active duty for a year. Neither twin had a driver's license because their parents were too poor to own a car.

Seventeen-year-old Bob Hammer, who had been unable to persuade his father to sign a permission form to let him join the Navy, Coast Guard, or Army because he was too young, found that Pearl Harbor changed all that. On December 8, with his father's approval, he enlisted in the Army. Hammer never forgot his dad's parting words: "I hate to see you go, Bob, but I wouldn't give 2 cents for you if you didn't."[14]

Seventeen-year-old Roland Pepin was a junior in high school. On December 7, 1941, he and his parents were reading the newspaper and listening to the radio when a news flash reported what had happened at Pearl Harbor. He decided at that moment to get into the armed services. "All of my classmates," he found out the next day, "including myself, could not wait to turn eighteen and graduate so that we could enlist and do our share to fight the war." There was a government program that allowed seventeen-year-olds to sign up and pick their branch of service, but they would not be inducted until they graduated. Shortly after Pearl Harbor, Pepin signed with the Army Air Corps. In mid-June 1943, he graduated from high school at La Salle Academy. On July 4 he celebrated his eighteenth birthday. On July 17 he was sworn into the military.[15]

Nearly all those who signed up with a promise to the Army Air Corps, and those who enlisted in the other services, wanted to fight. Now. At once. But the armed forces were not ready for them. C. W. Cooper remembered Lt. Galil Hannah, who came to Camp Wolters shortly after Pearl Harbor. Hannah had been born in Egypt and came to the United States when he was eleven years old. When he was seventeen his father gave his permission for him to join the Army. He went to

Panama, in the infantry, where he learned jungle warfare. Then it was back to the States to officer candidate school, where he earned his commission and was sent to Camp Wolters.

As Cooper recalled it, when Hannah reported, he didn't say, "When do we eat?" or "Where do I sleep" or "When do we get paid?" Instead he pounded on Cooper's desk and asked, "When can I go into combat?" Every day he came in to demand, "When can I go into combat?" Cooper reported each request to his commanding officer, who soon had enough. He told Hannah, "The next orders that come in, you're going to be on." The next orders were for a lieutenant to report to Attu, Alaska. As Cooper later put it, "Here this guy's trained in jungle warfare. He spoke Arabic fluently. He was perfect for North Africa or, failing that, Guadalcanal. And the Army sent him to Attu."[16]

Nearly all the young men who had signed up to join the Army Air Corps had to wait, often for a year or more, for the Air Corps to have enough airfields, airplanes, instructors, and barracks to start training them.

McGovern continued his education at Dakota Wesleyan. There he met and fell in love with Eleanor Stegeberg from Woonsocket, South Dakota. Among other attributes, including good looks, she had beat him in a debate in high school and outscored him in a test on current events at Wesleyan. In the first year of the war they got engaged, agreeing that they would not marry until the war ended. Stegeberg's family was poor, so after her first year in college she dropped out to work as a secretary for a lawyer.

A friend of McGovern's, Robert "Bob" Pennington, had joined the Army and was in training. He was dating Ila, Eleanor's twin sister, and wrote McGovern to ask about their father. In reply, McGovern wrote that "he is a very different sort of person. His life was practically ruined when their mother died as he loved her more seemingly than life itself. He is consequently a little inclined to be brusque and a little unfriendly when you are first introduced to him. If you can just dig beneath that reserve and aloofness, you'll find a heart there as big as your head. I think that the twins get that everlasting reserve of theirs from this same trait in their dad. Mr. Stegeberg, though, is one of the deepest men I've ever known." McGovern added that one night "I talked with him from ten o'clock to 2:30 the next morning. That experience did me a lot of good. From that day to this I haven't had a closer friend than Mr. Stegeberg."17

McGovern was no athlete but he became a star pupil and was elected president of his class. His chief extracurricular activity was debate. His partner was Matthew Smith, son of the dean at Wesleyan. In early 1943 the two of them went to the national debate tournament at North Dakota State University. There were over a hundred schools represented. McGovern and Smith won the contest. Driving the dean's car back to Mitchell, they were singing and carousing—or at least as much carousing as students at Wesleyan would do. They pulled up on the Wesleyan campus. It was February 12, 1943, and snowing hard. As McGovern remembered it, "There was Dean Smith standing there and when he saw Matt and me he just broke into sobs." In his hand he had a big envelope. It was orders from the Army Air Forces. McGovern and Walter Kriman, the student body president, were to report to Jefferson Barracks, St. Louis, in seventy-two hours. Smith said he would write a letter to the Army Air Forces asking that George and Walter be allowed to stay at Wesleyan at least until the end of the semester.

"No, Dean Smith," McGovern replied. "The time has come to go."

"Oh no, no, no, no . . ." the dean replied. Then he asked, "What will Eleanor say?" McGovern said he could handle that. He didn't mention his mother. Although not a pacifist, and very much opposed to Hitler and the Nazis, she hated to read of the losses. When the local paper reported that the Red Army had killed 60,000 Germans at Leningrad, or more than at Stalingrad, she read it and moaned. "Oh, dear," she would say, "isn't that awful. There must be so many sad homes in Germany tonight." When the report noted so many thousand Russians killed, she would cry out, "How do those Russian fathers and mothers stand it. . . . All those young boys. Isn't there some way that the heads of governments can get together and stop this slaughter?"

A few days after returning from the debate tournament, McGovern and Kriman packed a bag each and went to the Milwaukee depot to board the 6:00 P.M. train to Minneapolis. At the station, the student body from Wesleyan was gathered, along with the entire faculty. The cheerleaders were there, in their uniforms, along with the school band. "It was really an uproarious send-off," McGovern remembered. He felt it was a "joyful occasion," but only "if I could keep my eyes off my mother, who looked as though she were at my funeral. She could not believe that they were going to take her son off to this miserable war."[18]

CHAPTER TWO

Training

McGOVERN RODE THE TRAIN DOWN to Fort Snelling, Minnesota, where the following morning he was sworn into the Army. He took the oath and became a buck private. After a couple of days of just waiting around, it was south to Jefferson Barracks just outside St. Louis. The men called it JB. It was located in a series of ravines and hills. It was cold. When it wasn't snowing, it was raining. Mud was everywhere. JB, like most other AAF bases built during the war, was constructed according to Army Air Forces Chief of Staff General H. H. "Hap" Arnold's insistence that the bases be models of "Spartan simplicity." There were two dozen want-to-be air cadets in each tar-paper barracks. Their average age was nineteen.[1]

They were issued their uniforms, shoes, mess kits. For many of them it was their first time away from home, which made them susceptible to diseases. Illness became so prevalent that the cadets took to calling one street Influenza Valley, another Pneumonia Gulch. Nevertheless they were there to learn the difference between the right way, the wrong way, and the Army way of doing things, so they had little time to get acquainted. Instead they drilled.

The old sergeants were there to teach them how to keep their barracks clean, their uniforms ready for inspection at any time, how to march, shoot a rifle and a pistol, march some more, obey verbal commands. To the sergeants they were just another bunch of buck privates that needed to be shaped up. "And so the yelling and hollering began," McGovern said, "and the nonstop four-letter words."

The drilling was nearly continuous. If a man reported for sick call, and many did at first, the sergeants regarded him as—and called him—"a f—k off." McGovern was lucky. He was in good health, and his sergeant, named Trumbo, although he enjoyed drilling all the men—he called them "you smart college guys"—still had a streak of kindness in him. Sergeant Trumbo taught them close-order drill. He taught them to run as fast as they could, then throw themselves down behind a fence, a rise in the ground, or into a hole. How to put on a gas mask. And more. From dawn to dusk and into the night. They ate, then collapsed on their bunks. They woke up to reveille and started over again.

One Saturday night McGovern had the only experience he enjoyed at JB. He hopped a bus for the thirty-minute drive into St. Louis. Walking around alone, he found himself in front of the St. Louis Opera House. A uniformed attendant grabbed his arm and said, "Soldier, how would you like to hear a great American sing?"

"Who?" McGovern asked.

"Marian Anderson," the attendant replied. McGovern knew the name and the fact that the Daughters of the American Revolution had refused to allow her to sing in Constitution Hall in Washington because she was black. "Of course the professors at Dakota Wesleyan made sure we knew about that and properly condemned it and what a great woman she was." So McGovern said yes, sure. Anderson had asked that a representative of the Army, the Navy, the Marine Corps, and the Coast Guard join her on the stage. She had them stand in a semicircle behind her for the entire two-hour concert. She chatted with them between songs, which was a big thrill, but the biggest was hearing her sing.

"I don't think I'd ever heard such music and never again would hear anything so beautiful," McGovern recalled nearly a half century later. When she concluded with "America the Beautiful," the servicemen and everyone in the audience wept. Some were visibly sobbing. To everyone present, that was what America was all about. "That was one of the great moments of my life."[2]

The privates continued to march and otherwise learn the rudiments of soldiering. After thirty days, they shipped out, their destination colleges and universities all over the country—there were 150 schools involved—for five months of testing and ground school training. McGovern went to Southern Illinois Normal University in Carbondale. There it was dorms rather than barracks. McGovern was one of 125 living in Anthony Hall, all from the Great Plains and upper Midwest. The same number lived in other dorms. Many of those men were college students from New York City and they called the rural boys "shit kickers."[3]

The Army Air Forces had by then become what was called the largest single educational organization in existence. It had a total strength of just over 20,000 when the war began in Europe, representing a bit over 10 percent of the Army. By 1944 it was up to 2.4 million personnel in its ranks, almost one third of the total Army strength.[4] Nearly all of them had to be taught highly specialized skills, beginning with pilots. This put an enormous strain on the AAF. To respond, it had an apparently unlimited budget. "Everything is expendable in war," Eisenhower once said. He added, with a grin, "even generals' lives." And went on, "so long as you win."[5] The only limitation on the AAF's purchases was the capacity of American industry to manufacture airplanes of all types, plus supplies and equipment. In manpower, there were no apparent limits. The AAF built barracks and airfields. It rented college dorms and hotels. It hired civilian instructors. It spent more than $3 billion 1940s dollars in the course of the war. All this and more was done by a prewar cadre that had never seen more than a few aircraft flying in formation at one time. The AAF put the potential air cadets through a multitude of physical and mental tests before embarking on about as rigorous a training program as could be. During the first months of the war it wanted to graduate 30,000 pilots a year, along with even more thousands of bombardiers, navigators, engineers. By October 1942, the goal was up to 100,000 pilots a year, and proportionally more crew. The AAF determined that it needed one million air cadets to reach its goal.

For the men being tested, the most feared word was "washout." The process began immediately—slightly more than 50 percent of them failed either the initial physical or written tests and were packed off to the infantry. The AAF expected that result, and further that more than 40 percent of those left would fail to complete the courses of Primary, Basic, and Advanced schools.

To reach the required numbers, the AAF's policies evolved. On December 10, 1941, Chief of Staff Arnold dropped the requirement that all air cadets had to have completed two years of college—he substituted a qualifying test to replace the requirement. In mid-January 1942, he dropped the ban on married applicants for the air cadet program and lowered the minimum age from twenty to eighteen. The new policy greatly stimulated enlistment and for a year or more those inducted as aviation cadets greatly exceeded the AAF's capacity to train them.[6]

In November 1942, Charles Watry was eighteen years old. Congress was about to lower the draft age from twenty to eighteen. He and some others his age decided, "There was no way we were going to allow ourselves to be drafted into the infantry," so they presented themselves to the examining board, where they were given test booklets and answer sheets for the Aviation Cadet Qualifying Examination. The test would reveal how quick they were to understand directions and whether they could follow instructions accurately. There were reading comprehension sections and others testing mathematical and mechanical skills, judgment and problem solving, and leadership potential.

Watry passed and signed a paper signifying his intention to join the AAF as an aviation cadet. A couple of days later, on November 13, Congress, as expected, lowered the draft age. Watry was worried, since he was still not enlisted in the Army. He asked an AAF sergeant when he should report. Don't worry, he was told, it would be soon. He still worried.

On December 4, he was told to report for enlistment, and did. The next day, Franklin Roosevelt issued a presidential executive order terminating all voluntary enlistments, to be effective after December 13. McGovern was already signed up; Watry got in just under the wire. By then, there was a pool of more than 30,000 potential cadets, with another 20,000 officers and enlisted men awaiting training as well. The AAF was enlisting 13,000 men per month as air cadets, but it had only enough space, equipment, and instructors to train 10,000 a month, so 3,000 of the potential pilots were stuck in the enlisted reserves, doing what McGovern and so many others did at JB.

Watry was placed initially in the College Training Detachment program, really a holding ground, at Nebraska State Teachers College in Wayne, Nebraska. There were 300 men in his CTD. Most were in their late teens or early twenties and together, in Watry's judgment, "they were as talented a group as I have ever known." After that, it was on to the classification phase of training. They went through a day-and-a-half-long battery of tests, as did McGovern and all the groups at their various campuses. Developed by psychologists, the first part tested a man's general knowledge, graph and chart reading skills, understanding of the principles of mechanics, ability to read maps and photographs, speed and accuracy of perception, and understanding of technical information. The second part measured motor coordination, steadiness under pressure, finger dexterity, and the ability to react quickly and accurately to constantly changing stimuli. The third part was a private interview with psychologists, with such questions as "Do you like girls?" and "Do you wet the bed?"

Then there was another physical examination, "the most stringent possible." In Watry's words, "The physical exam is the single most critical event in a military (and commercial) pilot's career." Some of the flight instructors bragged that they could teach almost anyone to fly, but as Watry pointed out, "The number who can pass a flight physical is a far smaller group." AAF-experienced pilots took the exam every year (today's airline pilots take one every six months) and they always approached it with fear. To flunk meant you would never become a pilot, or continue to be one. A sign over General Arnold's door reinforced the point: "The Air Force's Business Is to Fly and Fight, and Don't You Forget It!" The men were tested on pulse rate and blood pressure before and after exercise, and much else besides.

The eye testing was critical. The men were tested on color perception, distance vision, near vision, accommodation, and other problems. The most feared of the eye tests was the one that caused the most rejections, depth perception, which was tested in a variety of mechanical ways. That was the one McGovern passed with ease. Some 20 percent failed and became washouts, departing the base that day, as the AAF figured it was not good for the man's morale to remain with those who passed. They still wanted to fly, so most of those who washed out volunteered for aerial gunnery training, radio operator training, or flight engineer training. By 1944 almost every one of the six enlisted crew members of a B-17 or a B-24 were washouts from the cadet program.[7]

In Kenneth Higgins's primary training he had civilian instructors, but an AAF officer, a lieutenant, would go up with him on his check ride. It was on a small, single-engine plane, a Primary Trainer 19 (PT-19) it was called. On the check ride, the magneto quit. The lieutenant told Higgins to make a turn. He couldn't. "I didn't have any power. The thing wouldn't go. We couldn't climb. I couldn't get the magneto working and I'm going into the mesquite trees." The instructor kicked the rudder and got the plane working again "and we came in sailing downwind and landed all right on the field. It came in hot, but we made it. I couldn't have done that in a million years, but he had flown for a hundred years."

The consequence was another check ride for Higgins, with another officer. "Lieutenant Gates, I'll never forget, he hollered at me all the time, beat my legs with a stick. So finally he said, 'Land this SOB and let me out.'" Higgins did, and Gates told him to take it up himself. "I can do that," he said, "and I hoot and hollered and was singing to myself as I soloed." So he graduated and went on to basic training, with a bigger plane. There he had an instructor who was teaching his first class "and he wasn't very good." After more testing, Higgins washed out. Still wanting to fly, he went to radio school.[8]

After the mental and physical exams, the men who passed were asked to list their preferences—pilot, navigator, or bombardier. Those who put down pilot—a vast majority—figured you needed a top score to qualify, but in fact the AAF took its navigators from those who scored the best. When a man finished his ground school, the AAF placed him in a training program, with top priority given to his aptitude for a type of training as revealed in his classification battery of tests. Second priority went to his personal preference. Third went to quota available (in 1944 the order of priority reflected the AAF's ability to attract young men—many quotas were already filled, so the priority became quotas first, then aptitude, and finally, if at all, individual preference).

The parents or wives of those who had passed received a form letter—stamped on the outside "GOOD NEWS" to allay fears that something bad or terrible had happened—that notified them that their loved one had been selected for pilot (or bombardier or navigator) training. It outlined the program he would be going through before receiving his wings. The last paragraph read, "A pilot occupies a position that requires sound judgment, a keen and alert mind, a sound body, and the ability to perfectly coordinate mind and body in the flying of the airplane. It is imperative that the men who fly our military aircraft possess these qualifications, for upon their skill will depend in large measure the success of our war effort."[9]

McGovern spent five months at Carbondale for his ground school training. The physical training program, and the academic studies, were "the toughest I've ever experienced." In the mornings, he studied meteorology, navigation, mechanical arts, all taught by college instructors. There were frequent quizzes and examinations, and thus more washouts. After a noon meal, the physical part began. Norm Campanella, a coach at Southern Illinois whose tumbling team had placed first in the nation, was the instructor. He quickly had them doing push-ups, pull-ups, sit-ups, knee bends, exercises of the waist, running in place, pushing forward with hands on a wall while pulling the head back. At the end of a few hours of such exercising, the men had to run five miles. There was no getting out of it—Campanella followed behind the slowest man in his aging Chevy. If a man said he had a stitch in his side, Campanella would say, "Try to run that out if you can."

The following day, more of the same. McGovern said that at first he could not see the point of pushing would-be pilots like that, but after it was over, he decided that Campanella "had us hard and in shape—every muscle in our bodies." Decades later he declared that Campanella had "made a bigger contribution to saving our lives than any other single person."

Almost every Sunday, McGovern went to the Methodist church. There were Catholics and Jews attending as well, partly for the sermons from a big, jolly, fat minister, partly because the minister formed them into a separate choir—some seventy-five men strong—and had them sing such songs as the Air Force hymn, or "The Little Church in the Wildwood," or "America the Beautiful." For a third reason, the minister had the families in his congregation take one of the men home, every one of them, for Sunday dinner—fried chicken, vegetables, bread, gravy, pies, and ice cream.[10]

In the fall of 1943, on completing the course at Carbondale, McGovern went to the San Antonio air base. There was more physical conditioning, but not much more—the AAF was simply holding him and the others until it was prepared to train them in flight school. McGovern's group included two or three All-American football players. There were lots of touch football games, done in military style—the instructors would divide the students into groups. McGovern would find himself opposite a guy who was a starter at Notre Dame or some fleet-footed halfback from Southern Cal. "And you really had to hustle just to keep from looking like a fool. When those guys touched you they'd hit you a belt that would knock you off your feet." He was at San Antonio for two months.[11]

Then it was off to Muskogee, Oklahoma, to begin to learn flying the Army way. There was a dirt runway there, at the edge of town, Hatbox Field. The instructors were civilians—the AAF didn't have enough pilots yet to use its own. McGovern had an old bush pilot, Herb Clarkson, who always had a cigar in his mouth and wore a leather jacket. "The instructor had dictatorial powers," he said. "Our fate was in his hands." In Clarkson's view, "McGovern was unusual in that I never saw him angry. A lot of them would show it, especially after I chewed them out, but McGovern never did."[12] The airplane was a primary trainer—PT 19—not much different from the Aeronca McGovern had flown in the Civilian Pilot Training program at Mitchell. It had two open cockpits with the student in front, Clarkson in the rear. The PT-19 had no canopy, so the trainee and instructor wore goggles and helmets. As he was one of the few who had soloed a plane, McGovern found the twelve weeks of training to be relatively easy and was generally rated first in his class.

On June 21, 1943, Charles Watry was officially appointed an aviation cadet. He moved to preflight training at a training base near Santa Ana, California, while other trainees went to the bombardier/navigator preflight squadrons. The appointment to the rank of aviation cadet put him on a par with West Point cadets and Annapolis midshipmen. He was paid $50 a month, plus $25 for flight pay. He got to trade in his buck private's uniform for an officer's uniform, without the commission stripe on the lower sleeves. He attended classes in navigation, mechanics, and the rest, and did the preflight training. When he finished it was off to primary school. Of the original 4,931 members of his class, 787 had washed out.[13]

Walter Malone Baskin was born on Christmas Day 1924 on a cotton farm near Greenville, Mississippi. When he was in his teenage years, an air show came to Greenville. Watching the graceful and colorful swooping and rolling stunts of the World War I airplanes, he was hooked. At the time of Pearl Harbor he was a premed student at Millsaps College in Jackson. He almost immediately signed with the Air Corps to be an air cadet. Like McGovern, he had to wait until February 1943 before the Army Air Forces called him into active duty. He did his primary training at Maxwell Field, Alabama.

Baskin described his day in a March 6 letter to his parents: "They really put it to us. We get up at 5:00 A.M.—shave, make-up bed, clean room and go to formation. Then we fall out and come back to the room and polish brass & shoes, and tidy up the room then fall back out to chow formation. After breakfast is lecture and then drill, then exercise, then more drill then dinner, then immediately after dinner we go to classes until 4:30 P.M. then drill 'til supper. After supper we have two hours to study—but we have no time to study—every night we must wash our tie, wash our belt, polish all our brass and bathe. We polish our shoes at least 10 times a day with polish."[14]

Baskin trained on an AT-10. "It really flies easy," he wrote his parents. "They don't pay much attention to how you fly here, it's procedure that must be perfect." In October 1943, he did his first solo in the plane. "There are few things in the world that can compare with the feeling of accomplishment in making the first solo" was a saying of the air cadets. Baskin was training, or marching, or taking classes from 7:00 A.M. until after midnight: "There has not been a minute we could call our own." Among many other things, he went into a chamber to prepare for flying at high altitude. Oxygen was pumped out of his chamber and he went "up" to 30,000 feet, where he stayed for an hour. He took off his mask so he could "get the feel" of oxygen deprivation. "That would certainly be a pleasant way to die," he told his parents. "You just drift off and feel fine all the time." Then up to a simulated 38,000 feet for fifteen minutes, to experience the "bends," which felt to him like a severe case of rheumatism. Some men were temporarily blind and dizzy. But all recovered.[15]

John G. Smith was born in 1923 in Chicago. As a boy, model airplanes were his hobby. By the time of Pearl Harbor, he was on the track team at Notre Dame, but he immediately signed up to be an air cadet. He was called to duty in February 1943 and was lucky—he was sent to Miami Beach for his basic, where he and the other trainees had their barracks in a resort hotel on the beach that the Army Air Forces had commandeered. Smith drilled, did KP and guard duty. He walked his post on guard carrying a wooden rifle. He remembered the first of many warnings he received on VD. After a movie with graphic lessons about what could happen, a chaplain warned the trainees at length about the temptations that would come, then concluded by saying he firmly believed that "no one here would give way to the weakness of the flesh." When he finished, the flight surgeon got up to say, "The padre is right, and I'm sure all you fellows will stay away from the girls, but . . ." and proceeded to give his VD lecture.

Following basic, Smith and his class went north to the University of Tennessee at Knoxville for the College Training Detachment program. They were billeted in a women's dormitory, four to a room. Smith felt that this was just marking time because the Army "had called up more people than the system could accommodate and had to find a place to put them." The high point in his CTD program came when he received the designation "aviation student." It did not mean anything in terms of rank but it was an assurance that if they did not wash out "we would eventually see an airplane." In May 1943, it was off to Nashville for classification. He remembered the psychologist's questions. In one case, a married interviewee was asked how many times he "got" his wife on the first night. One, the man replied.

"What was the matter?" the psychologist asked, then added, "I got my wife six times." The man blushed, thought, and replied, "But you see, sir, my wife was inexperienced."

Smith survived the classification period and went to his preflight training school at Maxwell Field. He learned Morse code, aircraft identification, chemical warfare, the use of gas masks, and more. He and the other 1,000 men in his class marched everywhere in formation. Those marches, and the retreats while the flag was lowered, helped give the men a sense of solidarity. Smith especially responded to the march in review by the entire class, with its saber salute and "eyes right." He never tired of it: "There was drama and a feeling of common endeavor."[16]

In late 1943 C. W. Cooper was executive officer in a company of the 2nd Filipino Infantry. The Army was building up teams of Filipinos to go back in the Philippines, so it would take a few men from the division almost daily to form up the teams. The division was shrinking in size, until it seemed it would almost disappear. Lieutenant Cooper wanted to get into the war, not train young men but lead them in combat. The AAF, by that time, was losing officers as casualties or POWs at an unsustainable rate in the Eighth Air Force stationed in England and flying missions over Germany. It badly needed replacements as pilots, bombardiers, and navigators. At Christmas 1943, Cooper saw a notice on the bulletin board asking for volunteers. He signed up at once.

Cooper was able to skip basic and go directly to classification at Santa Ana. He scored well and qualified for pilot, bombardier, or navigator. For his preference he put down navigator—he had a civil engineering education at Texas A&M and figured that was the best-related area for him to be in when the war ended. He got his wish and was sent off to San Marcos, Texas, for navigation school.[17]

Roland Pepin got through the basic class in Greensboro, North Carolina, and then it was off to Michigan State College for primary. More marching, more tests, more classification, but he also learned to fly in a Piper Cub airplane. On his first flight he felt a mixture of excitement and fear before taking off, but "the separation of wheels from the ground was the most thrilling moment of my then young life." He flew three hours once a week. The men had to solo to pass and about a fourth washed out. Pepin passed. After classification was complete, he chose navigation school, because at that time, late 1943, there was a three-month delay for those going to flight school while those going to become navigators got started immediately. He wanted to get started as soon as possible. He also feared the war could be over if he didn't get into it right away.[18]

Cooper, Pepin, and all other navigator trainees learned how to figure out where they were from dead reckoning (assuming position from the readings of the aircraft instruments), visual (plotting the position from viewing landmarks), loran (plotting the position from long-range radio signals), and celestial (finding the position from observation of the sun, moon, planets, and stars). Celestial was the most difficult to learn but also the most reliable, especially over oceans.

There was lots of ground school, but lots of flying in AT-7s as well. The trainee made twenty navigation flights, logging 100 or more flying hours. Training planes carried three students and an instructor, plus a pilot. Day and night flights were flown. There were point-to-point courses, problem missions such as rendezvous, search, and patrol flights. There were more than 50,000 students with a peak monthly output of more than 2,500.[19]

Cooper recalled being in the air when the instructor would say, "Put your head down on your desk." After an hour, he'd say, "Okay, find where we are and get us back to base." Cooper shot a fix on Polaris with his sextant to get the latitude of the plane, then used a radio beam and the radio compass, which would point toward the station. But generally he used dead reckoning. The plane had a device that gave him the wind drift. Over the intercom he would tell the pilot to make a correction, flying just off the straight line (called "crabbing into the wind") to where he wanted to go because of the effect of the wind. There were accidents. Cooper recalled that the man everyone thought of as the ace navigator in his class took his plane into a mountainside.

In May 1944, the Army Air Forces issued a brand-new sextant called the B-12. Celestial navigational errors diminished considerably with its introduction. It was so secret that the AAF issued each navigator his own sextant, to be guarded and kept in his possession always. In addition the navigators were issued celestial navigational tables—forty books—that covered the world.

Pepin graduated on July 31, 1944, a little more than a year from his induction. He had earned his navigator's wings and was commissioned as a second lieutenant in the AAF. Cooper was about to be graduated when his superiors called him in and said, "You've been getting sick on some of your flights." Cooper admitted it. They asked, "Are you sure you want to continue flying?"

"Sure," was Cooper's reply. In October 1944, he got his navigator's wings.[20]

Donald P. Kay was nineteen years old and a student at Penn State College on November 10, 1942, when he enlisted in the AAF to become an air cadet. He had wanted to be a flier all his life. In early February 1943, he joined John G. Smith in Miami Beach, lived in a hotel, ate his meals in the hotel dining room, and got through basic. Then off to CTD at North Carolina State College in Raleigh, then to Nashville to the classification center. He qualified and picked pilot as his preference. His primary pilot training was at Ocala, Florida, in a PT-17 Stearman. He managed to solo, but after four check rides he washed out. He still wanted to fly, so he said he would like to be a bombardier and was selected.[21]

First Kay went to aerial gunner school, a six-week course at Eagle Pass, Texas. All bombardiers were trained to take the place of any gunner—waist, nose, tail, in the top or the belly turret—and also to serve as armament officer. Then he went on to bombardier school. He did okay there until they began practicing at night. But he stuck to it, because "having washed out once, I didn't want it to happen again." He graduated and got his commission.[22]

Richard Rogers wanted to be a pilot, but as he put it, the AAF "had pilots out their ears. I don't think any of us in my group made pilot training. They needed bombardiers and navigators." He was sent to the bombardier-navigator school at San Angelo, Texas, where he took bombardier training, then gunnery school. Next came Biggs Field at El Paso. At least he got to fly—by August 1944 he had logged 252 hours in the air.[23]

Robert "Ken" Barmore, born December 27, 1921, was in junior college in Newark, New Jersey, in 1941, taking courses in meteorology and navigation and aircraft engines. In 1942 he signed up with the AAF, but before his first written exam "I was scared silly." He should have been—he failed. A month later he had a second chance, and he "wanted to get into aviation so badly" he studied. He passed. He was called up in February 1943 and sent to Nashville for classification. He had never been out of New Jersey in his life, so the twenty-four-hour train ride "was kind of a traumatic experience." From Nashville he went to Maxwell Field for preflight school, where he had his first ride in an airplane. Then to South Carolina for primary flight school.

Barmore began to fly. "My instructor wasn't very good, actually." Three of his five students washed out. "His idea was to go as high as the PT could go and get it upside down and then glide. You'd be hanging there with your feet up in your face. Boy I hated it. I knew right then and there I was never going to be a fighter pilot. I knew that." He passed his twenty- and forty-hour check and went on to Shaw Field, Sumter, South Carolina, for basic flight school.[24]

Robert Hammer was a sergeant in the Army. He volunteered for the AAF and went to the San Antonio Aviation Cadet Center. When he lined up for the first inspection, the St. Louis Cardinal baseball star Enos Slaughter was in front of him. Slaughter was asked why he had signed up for the AAF. "I thought I might get to stay in the States and play baseball," he replied—and he got what he wanted. Hammer's answer to the question was, "To get out of the States and do some fighting." He too got what he wanted. He went through the training, then into the air—his first time ever—in a PT-19. He had eight hours in the air and didn't like being a pilot. He fouled up his landing patterns and was washed out.

The base commanding officer called Hammer in and asked if he would like to be a navigator. Hammer asked how long the training time would be. The CO told him a few months. He asked what else was available. Bombardier—which meant an additional few months. Anything else? Radio operator—only a six-week course. Hammer picked radio operator. He was sent to radio school at Scott Field, Illinois, just east of St. Louis. There he learned the parts of a transmitter and receiver, made a receiver, and became proficient in Morse code.[25]

Nineteen-year-old Howard Goodner, like Hammer, didn't make it to pilot training, so he also selected radio. He went to school in Illinois, where he learned electronics, mechanics, code, and the workings of a radio. He mastered the internal electronics of the radio, built generators, studied vacuum tubes and amplifiers, transformers and transmitters. He learned to disassemble a set, then reassemble it blindfolded. Morse code was hard for him, as it is for most people. "The sounds come through earphones," he wrote his parents, "and they sound like a swarm of bees."

Goodner became so proficient that the Army Air Forces offered him a posting as a radio instructor. He was tempted, as it meant no one shooting at you and you got to stay in the States. "I would take the job," he told his mother, "but you stay here too long." So he declined, explaining, "I guess I just didn't want it. I couldn't take it and stay here while Tom [his brother] is across and all the others too. I guess if you were a boy you would look at it the same as I." She didn't.

Like all radiomen, Goodner went to gunnery school, in his case to Panama City, Florida. There he shot skeet with a shotgun, then progressed to firing from moving platforms, first with small arms, then with automatic weapons and finally heavy machine guns. He learned how to operate the power-driven turrets, how to sight and swing them and their twin .50 calibers. The total number of men who graduated from gunnery schools was nearly 300,000, more than for any other AAF specialty except aircraft maintenance.

Goodner completed gunnery school on January 12, 1944, finishing in the top 2 percent of his class. His superiors thought he should reapply for the air cadet program. He said no, because learning to be a pilot would take too long. He wanted to get into the war. "Don't worry," the squadron commander assured him, "you won't miss the war." Goodner again said no.[26]

George McGovern was in love, and terribly lonely. He and Eleanor had decided they would wait until the war was over before getting married. Through correspondence, the couple agreed to move the date forward to the day he got his wings. That resolution also faltered. When he was at Muskogee, they decided to get married as soon as possible. In a letter to Bob Pennington, McGovern wrote about his reasoning. He knew it was going to be "tough on Eleanor at times, but she's got plenty of spunk." Besides, "I honestly believe, Bob, it's the best thing for both of us that we get married as soon as we can.

There's just one reason why I think so, and that is we've simply got an old fashioned love affair on our hands, and it's pretty hard to stop love even for a war."[27] Why wait? Well, first because the would-be pilots had been told not to bring their wives to Muskogee because there were no rooms available for rent and the hotels were full. Besides, the men had to live on the post and could only be with their wives Saturday nights and Sunday until 6:00 P.M. Nevertheless, McGovern walked through town, knocking on doors, asking if the residents had a room for rent. An elderly couple said they did. A few days later McGovern got a telegram saying that his father had anemia and the Red Cross was recommending that he go home. He got a three-day pass.[28]

His decision to get married right away wasn't typical, but it wasn't unusual either. The men in the armed services knew they were going into a combat zone, whether in North Africa, Europe, or the Pacific, and there was a chance—maybe a good one—that they wouldn't come back. They wanted at least a taste of married life, and for those like McGovern who had a strict, religious upbringing, it would be their first, perhaps only, chance to experience a sex life with the woman they loved. Air cadet Walter Baskin wrote his parents in June 1943, "It seems that all these cadets have the marrying craze. All those who were not already married seem to be getting married as quickly as they can."[29]

McGovern took a train to Mitchell. His father had recovered, so the family, plus Eleanor, drove to her hometown, Woonsocket, and on October 31, 1943, Reverend McGovern presided at the marriage ceremony. The couple spent their wedding night in George's old room in his family house in Mitchell. The next evening they boarded another train and went off to Muskogee. Between them, they had one bag. The train was full, as most trains were throughout the war—soldiers, young mothers with crying children, and others—so the McGoverns sat on their bag. But as they changed trains in Kansas City, McGovern put the bag down to check in at the ticket office. Someone stole it. They looked but couldn't find the thief, and at noon they boarded their train. Again, no seats were available. "I looked at Eleanor and her lip was quivering—then she started to cry." McGovern did too—"We both just bawled." When they were drained, McGovern looked at his wife, and she at him. "We started laughing at each other. I said, 'Look, a suitcase full of what we had is not the world's biggest loss.'" Eleanor said her mother's wedding veil was in there and again there were sobs.

They got into Muskogee after midnight. McGovern had to fly at 6:30 A.M. on his forty-hour check ride. They had no pajamas, no change of clothes, no alarm clock. The couple who had rented McGovern the room got up, fixed some food, and talked. The young couple told them their problems, particularly the check flight. The old gentleman said he would take care of it. He set his alarm for 5:00 A.M. and drove McGovern to the air base.

As McGovern climbed into the cockpit for his check, he thought there was no way he could do it. He was sure he would be washed out. It turned out to be the best check he ever had. Many others had already washed out. Many others still would. McGovern felt that lots of them washed out "as we got into the flying part of it and they just couldn't execute—didn't mean they weren't capable, highly intelligent guys—but they just couldn't function and do the things you had to do in an airplane."

The senior base medical officer brought all the cadets, some 2,000 of them, into an auditorium for a talk on sex and VD. The men were young and wanted sex. The doctor said that when they got their wings and commissions they would have all kinds of opportunities for sex. He told them to be careful and always wear their condoms. The AAF didn't want any of them to be sick. "I know a lot of you are saying, 'That's not going to happen to me,' but my experience is that just about every man given the right circumstance is going to yield, and every one of you is vulnerable." McGovern thought, There's no way he's talking about me, I just got married, there's no way I'm gonna cheat on Eleanor. He had hardly had the thought when the doctor went on, "The most vulnerable guys are going to be you married fellas, because you're used to sleeping with a woman and you're going to miss it more than the single fellas." Not me, McGovern thought.[30]

"Here I was a new bride," Eleanor later said, "and George was a new bridegroom." They didn't see much of each other, but on occasion the wives could come to the lounge on the base. "The husbands were all carrying books," she recalled. "They insisted that we help them cram for the tests. They'd ask us to test them on this, and test them on that. It was interesting to look around and see all the wives with books in their laps, asking their husbands questions for the test."[31]

After Muskogee, McGovern went to Coffeyville, Kansas, where he again tramped the streets until he found a kind old lady to rent a room for Eleanor. He got to fly the Basic Trainer 13—a BT-13. It had a radial engine and was a powerful plane that he liked very much. It had a stick, not a wheel. "When you opened that throttle and started down the runway," he recalled, "that plane just fairly jumped." It had far more power and much more speed than the previous planes he had flown: "It brought you definitely to a different level of flying. It required considerably more skill to handle."

Not every pilot had that skill. It was at Coffeyville that McGovern saw his first pilot killed. The officer had pulled up too fast on takeoff and stalled into a nose drop. "He just hit the runway—just *bang.* I was standing not too far from there. The fire engines were out in what seemed to me to be nothing flat. But when they pulled him out of the plane his body was just like a lobster."[32] Cadet Charles Watry wrote that an accidental death led to a cadet saying, "That is the hard way out of the program." One of his classmates was practicing S turns along a road. A twin-engine plane was doing the same thing. They had a midair collision. One of the propellers of the twin-engine craft cut off the tail of the classmate's plane, which crashed, killing him. In total, the AAF lost 439 lives in the primary flight schools during the war. In basic school there were 1,175 fatalities, while in advanced training—flying bigger, faster airplanes, with more complicated training—there were 1,888 deaths.[33]

McGovern had the skill and the luck to survive and advance. He felt he was learning, gaining all the time, doing things he could not possibly have done three months earlier, including loops and spins and rolls. He had a lieutenant as instructor—no more civilian instructors. The military instructors were usually combat veterans, some of the best the AAF had. That is what McGovern thought of his lieutenant—one of the best.[34]

In the AAF, it was said, pilots often forget the names of those they flew with, but they never forget the names of their instructors. "Mine was really tough," Ken Barmore said. He had been negative toward his first instructor, a civilian, but now he had a military flier. His name was Lieutenant Chilton.* "Boy, I would have followed that guy anyplace." Once, in basic school, Barmore was doing solo acrobatics and went into a spin. "I couldn't get out of the darn thing and I was getting panicked." He thought he would have to parachute to safety. "Then for some reason it was just like my instructor was there, telling me, Now just calm down, pull the power back, neutralize the controls, go through your spin recovery procedure." He did, regained control, and landed without a hitch. "What happened?" Lieutenant Chilton asked. Barmore told him. "He was pretty happy that I had done what he wanted me to."[35]

After completing the three months at basic school, McGovern went on to advanced school. It was at that point that his class split, with the men being prepared to become fighter pilots going to one base, the bomber pilots to another. McGovern went to a twin-engine school at Pampa, Texas, in the Panhandle.

* Chilton was killed in France in 1944, flying a P-47 in combat.

The AAF used a combination of factors to make the selection. First was the current need for fighter and bomber pilots. Then came the aptitude of the student and his physique. Some men were too big for a fighter cockpit. Further, the AAF assigned to twin-engine advanced school all men with the physical capabilities to handle the heavy controls of the bombers. Finally, and hardly used at all in making the selections, was the cadet's own preference. More men wanted to be fighter pilots, but their numbers exceeded the demand for them.36

Before leaving to go to Texas, the McGoverns had "a little celebration" with the couple living in the next apartment. McGovern wrote Pennington, "Even Eleanor and I got thoroughly drunk. It was Eleanor's first time and my third. Believe me I've never seen anything funnier than Eleanor that night. She swears she'll never touch another drop, but I had so much fun watching her and listening to her rattle off Norwegian poetry that I'll probably talk her into it again. She's just as sweet drunk as she is sober, and much more of a comic."37

At Pampa, McGovern flew the AT-17 (Advanced Trainer 17) and the AT-9. The AAF had originally developed the AT-9 as a twin-engine combat attack plane, but did not like it and sold it to Mexico. When the war brought about a desperate need for training planes the Air Force bought the AT-9 back.

It was on the AT-9 that McGovern learned to fly with the instruments on a twin-engine plane. He had a gyro that showed the airplane's attitude, such as nose up or wing down. He learned to fly formation, how to do night flying. He shot landings, setting down, then taking off without cutting the engines or coming to a stop. All kinds of things. He would take off and his instructor would get him to look out the left window and then shut down the engine on the right. McGovern had to recover and get the plane back on the level and flying straight ahead with just one engine. Or coming in for a landing, the instructor would suddenly pull the power on the left engine, producing drag on that side. He would take the AT-9 away from the field and make McGovern find his way back—he had to remember the terrain sufficiently to get to the airfield.[38]

In pilotage, navigation techniques involved relating what was on the map to what the pilot saw on the ground. Railroad lines were most helpful—they were called the "iron compass." The names of small towns on water towers were excellent navigation aids. So were instruments. The trainees learned how to use them on a Link trainer, a small airplane set on a stand that could simulate actual flight. The inside of the Link was totally dark, except for the lighted instruments. John Smith recalled learning about vertigo on his Link, and later in real flying. "The semicircular canals in your inner ear are your primary balance mechanism," he noted. "They are tuned to your eyes and gave you a sense of balance. But if in a Link or a night flight, when your eyes lose their reference points, they can fool you." If Smith made a turn when he couldn't see, then returned to a straight and level path, his inner ear would not get the signal and would tell him he was still turning, so "instrument flying requires that you trust your instruments and ignore your senses." He also learned to use radio communications between the aircraft and the control tower.[39]

The hardest part was night flying in formation. "Beginners in formation always overcontrol," Watry pointed out, "fighting to hold the proper formation position with wild bursts of power, followed by sudden frantic yanking of the throttles rearward when it appears that the wing of the lead plane is about to be chewed up by the propeller of the airplane flying the wing position." Beginners tried to hold lateral position using only the rudders, but as Watry said, in that case "the airplane is likely to wallow through the air like a goose waddling to its pond." It was worse at night. The wingman would try to stay in proper position when all he could see was a white light on the tail of the lead plane. To Watry, it seemed his airplane "floated in a void." If there were no lights on the ground and clouds were overhead, there would be no indication of movement.[40]

Because of the number of accidents, Eleanor and the other wives, living alone except on the brief weekends, were worried sick about their husbands. Every time they heard a crash or a fire engine, they were almost petrified that their man had gone down.

McGovern worked hard at his training. He had to, as he realized from reports coming out of England about the Eighth Air Force and the stories he heard from returning veteran pilots about what combat was like. And he knew the dangers of flying from the number of accidents happening around him. In October 1943, air cadet Ken Barmore was in advanced, flying an AT-9, when he got word that two of his best friends from high school were killed in a B-24 crash at Elk, California, while they were on their last training flight before going overseas.[41]

Not all accidents were fatal, but some were, and none were comical except once when an air cadet pilot got lost in his formation on a black night. Others were also lost and trying to find the lead plane. "It was awful," McGovern said. "People were scared to death." So this one pilot saw a little white light ahead. He started flying toward it, thinking that was the light on the wing of the lead plane. After a couple of minutes, his co-pilot tapped him and said, "You're going 400 miles per hour." The AT-9 could only do 150 mph. The pilot realized that what he was doing was mistaking the light, which was in fact on the ground, as being from the lead plane, and he had his AT-9 in a sharp dive. He pulled back hard, figuring that would pull the plane up, but as McGovern said, "That's not the way it works—if a plane is going down and you pull the nose up, the plane keeps mushing down for quite a ways, until it loses its downward motion."

Exactly that happened. The plane hit the ground, a big pancake in a plowed field. But the pilot, thinking he had hit the lead plane, ordered the co-pilot to bail out. The co-pilot promptly did so only to discover that his jump from the wing to the ground was over in about three feet. He yelled to the pilot, "Don't jump, I'm in a cornfield." The pilots walked back to base. The next day a truck had to pull the plane out to a grassy spot where it could take off. That night, according to McGovern, "I've never seen a human being so mad or so scared" as the colonel in charge. He pulled the trainees into the briefing room—about 150 of them—and said, "I want you sons of bitches to turn around and look at the guy next to you, because you're looking at the biggest asshole you're ever going to see in your life—and so is he." The colonel said he ought to wash the entire class out. He called it the worst class ever at Pampa. "There isn't one of you that deserves to get your wings."

There were other problems. McGovern was now an air cadet, making $125 per month. Eleanor was supposed to get $75 of that, but because of some bureaucratic screwup, she didn't, while George received only $50. So she lived on the $50, as best she could, while he lived on the base. They were too proud to tell their parents that they needed help. Instead, Eleanor lived mainly on crackers and peanut butter. "She doesn't eat much anyway," according to George, and the peanut butter filled her up cheaply. That went on for three months. To buy civilian clothes and other necessities, and to expand her diet, she got a job as a legal stenographer with a law firm.

Just before his graduation, McGovern said he wanted to fly a B-24 but that he would be happy to be a B-17 pilot. At the ceremony, the colonel who had berated the cadets and characterized them as the worst class ever said that this was the finest class that had graduated from Pampa. The men found a manila envelope on their chairs. It contained their commission—"Second Lieutenant, Army of the United States"—and their wings. Another document rated them as pilots. Still another was a personnel order that required them to participate in regular and frequent aerial flights. Charles Watry considered that a bit redundant: "That's what we came to do—wild horses couldn't hold us back now!"[42]

Eleanor was at the airfield to pin on George's wings. The new and exuberant fliers marched past the reviewing stand, singing the AAF song, really belting out the line "Off we go, into the wild blue yonder."

McGovern looked at his assignment—Liberal, Kansas.[43] Eleanor went with him. "I became a camp follower," she later said. "Ten weeks here, twelve weeks somewhere else." She again rented a small room and saw her husband on Saturday nights and during the day on Sunday.[44]

Liberal, Kansas, meant McGovern would be learning to fly B-24s. He was pleased. Others were not. Watry had put down the two-engine P-70 night fighter as his first choice, the P-61 Black Widow as his second, and the B-25 two-engine bomber as his third. But like 262 out of 290 of his classmates, he was assigned to Troop Carrier Command. Troop Carrier flew C-47 transports, either dropping paratroopers or towing gliders. "It was a great disappointment to all of us." They wanted combat in modern warplanes, not hauling paratroopers in an airplane that had been around for years (it was the DC-3 in civilian use). The twenty-eight cadets in Watry's class of 290 who got their first choice of aircraft assignments were the only ones who had asked for four-engine bombers.[45]

Lt. Walter Baskin had the same fate as McGovern but was not happy. "I have been assigned to a B-24," he wrote his parents. "That's just about as far from what I wanted as anything could be, but I can still hope."[46] On his graduation, John Smith was asked to list his choices. Knowing that his list would count for naught, he nevertheless put down the A-20 Havoc, which although a bomber had near-fighter performance and a tight turning radius. It had a crew of three, enough to keep the pilot company but not a crowd to look after, as the B-17 and B-24 pilots had to. It had a relatively limited range, so the pilot wasn't up in the air all day. As for his other choices, Smith wrote, "If you are out of A-20s, it's all right, I'll just go home." He was assigned to a B-24.[47]

Whatever their assignment, the newly commissioned officers and pilots had something to point to with pride. Of the 317,000 men who entered AAF pilot training in World War II, that is, after passing their mental and physical examinations, 193,440 were successful in graduating from advanced. More than 124,000, or about two out of five, washed out along the way, most of them in primary, fewest in advanced.[48]

The AAF in World War II recruited and trained the world's largest air force. The training was exemplary. On average, before going into combat, the men had 360 hours of flying time. For German pilots and air crews, the average was 110 hours. For the Japanese, Italians, and Russians, it was even less. The three times or more experience in the air of the Americans showed up graphically in the results of air combat during the height of the air war, 1944 and 1945.[49]

CHAPTER THREE

Learning to Fly the B-24

"THERE'S SOMETHING ABOUT that big old, lumbering B-24 that I found reassuring," George McGovern said more than a half century after he had last flown one. The B-17 Flying Fortress, another four-engine bomber that became far more famous, was easier to take off, easier to fly, easier to land, and had other advantages, such as it didn't break up or sink when it crash-landed in the sea. But the B-24 was a man's airplane. It could be sternly unforgiving. It always required, and sometimes demanded, almost superhuman strength to fly. On a long mission it could wear out even the strongest pilot. "I've seen pilots at the end of the mission that were so exhausted they literally had to be lifted out of the pilot's seat by their crew," McGovern recalled, because "they couldn't get up." He thanked God for Norm Campanella, who had gotten him into top shape at his Civilian Pilot Training exercises.[1]

The B-24 bomber was the hardest plane to fly. One pilot, Guyon Phillips, later said he "never knew a pilot who asked to fly the Lib [short for the Liberator] as a choice. There were so many other planes that were more preferable to fly." He continued, "You could never trim the son-of-a-gun, and had to horse it around constantly." Formation flying for several hours gave his left arm a workout. He steered with that arm, using his right arm for the throttles and switches. After the war Phillips found that he could arm-wrestle his college roommate, a big football player, left-handed, "but stood no chance with him right-handed."

Phillips also learned "to make no sudden moves in a B-24," because response time had to be calculated.[2]

Until 1944 the B-24 was the biggest airplane in the American fleet, and the most expensive. More aluminum was used to build the Liberators than any other craft. "The B-24 has *guts*," said the AAF in its instruction manual for pilots. "It can take it and dish it out. It can carry a bigger bomb load farther and faster, day in and day out, than any airplane that has passed the flaming test of combat." It could be sluggish, though. One pilot noted, "That plane took its own good time to do whatever it was going to do." It could take punishment as well as the B-17, a statement that no B-17 pilot or crew would agree with—but in operations, B-17 losses were 15.2 percent compared to the B-24 operational losses of 13.3 percent. Still, when the B-24 lost a single engine, "You were right now in trouble." In particular, its new wing, designed by Consolidated engineer David R. Davis and called a "Davis wing," had a distressing tendency to fold up and break off when hit by a shell.[3]

There was not just one B-24 model but rather a series of modifications. After it reached the production stage at the beginning of the war, numerous changes were made to enhance performance, changes that increased speed, altitude, range, firepower, armor, and payload. So too with almost all the AAF airplanes, which in the fighter and reconnaissance category were by 1944 equal to the enemy's best, due in part to their heavy and rugged construction. The United States did lag far behind Germany in jet planes and guided missiles, but in heavy bomber and transport planes the American superiority was beyond any challenge. And it was way ahead in numbers.

In 1939, the Army Air Corps had 1,700 aircraft and 1,600 officers. When in 1941 President Roosevelt called for the production of 50,000 military planes per year, people thought him crazy. By March 1944, over 9,000 were built in one month, 110,000 in that year. In total, the United States produced almost as many aircraft as did Britain, the Soviet Union, Germany, and Japan combined, and greatly exceeded them in total airframe weight. By March 1945, a total of 7,177 American bombers were flying combat missions in Europe, thousands of others in the Pacific.

To keep all those planes flying, the AAF had seven men on the ground for each one who flew. Seven hundred thousand graduated from courses in maintenance alone during the war. Its clerks, telephone operators, and other support personnel, mainly civilians, numbered more than one million, half of them women, many African-Americans, others handicapped.[4]

The AAF was not built for defense. Its strategic goal was to carry the war to America's enemies in their homelands. Its fighter force existed for many purposes, such as photographic reconnaissance and tactical support of ground troops by attacking enemy troops and columns, trucks, bridges, and trains on the ground, but primarily it was in combat to protect the heavy bombers from German or Japanese fighter aircraft.

The Liberator had a wingspan of 110 feet. The Davis wing's cross section was shaped like a raindrop and mounted against the top of the fuselage. It provided outstanding lift and carried self-sealing fuel cells. The fuselage was sixty-six feet long, eighteen feet high. Without a load the Liberator weighed 32,505 pounds. Its maximum weight with a full bomb load was 60,000 pounds. After improvements, it carried ten .50-caliber machine guns—two in the nose, two in the top turret, two in the tail, two in the bottom turret, all power-operated, and one manually controlled .50 caliber on each side of the waist. It could reach slightly more than 300 miles per hour, fly as high as 32,000 feet, and had a range of 2,850 miles—all exceeding the B-17's capabilities. It had four engines, mostly Pratt & Whitney rated at 1,200 horsepower, each with a turbo supercharger that increased the mass air charge of the internal combustion engines and was used to compensate for the lower density of air at high altitudes. The propeller blades were as large as a man.

The B-24 had a tricycle landing gear, with one wheel under the nose—replacing the B-17's tail wheel—with the two main wheels under the wings. It had an extensively glazed greenhouse nose. It had two bomb bays, each of which could match the B-17's single bay for capacity, and roll-up bomb bay doors, which eliminated buffeting caused by standard doors, which opened below the plane into the airstream. Its original 8,000-pound payload could be configured in four ways—four 2,000-pound bombs, eight 1,000-pound bombs, twelve 500-pound bombs, or twenty 100-pound bombs. With improvements, the payload rose to 12,800 pounds.[5] The improvements obviously increased the plane's lethality, but they did render it less stable.

Both the Eighth Air Force and later the Fifteenth Air Force flew both B-17s and B-24s. In the Pacific, by 1943 the B-24s had totally replaced the B-17s.

The B-24s were called "Flying Box Cars" because, according to some, they were the boxes in which the B-17s were shipped overseas. Others called them "New York Harbor Garbage Scows with Wings," or "Spam Can in the Sky." Additional nicknames were "Banana Boat," "Flying Brick," "Pregnant Cow," and "The Old Agony Wagon." The most distinguishing feature of the B-24 was its twin tail, much scoffed at by the men who flew the B-17s—as, indeed, was almost everything about the B-24. But it could carry a larger bomb load for longer distances than the B-17, with a crew of the same size—ten men. The AAF official history described it as "an ungainly-looking ship on the ground, but it had a grace of its own in the air."[6]

————

It was almost universally agreed that the B-24 was the hardest plane to fly. The AAF knew that and its training program reflected the fact. "I don't think there's a person alive that could fly a formation of B-24s for ten, twelve, thirteen hours that wasn't trained the way we were," McGovern declared. "I don't think he could do it."[7]

The first time McGovern climbed onto the flight deck and sat at his seat, he was confronted by a bewildering sight. There were twenty-seven gauges on the panel, twelve levers for the throttle, turbocharger, and fuel mixture, four on the pilot's side on his right, four on the co-pilot's side on his left. The wheel, or "yoke" as it was called, was as big as that on a large truck. There were over a dozen switches, plus brake pedals, rudders, and more.

Beyond familiarizing himself with the instruments on the flight deck, McGovern was going to have to learn about the remainder of the craft, from the wheels to the nose to the trailing (when in flight) aerial, to the top and ball turret, and everything inside. Before taking off, he had to do a visual check of the entire plane. Further, he needed to know the responsibilities and operations of every crew member, and be capable of doing each of their tasks, from the gunners to the radioman to the engineer to the navigator to the bombardier. Every one of these men were, like the pilots, cramped into the smallest possible position, because in the B-24 no space was wasted.

After he got his wings and commission, McGovern went to the AAF base at Liberal, Kansas, for transition training. This would be the next to the last stage of his becoming a B-24 pilot. Because of the heavy losses the bombers had suffered in Europe, particularly on the August 1, 1943, mission against the oil refineries in Ploesti, Romania, the pilots' training time was cut back by a month. The program involved not only learning to fly a complex, high-performance aircraft, but also the acquisition of flying techniques and complete knowledge of the plane and the functions of the crew, all preliminary to operational unit training. In addition, the program involved ground instruction in equipment and practical maintenance, weather, radios, aircraft weight and balance, bombing approach procedures, and the general duties of a pilot.[8]

In October 1943, Lt. Walter Hughes completed his basic training. He applied for multiengine advanced flying school, partly because "my temperament was not really suited to being a hot pilot," but also because "the grapevine reported that those who applied for single-engine school ended up in bombers anyway, but as co-pilots." He went to the AAF field at Marfa, Texas, where he was handed a release that began, "This is not a sporting man's war—get hard, get tough, and get mean!" Then it was off to B-24 school at Kirtland Field, near Albuquerque, New Mexico. He rushed to the flight line to see his first B-24 and was awed: "It was HUGE." It had 4,800 horsepower and all the planes he had flown before had 450 horsepower. When the plane moved on the ground, "it waddled." On his first flight, when the instructor pushed the throttles forward, Hughes was smashed back into his seat, which "sent tingles through every nerve." But the real thrill "came when I did it myself." Engine power control was complex, including throttle, fuel air mixture, propeller pitch, and turbocharger setting. Takeoff required 2,500 revolutions per minute; climb power was 2,400 rpms. There were a number of cruise settings. And much more.[9]

The first time he flew in a B-24, Lt. Donald R. Currier, a navigator, recalled, "I was completely amazed by its monstrous size, its four mighty engines, and all of the many instruments on its flight display."[10]

McGovern would have one instructor through the program, and he was crucial. When he arrived in Liberal and got Eleanor settled in a room and himself in the barracks, a colonel told him that he would find his name in the operations room on the blackboard underneath the name of his instructor. Along with his classmates, he ran to the board. Each instructor had four students chalked in below his name. McGovern's name was right at the top on his list. He saw that First Lieutenant Ray would be his instructor and wondered if he was related to Norman Ray, the man who had talked him into taking flying lessons back at Dakota Wesleyan.

As McGovern was wondering if Ray was related to his college

friend, the instructor came into the room, and it was Norman Ray himself. Ray had joined the AAF immediately after completing the course at Wesleyan and been in the service for a year and a half. When he completed his training he was so good a pilot that the AAF, instead of sending him overseas, had made him an instructor on the B-24 bomber.* "Didn't surprise me," McGovern said, "because the guy just ate, slept, and breathed flying."

Ray barely smiled at McGovern (who found out later that Ray had asked for him to be his student). McGovern thought, I can't call him "sir," it will make me feel ridiculous. But he thought again and said, "Well, sir, I'm glad that I got assigned to you."

Ray replied, "Well, don't think it's going to be easy, because it isn't. This is a tough course here and you're not going to find many easy hours here at this field with this airplane." He gave McGovern a hint of a smile but no flash of recognition at all. "And I can tell you," McGovern said, "he never gave me one tiny little break—not a bit. If everybody else had to do a maneuver ten times, I had to do it fifteen."

McGovern had a lot to learn, Ray had a lot to teach. "He was just smooth as glass," McGovern recalled, "the way he could move that bomber around." Ray taught McGovern how to read all those gauges, how to use the switches, how to manipulate the flaps and use the rudders, how to take off and land, how to keep the plane level, how to bank it, how high and how fast to fly it, and that there was nothing more useless to a pilot than altitude above, runway behind, or gasoline down at the airfield. Whenever McGovern made a mistake, or hesitated, Ray gave him hell.

Once on a night flight Ray was teaching him how to use the radio

---

*Ray pestered the AAF with requests for combat duty and finally got his wish. In early 1945 he joined Col. Paul W. Tibbetts with the specially trained 509th Composite Group flying modified B-29s. Tibbetts had once been General Eisenhower's pilot and had the reputation of being the best flier in the AAF. The 509th carried the atomic bombs. Ray was scheduled to be the pilot on the fifth run, had more than two been necessary to bring about Japan's surrender. He stayed in the Air Force and became a colonel.

compass on the B-24, how to get back to base and how to pick up another base and other points, how to navigate with the help of the instruments, and so on. He went over the procedures with McGovern several times, then when they were fifty miles or more away from Liberal, he sat back in his pilot's seat and said, "Okay, take me home."

It was a dark night. There were no lights on the ground. McGovern almost froze. He couldn't remember anything. Nothing worked.

"Well, George," Ray said, "let me put it to you this way—you either take us back to that field or I'm going to wash you out." There was no hint of a smile. As McGovern remembered it, Ray continued, "I can't in good conscience graduate you from here and say that you're ready to fly a four-engine bomber with ten human beings on board—I'm just not going to do it. If you can't find that field, then just go get your things and you're through with the Air Force unless there's some other post you want here, but it isn't going to be flying, it's not going to be as a pilot."

McGovern thought about all the work he had put in, all that time, and about how Ray was one of his good friends from college, and here he was telling McGovern that he was all through. He couldn't believe that Ray was going to do this to him. He looked at Ray again and could not detect any yield or compassion.

Ray asked McGovern a couple of questions about his instruments, "sort of elementary ones," McGovern recalled. Then it clicked. McGovern remembered what he had been taught and what he needed to do, "and after the second question I knew exactly how to do it." He set a heading, "and boy was I glad when the lights started to twinkle ahead and I could see those runways coming up out of the darkness."

It was just as Ray had warned, hard flying. "I can't recall once that he ever let his guard down." At a function after the war, Ray told Eleanor that "all I was trying to do was to keep George alive in combat. I figured that the harder I rode him, the better his chances of surviving missions over enemy targets."[11]

For Lt. John Smith, transition school was at Maxwell Field, Montgomery, Alabama. There he immediately learned that the B-24 was "a giant step up" from the airplanes he had flown in advanced training. His instructor was Lt. Robert Baskerville. Smith rode together with three other pilots, taking turns at the controls. Baskerville said it saved time and gave them a chance to learn from the other guys' mistakes. They began by learning how to take off and how to land, mainly by doing touch-and-go landings until Baskerville was satisfied they were not going to kill him or themselves, then went on to cross-country navigation flights.

Smith's second cross-country flight "was the most important trip of my life." Baskerville arranged a trip from Maxwell Field to Mitchell Field, near Milwaukee, Wisconsin, to pick up a bomb bay load of beer. Smith called his girl friend, nineteen-year-old JoAnn Stanton of Chicago, and arranged to meet her during the beer run. She was there. He asked her to marry him. To his surprise and joy, she said yes.[12]

After completing transition school at Liberal, McGovern moved on to Lincoln, Nebraska. It was mainly a holding base and Eleanor recalls it as "the one fun time we had" during their nomadic times from 1943 to 1944. George was doing no flying and aside from his ground school classes in first aid, "global sanitation and hygiene," and other things, he had free time. Eleanor's twin sister, Ila, came down from South Dakota for a visit. Eleanor lived in yet another rented room while George lived in the barracks.

To his friend in the Army, Bob Pennington, now stationed in England, McGovern wrote, "I should have gotten married a year ago. I don't see how anyone could be any happier than Eleanor and I are. When we're together on weekends, the time just seems to race away." A week later he wrote, "Having her here has really made an awfully big improvement in my morale. Of course those days when I can't see her go by pretty slowly, but then all the days were like that before we got married. Eleanor seems to be happier than she has been since I've known her, so things are really working out swell for us. If being married under the handicap of a war is so wonderful—it must be nothing short of marvelous in peace time. Bob, let's hurry up and get this thing over with so we can really start living again."13

At Lincoln, McGovern found out who was on his crew. The commanding officer called all the pilots together and gave them a list of the crews they would have, with the man's name, the position he was going to fly, his age, and the town he was from. McGovern drew Sgt. Isador Irving Seigal as his tail gunner. Other gunners were Sgt. William "Tex" Ashlock from Hereford, Texas; Sgt. Robert O'Connell, nose gunner from Brattleboro, Vermont; and Sgt. William McAfee, ball turret gunner from Port Huron, Michigan. ("I always thought the ball turret was the most terrifying place to ride on that plane," McGovern later said. "You're just suspended there above the earth in a glass compartment." One compensation: the ball turret gunner had a fabulous view.) Sgt. Ken Higgins was the radio operator.

All these men were sergeants because the AAF learned early that when the crews of the B-17s and B-24s of the Eighth Air Force bailed out over enemy territory and were taken prisoner (although many of them managed to evade and escape the Germans via Spain thanks to the French underground), the stalags where they were imprisoned were run by the *Luftwaffe*. It was German practice to treat sergeants who became POWs different from and better than corporals or privates. Further, *Luftwaffe* chief Hermann Göring, who had a romantic view of the "knights of the sky" after his World War I experience as an ace, insisted that the stalags holding downed airmen be superior to stalags that held infantry. So the AAF decided that any man who flew over enemy territory should be a sergeant or an officer.

Sgt. Mike Valko was listed as McGovern's flight engineer. He was from Bridgeport, Connecticut. McGovern was startled when he saw Valko's age—thirty-three—and thought, There is no way an old guy like that is going to listen to me (McGovern was twenty-one). That day McGovern started growing a beard and a mustache so that he would look older.

Lt. Sam Adams, from Milwaukee, would be McGovern's navigator-bombardier (by this stage of the war, the two functions were done by one man). Lt. Bill Rounds would be the co-pilot.

McGovern knew their names, ages, and hometowns, but he had not yet met them. Meanwhile he and Eleanor had a bit of a chance to enjoy married life.

One thing, though: she wanted to get pregnant. He asked her, "Eleanor, don't you think that it would be better to wait until the war is over?" He was going into combat. He thought he would have thirty-five missions to fly and that there was a good chance he might not come home.* There was also a chance that he might, but considering the casualties the Eighth Air Force was sustaining, which were growing alarmingly close to nearly one half of the combat crews, it was a shaky proposition. In addition, her father had told George he hoped the two of them were not thinking about bringing a child into the world when George was going into combat. But that same point was a motivation for Eleanor. As he said a half century later, "If there was any doubt at all about my coming back she wanted to be sure that she had a child, a part of me."

To Bob Pennington, McGovern wrote that "Eleanor's never even breathed a whimper or complaint of any kind. I've never known a person like her. She will never stop going up in my estimation. I love her more every time another day goes by. I really believe we'll be more in love and more romantic on our golden wedding anniversary than we are now. Ain't love grand?"14

Then he thought, Well, if that is what she wants, why not? She has followed me to every post I've been at, every time I moved she's been

---

* The number of required missions was raised to thirty-five from the twenty-five originally assigned.

willing to be there and if this is what she wants, so be it. She said it was what she wanted and that now was the time to do it. He decided to go ahead, and it was done. McGovern wrote Pennington after Eleanor became pregnant, "I'm proud of the prospect of being a dad, Bob. It's one of the warmest and best feelings I've ever had. Eleanor is happier than I've ever seen her before."15

Lt. Walter Shostack, like McGovern, learned to fly a B-24 in Liberal, Kansas, then went on to Lincoln, Nebraska, to meet his crew. They consisted of a tail gunner from Lubbock, Texas, Bob Brewer; an engineer named Jack Keppo from Roswell, New Mexico; a radio operator, Alexander Dubbets, from Akron, Ohio; an ex-Canadian pilot named Charles C. Shrapshire III as the belly gunner; a navigator from Illinois, Lijo Strander, Jr., who insisted on being called Joe; a bombardier from Dover, Delaware, named Edward "Eddie" Rider; and a co-pilot from Windsor, Connecticut, named Joseph Delinski. Shostack was a Russian immigrant. Wherever they came from, they were all in the AAF now, and that fact was paramount. They, and other airmen, struck Shostack as "a cross section of the United States. They were good and bad and stupid and bright and immoral and moral, each slice of humanity." But, he added, "the one lesson we all learned was that you took care of your buddy because he was going to take care of you." They trained together with McGovern and his crew and hundreds of others at Mountain Home, Idaho. It was during this training that Shostack lost one of his high school classmates, Richard Schorn, when Schorn flew his B-24 into the side of a mountain, a not-uncommon hazard.16

Lieutenant Roland Pepin, the navigator, joined his crew at March Field in Riverside, California. The men came from all parts of the country. From the time they got together, "we lived, slept, ate, worked, and played together. We would share our lives until death or the war's end." Nineteen-year-old Pepin was the youngest member. Lieutenant Duncan was twenty-six years old. To Pepin that seemed "ancient," but the two men formed a close bond. "Duncan liked to drink," Pepin recalled, "and I didn't, so I made sure he kept out of trouble."

They flew training missions all around the California coast and out over the Pacific. All the crew practiced their individual skills, bombing runs, takeoffs and landings, air-to-air gunnery, navigation, radio work, and whatever else it took to make them combat-ready. After some months of this they got orders to go to Europe. First, though, they had a ten-day leave. Eight of them pooled their money and went to a resort at Lake Arrowhead, where Pepin said they "had a first-class bang-up time. We lived as kings and crammed all the pleasures one could have into our last fling before joining the battle. Duncan, who had a lot of manly experience, rewarded his young watchdog (me) by making sure I learned about life quickly. I fell in love at Lake Arrowhead. I fell in love several times in California before it was time to say goodbye to Chris, Susan, Lori, and Amy."17

It was critical for each crew to develop and maintain a close bond. They lived together, sergeants in one place, the officers in another. Irritating habits could magnify and ruin their relationship, things like their accents, the music they liked, the curse words they used, their taste in women and liquor and books or comics, their politics, their bragging or their being unusually modest, their way of washing or brushing their teeth, the way they wore their clothes, the packages they received from home, how they played sports or which sport they liked, their jokes, what made them laugh or cry, anything and everything.

They were on their way to being men at war. They would need to have a closeness unknown to civilians, no matter what the civilians did. Their lives would be at stake. Every one of them had to depend, absolutely, on everyone else doing his job right. They had to not only get along with one another but also to have unquestioning faith in each other. Yet they were thrown together. Before being assigned to their crew, most if not all of them had never known anyone else in their airplane. All they had in common was being in the AAF, an unquenchable desire to fly, a never or seldom spoken patriotism, and—overwhelmingly—being young. Most were twenty-two years old or younger.

Lt. Donald Kay, a bombardier, met his crew at Biggs Field, El Paso, Texas, in April 1944. The co-pilot assigned to the plane was a married man but "he was trying to set a record for sex in his first week and scared the hell out of the rest of the crew." The sergeants got together and came to Kay and the navigator to ask them to tell the pilot that the co-pilot had to go. They gladly did so and shortly thereafter he was replaced. One of the waist gunners was an alcoholic "and we dumped him too." The crew, as finally assembled, came from Kansas (pilot), Illinois (co-pilot), Indiana (navigator), Connecticut (Kay, the bombardier), and the sergeants from Wisconsin, Mississippi, New York, West Virginia, and New Jersey.

Of the seventeen original crews that began training when Kay's crew did in May 1944, only six finished the war. In Europe, his 465th Bomb Group lost thirty-five crews. His was the only one of the four crews that arrived in Europe on July 22, 1944, to finish. Of the other three bombardiers, two were killed in action and the other became a POW.[18]

———

Lt. Walter Baskin had hoped to be a fighter pilot, but to his dismay was assigned to a B-24 as a co-pilot. Beginning in January 1944, he trained at the air base in Blythe, California. His letters home reveal how tough it was. January 3: "We have been flying this B-24 day and night since we got here and they keep us pretty busy. It's 9:00 P.M.

now and I have to go to Link from 10 to 11 to-night. Then get up pretty early in the morning so you can see that sleep doesn't mean anything around here. All you do is work and if you don't work there's nothing else to do so you just work."

The AAF did not have enough B-24s for the demand. February 10: "When we are scheduled to fly we have trouble getting an airplane that will fly. There are plenty of planes here, but they are old and over half of them are always on the ramp being repaired. We had a nice scheduled cross country flight all fixed up to go to Santa Maria yesterday, but one of the engines was throwing so much oil that we wouldn't take it up." Still the crew kept busy. February 11: "Every third day we go twenty hours straight and the two days in between are seventeen hours long. . . . We fly every day and sometimes we don't get home 'til 3 A.M. but we still get up and go again. I believe combat will be a rest after this."

On March 2 he wrote: "We are winding up our training here and the last part will be almost entirely devoted to formation flying. When you get to combat if you can't fly formation you are just a 'dead duck.'" As Consolidated, Ford, and the other makers of the plane began to turn them out in record numbers, Baskin's craft improved. He was glad to tell his parents, "This ship is brand-new and has just twenty-eight hours of flying time on it. It is going to carry us a long way and then bring us back, so it gets first consideration in all cases."

He liked his fellow officers. Baskin came from a Mississippi cotton farm. The pilot, Lt. Russell Paulnock, was the son of a Pennsylvania coal miner. Baskin described Paulnock as "a good boy and a cautious pilot." The bombardier was Lt. James Bartels, from Cleveland, Ohio, the son of a preacher. He was married and his wife was at Blythe with him. The crew had been practicing dropping bombs and Bartels was "a right good bombardier." The navigator was Lt. Earl Barseth. "He is from New England and a typical Yankee," Baskin wrote.

In mid-March, Baskin's B-24 made cross-country trips. He wrote his parents on March 13, more or less unbelievingly, "Last week we flew over the Grand Canyon and Boulder Dam and that is really a beautiful sight. We flew for hours over stretches of desert and waste land where *nobody* lives."

In one letter, Baskin declared that "this B-24 is not my dream ship," but he confessed "it certainly packs a wallop."

In April, his training completed, Baskin joined McGovern at Lincoln, Nebraska, where his plane was weathered in for a few days. Then in the middle of the month the sky was clear, so it was off to Florida in formation with his bomber group on its way to Europe. Co-pilot Baskin was flying when the plane passed over his farm near Vaiden, Mississippi. Baskin pealed his Liberator out of formation and buzzed the place. He scared the wits out of all the chickens, cows, pigs, and mules and saw his dad standing in the backyard, puffing on his pipe, watching. Then he buzzed his school, practically at window level, to give Bobby, his little brother, a big hello. Bobby, hearing the plane roar, jumped up from his desk saying, "That's my brother," and ran out to the playground to wave goodbye to his big brother as Baskin flew off on his way to combat. The chickens didn't lay and the cows went dry for a week, and Bobby got suspended from school.

For Baskin it was fun, but it wasn't like being the pilot of a fighter airplane. As he wrote his parents, "This co-pilot job is not what I was raised to be."[19]

———

Ken Barmore had his first look at and ride in a B-24 on December 30, 1943. He was a co-pilot. His pilot was Lt. Jim Connelly, from Texas, "who was just the greatest guy." Riding with them at first was an instructor who was an American but had joined the Royal Air Force before Pearl Harbor and flew a Wellington bomber over Europe. After America entered the war he came home to join the AAF, and Barmore felt "we were real lucky to have him, he was a neat guy." To Barmore's discomfort, he didn't get to do much of the flying: "They just threw the co-pilots in the right seat and learn as you can." He tried and tried again to move over to the left seat, but he had not gone through transition school so his chances "were practically nil." He did a lot of formation flying and bombing practice. "I got to feeling pretty comfortable in the airplane" but Connelly would seldom allow him to take off or land.[20]

———————

Radioman Sgt. Robert Hammer met his fellow crew members at Mitchell Field, New York, then went with them to Georgia for flight training on their B-24. Formation flying for his pilot and indeed all the other pilots was difficult. Much of the air time was devoted to learning how to do it, despite a high accident rate. Three B-24s were lost during practice, killing thirty men. On one occasion while flying in formation, Hammer was sending blinking signals from the waist window to the radio operator in the plane to the right. He had just signed off when another plane was sucked into that plane by the prop wash. It tore the fuselage in half. Hammer saw men, including the radio operator he had just communicated with, flying in one direction and their parachutes in another. All ten were killed, but the other plane managed to land safely.

After Hammer's plane landed, and just before debriefing, his pilot came up to him with tears in his eyes. He asked if Hammer didn't think they were making the planes fly too close together. After the debriefing his pilot was grounded for his emotional response. Other men were lost, including the originally assigned navigator, who took the plane into a gunnery area on the East Coast on a night mission. Hammer commented, "We had been shot at before even getting out of the States." With the replacements, the crew flew to New Hampshire, got a new B-24, and flew it to Gander Field, Newfoundland, then off to Europe.[21]

———————

Sgt. Howard Goodner, a radioman, was sent to Buckley Field, Colorado, to be assigned to a crew. There he took refresher courses in communications, target identification, and first aid, but they were mainly to kill time. In June 1944, his orders arrived, sending him to Westover Field, near Springfield, Massachusetts, a long train trip. There he met his fellow crew members.

Goodner's pilot was Lt. Richard Farrington, from St. Louis, a tall man who exuded self-confidence. Farrington had enlisted when he was nineteen years old and had not yet reached twenty-one. The co-pilot, Lt. Jack Regan, was twenty. From Queens in New York City, he was nicknamed Abe because of his deep voice and uncanny resemblance to the young, beardless Lincoln. The bombardier, Lt. Chris Manners from Pittsburgh, was twenty-three. The sergeants came from all over and ranged in age from eighteen to twenty-eight. Eighteen-year-old Albert Seraydarian, an Armenian-American, was from Brooklyn. His "dem's" and "dose's" and other Brooklynese were so thick the southern-born Goodner could barely understand him. His nickname, unsurprisingly, was "Brooklyn." Another gunner was eighteen-year-old Jack Brennan from Cliffside Park, New Jersey. The nose gunner was Harry Gregorian, like Seraydarian an Armenian-American, but from Detroit. The flight engineer, Jerome Barrett, twenty years old, came from New York City. His father owned a chemical company that occupied two entire floors of Rockefeller Center and his next-door neighbor was Broadway star Ethel Merman. Goodner liked him at once—the two boys, one from Central Park West, the other from Cleveland, Tennessee, hit it off at once. Bob Peterson, the ball turret gunner, was the "old man," married with two kids.

In this way Americans from all over the country, from far different backgrounds, got to know one another. For every one of them, as for McGovern and his crew, or Baskin and his, or Barmore and his, it was a broadening experience. As was the war, which had taken them to various parts of the United States in travels most of them never thought they would have, and was about to take them off to Europe.22

Except for the pilot and co-pilot, most members of the crew had never before been in a B-24, and they had much to learn. The crews found that just entering their B-24 was difficult. As Thomas Childers described the process in his book *Wings of Morning*, "The bombardier, navigator, and nose turret gunner were forced to squat down, almost on hands and knees, and sidle up to their stations through the nose- wheel well of the ship." Inside, the three men had to squeeze themselves into a cramped compartment. The bombardier squatted on a small seat right behind the gunner, where he hunched over the bombsight or simply sat on the floor. The navigator sat at a tiny retractable stool, really too small to sit on, with the navigator's table holding his charts in front. It was little more than a thin shelf on the bulkhead that separated the nose from the flight deck. At eye level, he could see the feet of the pilot and co-pilot.

Childers goes on: "The other crew members entered the plane by crawling up through the open bomb bay doors, about three feet off the ground. Once inside they would stand upright, step onto the narrow catwalk, then move forward onto the flight deck or back into the waist." The radioman sat at a small desk facing his radio sets, just behind and below the co-pilot. The engineer stood between the pilot and co-pilot at takeoff, helping to monitor the engine and fuel gauges. In the air he took his position behind the pilot and just across from the radioman. When required, he climbed into the top turret, where he stood, his feet on a metal bar inches above the radioman's head.

The waist gunner, the ball turret gunner, and the tail gunner used the catwalk to get to their positions. The tail gunner, standing on a tiny platform, slipped his legs into the turret. There was not enough room for him to wear his parachute. The waist gunner—two before mid-1944, one thereafter as the danger from enemy fighter planes diminished—stood. At altitude the bitterly cold wind howled through the open windows of the waist, making this position and that of the ball and tail turret gunners miserable, covering them and their guns with a thin veil of frost.

The ball turret was, as McGovern said, the most physically uncomfortable, isolated, and terrifying position on the plane. "The gunner climbed into the ball, pulled the hatch closed, and was then lowered into position." They were suspended beneath the plane, staring down between their knees at the earth. Although all ball turret gunners were small, few of them had enough room to wear a parachute. If a bailout was necessary, they relied on the waist gunner to engage the hydraulic system to raise the turret and help them out and into their parachutes. That is what is called trust.

Adding to the extreme discomfort, the B-24 was not pressurized and at above 10,000 feet the men had to wear their ill-fitting rubber oxygen masks for hours at a time. They wore electrically heated flight suits, plugged into rheostats, but when the system shorted out or was damaged the suits were useless. Thus the men wore in addition layers of bulky clothing, which made movement within the claustrophobic aircraft even more awkward and agonizingly slow.

At all AAF bases where B-24s were involved in the training, the pace was intense, the practice flying seemed endless. Most dangerous was formation flying at night. Sergeant Goodner told his parents, "The B-24s are nice ships, but we lose a lot of them. Since I got here we have lost seven ships." Once when the squadron commander of a night flight, a veteran of thirty-five missions over Germany, called out to the pilots in the formation, "Close it up, close it up," Lieutenant Farrington edged his plane closer and closer. Goodner heard the waist gunner mutter on the intercom, "Jesus, I can shake hands with their tail gunner now."[23]

A week after arriving in Lincoln, McGovern met his crew. His beard and mustache were just getting started. He was worried about "whether or not I could convince the crew that they were safe in the hands of a twenty-one-year-old pilot."[24] His co-pilot, Ralph "Bill" Rounds, wanted to be a fighter pilot. "Everything about the guy said fighter pilot," one of his friends recalled.[25] But the AAF decided against it and washed him out of fighter pilot training. His superiors told him that if he wanted to fly it would be as a co-pilot on a B-24. He took the option.

At first, McGovern was a bit concerned, because when Rounds had the controls "he'd try to fly that B-24 like a fighter plane. He'd whip it around and the crew was scared to death of him." But as the practice runs went forward, McGovern came to have great respect for his ability, because Rounds became "a very good formation flyer—he could tuck that wing right in there and just hold it."

On the ground, McGovern discovered just how different the two men were in their personalities. "He was a clown if there ever was one," McGovern said of Rounds. "You couldn't be around him without laughing." Rounds was a rollicking, fun-loving adventurer, with an eye for the women. McGovern marveled at the speed with which he "could move from the air base to the business of heavy romance with total strangers." He would listen to Rounds's accounts of his "spectacular multiple achievements in a single evening that were vastly beyond my area of experience."

Once they were in a car in town, with Rounds driving and McGovern in the backseat. Rounds spotted two young women and immediately opened the front door and jumped out of the car in pursuit. He forgot to put on the hand brake and the car continued rolling down the street. McGovern climbed into the driver's seat and narrowly averted hitting a parked truck. By the time he got the car stopped, "Bill was back with a girl on each arm."[26]

Despite their divergent personalities, the two men would be living together, fighting together, and it was critical that they like and respect each other. They did. Rounds said later that "I was very pleased with everybody when our crew made up, but George was kind of a big daddy, a big brother type." Rounds got to know Eleanor. McGovern called her "Bunny," he remembered—a temporary nickname—and Rounds thought "she was just a slick little gal. We just all loved Eleanor." He was aware of their differences. "I was a single guy and sort of out on the prowl," he said. "George was never one to put a damper on a party, but I never saw him drink much." On June 27, he wrote his parents, "McGovern's a very nice, refined, quiet man and I know that we will make a fine team."27

On September 1, 1944, McGovern also wrote to Rounds's parents. As a reassuring note, he opened, "Scarcely a day goes by that Bill doesn't quote his dad on some subject, or voice an opinion of his mother's." Continuing, he admitted "we were all very green when we first started out here. . . . We are working with a great bunch of boys. Our crew spirit is growing every day." As for their son, he wrote, "I couldn't have asked for a better man to fly with than Bill. He hasn't complained about being assigned to a B-24 and was good in flying formation. I feel I have had more than my share of the luck in getting a good co-pilot." As to what lay ahead, "I guess the only way to look at the matter is to realize that the sooner we go overseas and finish our missions the sooner we'll be back in the U.S.A. for good. That's the thing we all want the most."28

The other officer in McGovern's crew was the navigator-bombardier, Lt. Sam Adams. He was McGovern's age and intended to go to a seminary after the war to study to become a Presbyterian minister. He was quiet in manner, intelligent, well-read, intense. He and McGovern hit it off immediately and they became close. "He was a very deep guy," McGovern said. "I could really talk to him."

Sgt. Bill McAfee, the ball turret gunner, was happy-go-lucky by nature and already popular with the rest of the crew. Sgt. Ken Higgins, the radioman, had a wit that could deflate pomposity no matter the source. Sgt. Bob O'Connell, the nose gunner, showed at a poker game the night they all met that he was the gambler of the crew. "Bob wasn't any older than any of us," one of the crew said, "but when he played poker, you would have thought he was thirty." Sgt. Bill Ashlock, Tex, the waist gunner, had a soft drawl and a competent manner.

The flight engineer, Mike Valko, was the sergeant who, because of his age—thirty-three—had caused McGovern to worry about being his commander. He turned out to be not only the oldest man in the crew—by ten years—but the shortest, at less than five foot five. He had grown up the hard way in Bridgeport, where he had held a variety of jobs, including roustabout at a carnival. He claimed that he could have done better in life had he been a little taller. He had started drinking at a young age and he continued to imbibe. Still, McGovern found that "he was submissive to the slightest wish I had. He just couldn't do enough to please me." McGovern shaved off his beard and mustache.

Sgt. Isador Seigal, the tail gunner, was the eccentric of the crew. He slept with a loaded .45 pistol under his pillow and was seen walking around the barracks with a bayonet strapped around his middle but otherwise naked. With six enlisted men crowded into one tent, such bizarre behavior was not always welcome.

In late June 1944, after a couple of weeks at Liberal, the McGovern crew went to Mountain Home, Idaho, where again their training time was cut by a month in order to get them into combat faster. They practiced formation flying, night flying, practice bombings using sandbags with a small powder charge and a detonator to indicate where they were hitting, landings and takeoffs, and flew and flew and flew. With the other planes in their group, they would go in formation to the initial point, or IP, where they would make a sharp, sometimes 90 degree, turn. The technique was used to get them over the target in a tight formation so that all their bombs—which were released by Adams when he saw the lead plane's bombardier drop his bombs—would come down in the same place or at least nearby. A further purpose of the technique was to fool the enemy as to their destination. After departing the IP no turns or evasive maneuvers could take place regardless of weather, enemy aircraft, or ground fire.

After crossing the IP and turning, Adams with his Norden bombsight had control of the plane—although McGovern could override him if necessary—and the requirement was to fly straight and level and wingtip to wingtip to make a good pattern. The Adams-McGovern team became proficient at it.29

Eleanor and George lived in a barracks for married men, so for the first time they had a room together. Because the formation flying was so demanding and led to so many accidents, Eleanor worried about her husband. She was right to. Twice as many air officers died in battle than in all the rest of the Army, despite the ground force's larger size. In addition, in the course of the war, 35,946 airmen died in accidents. That was 43 percent of all accidental deaths in the wartime Army. In 1943 alone, 850 airmen died in 298 B-24 accidents training in the States, leaving the survivors "scared to death of their airplanes." Those in training always knew that pilot error could result in death for an entire crew. Wives, girlfriends, and parents of the fliers were at least apprehensive, if not terrified, of the risks their loved ones were running. "We'd hear sirens and we always knew what they meant," Eleanor said. "There were a lot of crashes because they were training these men so rapidly." She became ill—possibly morning sickness, possibly from worry—and had to be hospitalized for a few days.30

Once, while flying in formation, McGovern's squadron was practicing warding off an attack. A two-engine B-25 dove on the B-24s. The B-24 pilots expected the B-25 to go under their formation, but instead the plane keep coming and collided head-on with a Liberator. There was an explosion that took out two other B-24s. Four bombers were just gone. Fortunately they did not have full crews in them—only the gunners and the pilot—but twenty-four men were dead. McGovern got back to his room, badly shaken, but what happened next made everything worse. Everybody at Mountain Home knew about the crash but no one knew who had been killed. The base chaplain had the duty of informing the wives of the married men. "It was just the most awful night of my life," McGovern said. The chaplain, carrying a list of the men killed, came into the married men's barracks and started knocking on doors. As soon as the wife opened the door and saw him, she screamed. "Just these awful cries of anguish." Some of the widows were pregnant. A half century later, McGovern said "I can still hear them yet."

McGovern had other problems as well, personal ones with his crew. Seigal was constantly suffering from airsickness. "I was scared every minute I was up in the plane," he acknowledged. McGovern talked to him and settled him down—some.

McGovern knew his plane. "I could do a little of everything," he said. "I knew when the crew were screwing up." Once Valko made a serious mistake. Standing between the pilot and co-pilot, he decided to experiment by hitting the "crash bar," which had the effect of grounding out all four engines on the plane. McGovern immediately flipped the switch back. Fortunately, the engines caught after the big plane had made a sickening lurch. Rather than chewing Valko out in front of the crew, he waited until they were on the ground before talking to him.

A few days later, Sergeant Valko reported to McGovern that the crew feared Seigal might do something drastic with his pistol. McGovern made Seigal turn it over, along with a knife, and sent him to talk to the base psychiatrist. He did and was declared mentally healthy, but from then on there was intense hostility between Seigal and Valko. Regardless of McGovern's involvement in this matter, Seigal admired him. "Most of your officers at the time," he said years later, "weren't too impressive, but McGovern was mature, a person who commanded respect. From the day I first met him I liked him."[31]

Whatever the truth of Seigal's judgment of AAF officers in general—and most would dispute it, especially as it applied to pilots—in fact McGovern was one of a large group of men who had been better trained for war than any other. The pilots and their crews were in training longer before being sent to war than even the men in the Navy and especially those in the infantry.

Most airmen who survived combat complained after the war that they had not been properly prepared for its test—but then so did those in the Navy and the officers and men of the infantry, with better reason. Nothing can actually prepare a man for combat, the supreme test, but the AAF put more time, effort, and money into doing so than the other services could or would. McGovern and his fellow pilots, like their crews, had mastered techniques and developed unsurpassed professional skills. They were healthier than most other servicemen to begin with, and more so at the end of training. They had volunteered for combat. They regarded themselves—and were so regarded by others—as the cream of the crop.

And they were. The AAF taught them to regard themselves as technicians and professionals. AAF psychiatrists commented that whatever their shortcomings, the airmen that made it through the training were masters of "this super-toy, this powerful, snorting, impatient but submissive machine." The heavy bomber especially "enables the man to escape the usual limitations of time and space." Flying created "a feeling of aggressive potency bordering on the unchallenged strength of a superman." The men of the AAF flight crews "very much enjoyed the business of flying an aircraft," which gave them "an overwhelming sense of the vastness of the universe."[32]

In McGovern's case, as with his crew, as with thousands upon thousands of others, the AAF in World War II had proven itself not only the largest educational establishment ever created, but the best.

Each crew thought of itself as the best of the best. McGovern wrote to Pennington, "I've really got a top-notch crew. They were all pretty green at first as was their pilot, but we're getting hot, I believe. . . . Incidentally the boys have decided that since I'm the only married man on the ship we should name it after Eleanor, the 'Dakota Queen.' The boys seem to think a lot of Eleanor."[33]

In September 1944, the AAF judged that the McGovern crew was ready. Orders took them to Topeka, Kansas, where the AAF put them up in the Jay Hawker Hotel. Bill Rounds's father came over from

Wichita and gave them a banquet. McGovern at that time was not much concerned about domestic politics—his father was a Republican—but he was surprised at the vehemence of Mr. Rounds's convictions. Mr. Rounds took an immediate liking to Eleanor, but because of the intensity of his feelings toward the president and Eleanor Roosevelt, he would not call her "Eleanor." He explained to McGovern that "I can't say that woman's name!" All through the evening, he called her "Helen."

Still, it was a happy occasion, made more so by a rumor Bill McAfee picked up from an AAF friend stationed in Topeka and spread around. It was that their group had been selected for antisubmarine patrol off the coast of New York and New Jersey. That made Eleanor "deliriously happy" because her husband would be stationed in Newark or New York. But it turned out to be the bane, the constant companion, of all men at war—just a rumor.[34]

Instead, orders took the crew to Camp Patrick Henry, outside Norfolk, Virginia. There they prepared for shipment overseas. There being no new bombers available to fly over—as most crews going to Europe did, via South America and Africa—they would go by ship. (Lieutenant Shostack and his crew flew a brand-new B-24 from Kansas to Gander, then to the Azores, then to Marakesh, Africa, and finally to Italy. They carried pistols and 2,500 cases of K rations. They flew just a few feet over the ocean, "a fascinating trip," Shostack said. But when they got to Italy, "nobody wanted the K rations.")[35]

The library at Patrick Henry was a good one, with well over a thousand paperbacks—then something new in book publishing, given free by the publishing houses to the armed services—and McGovern sat in the reading room devouring all he could. He found some hardback books people had donated, including a big, thick volume by Charles A. and Mary R. Beard, *The Rise of American Civilization,* another by Burton Hendrick, *The Men of the Confederacy,* one edited by Norman Cousins called *A Treasury of Democracy.* Those books he liberated, intending to send them back after the war, and stuffed them into his duffel bag to read when he got to his overseas air base.* He was not alone—many others in the various armed services brought books with them to war, to read when they could—thus the soldiers of democracy.

The ship was a captured German passenger ship, which sounded good until the men going over saw it. "It was basically an old tub," one of them recalled. It had perhaps 4,000 AAF men aboard, so it was crowded. There were six decks, each with six rows of bunks. A valuable cargo and then some—all these men had cost the American government a considerable amount to train for action. It sailed alone, although usually with American airplanes, operating from aircraft carriers, overhead to protect it. Still the ship took evasive action to avoid German submarines. It was the first time McGovern and most of the other men had ever been at sea. Fortunately there were no storms. Further, there were no classes, no training of any kind. To stay in some kind of shape, the men walked around the deck, endlessly.

The ship took nearly a month to get to its destination, Naples harbor, Italy. McGovern and his crew members were going to join the 741st Squadron, 455th Bomb Group, Fifteenth Air Force, stationed on the other, Adriatic side of Italy. There the McGovern crew would meet its B-24 and the veterans and the replacements, including Shostack and his crew.

---

* After the war McGovern wrote the librarian at Patrick Henry saying he had a guilty conscience and needed to clear it by returning the three books. The librarian wrote back: "Dear Lt. McGovern. First of all, let me congratulate you on your remarkably good taste in the books you borrowed. Secondly, somewhat sadly I must tell you that the library has been disbanded and the books given away. . . . This letter is my gift to you of those books." McGovern still has them in his library.

CHAPTER FOUR

The Fifteenth Air Force

WORLD WAR II WAS THE GREATEST CATASTROPHE in history. More people were killed, more buildings destroyed than in any previous or subsequent war. It brought terror and death to millions of civilians, women, children, old men, more millions of soldiers killed in their teens or twenties.

It was airpower that made it so destructive. That airpower was the result of technological improvements in aircraft. Paradoxically it was also the result of the human desire to escape the slaughter of the trenches along the Western Front in World War I. Yet by the end of World War II airpower had brought about more destruction and death than had ever before been experienced. H. G. Wells had predicted that something like it would happen. In *The War in the Air* (1908) he wrote of his nightmare vision, that airpower would become both the product and the downfall of Western civilization. He gave it as his view that aerial warfare would be "at once enormously destructive and entirely indecisive."

Wells was only half right. Aerial warfare *was* enormously destructive but it was also absolutely decisive. Far from destroying Western civilization and its greatest triumph, democracy, the war saved it. Millions of people from countries around the world participated, using many different types of weapons, but none of them contributed more to this result than the airmen.

At the end of World War I, one of the inventors of the airplane, Orville Wright, expressed his view that "the aeroplane has made war so terrible that I do not believe any country will again care to start a war."[1] He too was wrong. Far from making war unthinkable, the airplane contributed to making it happen.

The rifle, machine gun, and artillery, not the airplane, had been decisive in World War I. The four-year stalemate in the trenches was so massive, deeply determined, and resistant to change that whatever advantage superior airpower offered was insufficient to break it. The nations at war did make efforts to win it through bombs dropped from airplanes. The Germans dropped a few bombs on Paris during the war's first weeks, while the British struck Zeppelin sheds in Germany a month after the conflict began. In 1915 a Zeppelin bombed England. Austrians and Italians bombed each other's cities. The French attacked German military and industrial targets from the air. By war's end, bombs had hit every belligerent country's capital in Europe except Rome. None of this destruction had any noticeable effect on the course of the war, nor could it break the horrible stalemate. As the Italian soldier and prophetic airpower strategist Giulio Douhet put it, even a rare offensive success on the ground so exhausted the victor that "the side which won the most military victories was the side which was defeated."[2]

That is what gave air war its appeal. Douhet was its first advocate. In his *The Command of the Air* (1921), which was widely translated, he saw heavy bombers as a way to leap over the trenches to bring about decisive results in a breathtakingly short space of time. A large bomber force, in his view, would in a few days lay waste the enemy's cities and cause the civilian population to demand peace at once. In Britain B. H. Liddell-Hart, like Douhet a soldier in World War I, became a military critic and historian. In his *Paris, or the Future of War* (1925), he explained that "aircraft enable us to *jump over* the army which shields the enemy government, industry and people and *so strike direct and immediately at the seat of the opposing will and policy*."[3] In America, General

William "Billy" Mitchell tried to popularize the same theme. He suffered a court-martial for his attempts to make the Army Air Corps into the country's chief armed service, but his appeal was nevertheless wide and deep. As Michael Sherry wrote in his magnificent work *The Rise of American Air Power*, "Air war, like no other weapon in the modern arsenal, satisfied yearnings for blood and punishment among peoples deeply wounded by war and deprived of decisive victories."[4]

Charles Lindbergh added greatly to the appeal, especially among Americans. He had been trained in the military. Although he wrote in *We* (1927) that he and his fellow pilots had flown only "for the love of flying," his feat involved far more than just risk taking and fun. He embodied at once the promise of the machine age and the virtues of frontier individualism, both of which appealed beyond measure to an American people who were more frontier-minded and technologically oriented than anyone else. To them, airpower carried the danger to Western civilization that Wells had prophesied but also a way for their country to act decisively in the next war without having to send millions of young men into the trenches. As Sherry puts it, the airplane was both peril and promise.[5]

In the decade before World War II broke out, Hap Arnold and many others in the Army Air Corps strove without letup to make airpower—and especially bombing from the air—the principal weapon of the armed services. They failed. But when America entered the war, they had an opportunity. Although the country hardly put its entire effort into what they called a strategic bombing campaign, after Pearl Harbor it extended itself in that direction to a remarkable degree. The B-17 and the B-24, both developed and manufactured before America's involvement, became the sine qua non of the AAF. The B-17 got the name Flying Fortress, but that could be applied to both airplanes. They bristled with .50 caliber machine guns that were judged sufficient—when the planes flew in formation and therefore could jointly defend themselves from any enemy fighter attack—to justify the idea that the bomber would always get through.

The goal was precision bombing that would destroy key enemy targets. The British tried that at the outset of the war, only to discover that daylight raids were far too costly because of German fighters, so they went over to night bombing, making German cities and their civilian population the target. Terror bombing, in short. Neither Arnold nor any other high-ranking member of the AAF was willing to adopt such a policy. They continued to insist on precision, i.e., daylight, bombing. Arnold spoke frequently on what bombers could do. He said they were so fearsome that "in 60 seconds, the cumulative effort of a hundred years can be destroyed." Airpower, he declared, "is a war-winning weapon in its own right." He called bombing "cheapest on all counts," and "by far the greatest economizer in human lives."[6]

To make strategic bombing a reality, the AAF created the Eighth Air Force, under Gen. Ira Eaker, based in Britain. The heavy bombers of the Eighth struck the first offensive blow against the Germans in the summer of 1942, in order to show an American contribution to the European war, but they had been rushed into battle prematurely. In 1942 strategic bombing was a high priority but a distant reality. Not until 1943, and then in far smaller numbers than the AAF hoped, planned for, and advocated, were bombers from the Eighth able to penetrate German airspace.

Despite its early failure to live up to its promises, the AAF conducted an extensive propaganda campaign. One writer who took part was John Steinbeck, who was working for the AAF when he produced *Bombs Away: The Story of a Bomber Team* in November 1942. Steinbeck wrote that the men of the AAF sprang from the frontier tradition of the "Kentucky hunter and the Western Indian fighter." He presented the airman as both individualist and a joiner, a relic of the past and a harbinger of a new era, a free spirit and a disciplined technician, a democrat and a superman, "Dan'l Boone and Henry Ford."[7]

That same month, British and American forces invaded North Africa, and many of the bombers stationed in England were diverted to that battlefront to support the ground troops with tactical bombing. Nevertheless the Eighth continued to grow and to bomb. It was taking stupendous losses, but the commitment to strategic bombing continued, to the point that it almost seemed the AAF found it preferable to bomb badly rather than not at all.

The British thought the Americans mad to continue daylight bombing. The Americans thought the British were almost criminal in their insistence on night bombing. Both sides continued their own methods anyway, so desperate were they to hit at the Germans some way, somehow. On the ground, until mid-1943, except in North Africa, no American soldiers were firing their rifles at German soldiers. Red Army soldiers were inflicting huge casualties on the German army while suffering terrific losses. In July, the Western Allies invaded Sicily. In September, they invaded Italy. These invasions were supported by the Twelfth Air Force based in North Africa.

The Eighth Air Force's heavy bomber offensive was an impersonal sort of war, monotonous in its own peculiar way. Day after day, as weather and the available force permitted, B-17s and B-24s went out, dropped their bombs, and returned to England. The immediate results of their missions could be photographed and assessed by intelligence officers. The bombers were scored in categories that sound like high school grades—excellent, good, fair, poor. But missions, or a series of them, were rarely if ever decisive, in large part because the Eighth Air Force didn't have enough bombers, but also in part because of enemy reaction. The Germans could repair damage almost as fast as Civil War troops could repair railroad tracks torn up by the enemy, and they could—and did—decentralize their industry. So for the airmen there was little if any visible progress, nothing like the gains that could be shown on maps when the ground forces pushed Erwin Rommel's Africa Korps across and then out of North Africa.

Eighth Air Force bomber crews, the official history states, "went back time and again to hit targets they thought they had already demolished. Drama there was with each sortie, and plenty of it, as the American public was never allowed to forget, but as for the big picture there was none. Indeed, the 1942–1943 offensive from the air was flat, repetitive, without climax." Arnold's claims were hollow. The bomber crews felt no sense of accomplishment, at least until they had flown their twenty-fifth mission and were allowed to go home. There was no enemy surrender, hardly any diminution in the firepower of his army or in the size of his air force or ack-ack defense.[8]

In their official history of the AAF, editors Wesley Frank Craven and James Lea Cate and their team describe what it was like for a pilot: "A nineteen-year-old boy takes off with his crew. He must fly from his base, often at great distance from the target, through weather which frequently makes precise navigation difficult and through opposition from fighters whose passes are incredibly swift. He arrives over the target at as nearly the set minute as possible and performs his deadly task.... Even without the emotional strain of the battle, the boy would find it impossible on his return to give to his interrogating officer an accurate and detailed report of his own experiences, and the story of a large mission must be compounded of hundreds of such imperfect individual reports."[9]

Losses to enemy defenses mounted, to the point that it was widely speculated that the high casualty rate suffered by the Eighth Air Force might deprive the United States of the elite of its youth in much the way that Ypres and Passchendaele and other World War I battles had done to England. For those in combat, the risks were higher in the AAF than in the American ground forces. In total the AAF, about one third of the U.S. Army, took about one ninth the battle casualties of the entire Army, but most AAF men were mechanics or command and staff officers, staying on the bases in England that were relatively safe, especially as opposed to the foxholes of infantry soldiers. But the AAF had a far higher proportion of officers in action than did the Army as a whole—including fighter pilots, about half of all flying personnel were officers—and twice as many AAF officers died in battle than in all the rest of the Army. On average, almost 4 percent of the bomber force were killed or missing in action on each mission. The mean number of missions completed for the Eighth Air Force was 14.72, meaning more than half its crews never got much past the halfway point in compiling the twenty-five missions required to go home.

Many crew members, including pilots, were wounded even though their planes got back to base. They were hit by flak or German machine guns. When flight surgeons talked to one squadron commander who "flopped on us" after some brutal missions, they learned he "was not worried about *himself.* He had not gone yellow; he was perfectly willing to see himself expended. But he simply couldn't bring himself to the point of taking another crew into combat, and then losing some of them. It had happened too often." This came about because the men were so close to each other, "so bound together by a common purpose and a common fate."10

For British bomber crews, a sense of helplessness destroyed the airman's hope that he would gain mastery of his fate as he accumulated skill and experience. Something similar happened to American crews, but at least by late 1943 they had the satisfaction of a declining loss rate as they gained experience. Further, there was the possibility that half of their number could successfully bail out of a stricken bomber on its way down. Still, they had to keep flying until completing their quota of missions. One Eighth Air Force doctor saw his task as "to help the men carry on to the limit of their capacity, and then perhaps fly a few more missions." AAF psychiatrists acknowledged that among the crews "a hair divides the normal from the neurotic, the adaptive from the nonadaptive."11 The strain was compounded the more missions were flown: the role of blind chance when attacked by fighters or by flak; the inherent danger of flying wingtip to wingtip in formation; the loss of comrades; the cumulative impact of repeated missions, often over the same target; the sense of helpless confinement whether on the flight deck or in a ball turret.

Danger began at takeoff. The aircraft were so heavily loaded with bombs and gasoline that the slightest mechanical or human failure could abort a mission or destroy the plane and kill the crew. Then came the long flight, the success of which depended on the most careful calculations of altitude, speed, and fuel consumption, plus avoiding or driving off enemy fighters. The conditions inside the plane added immeasurably to the danger. More men were disabled by frostbite than by combat wounds. They would come on board wet or sweaty, or perspire heavily when under attack, or urinate in their suits, causing their hands, feet, and other body parts to freeze. Anoxia from shortages of oxygen compounded the threat of frostbite and posed a serious danger in and of itself. The pilot and his crew also had to cope with damage to or malfunctions of the plane, or unpredictable changes in weather.

Even so, the pilots and crews had the strongest possible attachment to their airplanes. "He loves them for their strength and beauty," one commentator wrote of a pilot in 1944. "He looks upon them as extensions of his ego, or friends whose temperaments are more vivid than those of most human beings he knows."12

But in 1943, despite all the effort the Americans put into the air war, there was little sense of progress.

On August 1, 1943, the Eighth Air Force carried out what its official historians later called "one of the outstanding air operations of the war."13 Those who participated in it could not agree. It came about because of the frustration of the AAF generals, who felt certain that if they could just find and destroy the key German industry, the one on which everything else depended, they could win the war. They tried electrical generators, ball bearing plants, aircraft factories, and other targets, but nothing seemed to work. Then they came up with the idea of hitting Germany's fuel refineries. Surely without gasoline the Germans would have to quit.

The prime target was Ploesti, in Romania. The oil refineries there produced 60 percent of Germany's crude oil and crude oil provided two thirds of Germany's petroleum resources. In April 1943, General Arnold ordered the Plans Division of Headquarters, AAF, to study Ploesti and prepare an attack. Col. Jacob Smart originated the idea of a minimum-altitude, mass attack to be flown from the recently captured airfield near Benghazi in Libya. In early June, General Eisenhower, in command of the Allied forces in the Mediterranean, approved Smart's plan. The code name was TIDALWAVE. The bombers would be B-24s, with two groups coming to Libya from the Eighth Air Force, three from the Twelfth Air Force. A group usually consisted of six bomb squadrons of six bombers each, for a total of thirty-six bombers. The B-24s would carry both 1,000-pound and 500-pound demolition bombs, a total of 311 tons, plus 290 boxes of British-type and 140 clusters of American-type incendiaries. The planes would be equipped with two auxiliary bomb bay tanks, giving each bomber a fuel capacity of 3,100 gallons.

In the last ten days of July the five groups were pulled out of operations in Sicily (invaded by the Allies on July 10) to undergo intensive training near Benghazi. The B-24s flew and bombed from minimum altitude. They hit a dummy target laid out in the Libyan desert that looked like Ploesti. They hit it again and again, until one crew member decided "we could bomb it in our sleep."[14] They kept a tight formation. They studied great quantities of data dealing with the route to be flown, enemy defenses, and the dozens of other items that had to be clearly understood and appreciated. On July 28 and 29 the entire task force participated in two mock missions. According to the experts, the bombers "completely destroyed" the targets in less than two minutes.

Shortly after dawn on August 1 the 177 bombers, carrying 1,725 airmen, took off, passed the island of Corfu, then swung northeast—across the mountains of Albania and Yugoslavia. But dumb luck struck—towering cumulus clouds destroyed the task force's unity. Radio communication might have restored it, but orders were for radio silence to preserve surprise. The initial point was sixty-five miles from Ploesti. The planes dropped down to 500 feet. They encountered severe fire from ground defenses and from enemy fighters. In spite of the opposition, the B-24s dropped down to 100 to 300 feet. At anything less than 1,000 feet the bombers were in danger of being turned wrong side up by the tremendous updraft from their own bombs exploding. They came over the target badly mixed up and after the first group the remainder had to drive straight through intense flak, explosions from the ground, flames, and dense black smoke that concealed balloon cables and towering chimneys. Turning away and heading home, they were jumped by enemy fighters. Their attacks continued even when the Liberators got over the Adriatic.

The AAF generals judged the Ploesti attack a success. Photographs apparently showed that 42 percent of Ploesti's refining capacity had been destroyed. But by no means was this decisive, because the Germans made up for the lost refining capacity by activating idle units at Ploesti and by speedy repairs to damaged plants. And not until the late spring of 1944 was Ploesti hit again, this time from high altitude.

American losses were so heavy that the final judgment must be that the Germans won the battle. Fifty-four planes were lost, almost one third of the attacking force. Lost too were 532 airmen. Not all were dead; some had bailed out of their B-24s as the planes went down. Most of them became POWs. News of the raid and the losses the AAF had sustained spread, even across the Atlantic. McGovern was in training at the time and discussed it with his fellow air cadets. "It aroused anxiety on the part of every pilot," he said, "because we realized this was an enormously costly mission. We knew we had to fly twenty-five or thirty-five missions and guys were saying, 'How are you going to survive if you have to go up thirty-five times against that kind of thing?'"*

---

* The total was up to thirty-five by this time.

On August 13 the surviving bombers on loan from the Eighth Air Force participated in a mission against the airplane factory in Wiener Neustadt—another key target. On August 17 the Eighth Air Force from England flew a mission to the Schweinfurt ball bearing plant and another to the aircraft plant at Regensburg. Both targets were in Germany. In what proved to be a fantasy, the AAF considered them "key" targets that, if destroyed, would force Germany to sue for peace. Instead, the Germans downed even more B-17s and B-24s and managed to recover from the damage.[15]

_____

It was because of Ploesti, and the heavy losses on many other raids, that the AAF sped up the training time for McGovern and his crew and all the others preparing to enter the battle. By the late summer of 1943 American industry was producing enough planes but there was a bottleneck: not enough combat crews. The Eighth Air Force had nowhere near enough pilots to fly the B-17s and B-24s available in England. General Arnold noted, with great concern, that not even by December 1943 would the AAF be able to provide replacements and reinforcements enough to allow the Eighth to operate at full strength. Neither could the other air forces, in the Pacific or North Africa. Planes without pilots and crews were as useless to the AAF as runway behind a landing airplane.

Progress was being made on the ground. After the Allies had taken Sicily and in September had invaded mainland Italy, the American Fifth Army was moving north along the west coast after some frightfully rough going at Salerno, while the British 1st Airborne Division had taken Taranto and Brindisi on the east coast and quickly captured Bari on the Adriatic. The British Eighth Army meanwhile was driving north. By October 5 the Americans had captured the port at Naples while the British had taken Foggia, which was surrounded by now defunct German and Italian airfields. Italy, after overthrowing Mussolini, had surrendered, but the country was immediately occupied by German troops, who used Italy's rivers and mountains to form a formidable defense across the country.

Still, southern Italy was in Allied hands. That opened opportunities for the AAF. From the airfields around Foggia, American bombers could participate in the Combined Bomber Offensive (CBO). Italian-based bombers could hit targets in the Balkans, Czechoslovakia, Austria, and southern and eastern Germany. Ploesti's oil, the Danube River supply route, Wiener Neustadt's industries, and others would be within range of B-17s and B-24s. Along with fighter aircraft, the heavy bombers could support Allied ground armies as they continued their drive north up the peninsula.

There were more advantages, or so it was argued among the Allied high command. Basing a large heavy-bomber force in Italy would ease the congestion in England brought on by the airfield requirements of the Eighth Air Force. Better weather conditions in Italy than in England would make it possible to strike more blows against the enemy. From Italy two of the largest German aircraft factories, which together produced 60 percent of the enemy's fighters, would be in range. The Germans would be forced to move half of their fighters to the southern German front, thus relieving the hard-pressed Eighth Air Force. American bombers flying from Italy would enjoy the shield of the Alps against the German radio warning system. Further, a major new base around Foggia could be quickly brought into being by stripping the six groups of heavy bombers assigned to the Twelfth Air Force in Libya. Those groups would serve as a nucleus for the new force, and fifteen additional groups could be diverted from current allocations to the Eighth.

Despite these points, Gen. Ira Eaker had strenuous objections to the plan. He was naturally alarmed at the prospect of losing bombers previously earmarked for his Eighth Air Force. He said sending them to Italy would violate the basic principle of concentration of force. He doubted that the necessary fields could be provided in Italy and wondered where on earth the AAF would get the ground crews necessary to keep the bombers flying. And he questioned the weather argument. He said that the critical factor in daylight attacks was weather over the target in Germany, not weather in England. He pointed out too that the Alps would constitute a serious obstacle to the safe return to base of damaged aircraft.[16]

General Arnold ignored Eaker. In mid-October he sent Eisenhower a directive for the establishment of a new air force in Italy with a primary mission of strategic bombing. Gen. Carl Spaatz would take command of the United States Army Strategic Air Forces in Europe, while Gen. James "Jimmy" Doolittle, who had led the famous B-25 attack on Tokyo in 1942, would replace Eaker as commander of the Eighth. The new force, to be called the Fifteenth Air Force, would be commanded by Gen. Nathan Twining. Eisenhower agreed.

At the end of November, with an advanced echelon already established at Bari, on the Adriatic south of Foggia, staff officers and other supporting personnel began moving to Bari. On December 1 the Fifteenth Air Force opened its headquarters there, where it would stay until the end of the war.

That fall, to prepare for the coming of the heavy bombers, engineers began the construction of heavy bomber fields around Foggia. In spite of great difficulties imposed by rain and mud, insufficient equipment and personnel, and poor transportation, plus bomb damage to the airfields previously used by the Germans, by the end of December the engineers were completing construction on more than forty-five airfields (including ones for medium bombers in Sardinia and Corsica). The work ranged from repairs and drainage to putting down paved or, more often, steel-plank runways. And they laid pipelines for aviation gasoline from Bari to Foggia.

Thus was the Fifteenth Air Force born. Initially it consisted of six heavy bomber groups and two fighter groups, but it would soon become the second largest air force in the world, behind only the Eighth in total numbers of planes and personnel. By April 1944, it had twenty-one heavy bomber and seven fighter groups.

Even on "moving day," December 1, 1943, the Fifteenth struck a blow, bombing ball bearing factories, bridges, and railway facilities in northern Italy. But the next night, the *Luftwaffe* sent a flight of bombers to Bari. About thirty Allied ships were being unloaded and when darkness fell lights were turned on to keep the unloading on schedule. At 7:30 P.M. the German bombers struck. In twenty minutes, without loss to themselves, they left nineteen transports destroyed and seven severely damaged. Two ammunition ships received direct hits, as did a tanker carrying oil, causing an immense fire. Over 1,000 workers were killed and it took several weeks to bring the port back to full operation.[17]

Welcome to the war. The Fifteenth went to work anyway. Just before Christmas 1943 it carried out a mission against the Messerschmitt plant at Augsburg. In the new year, it supported American landings at Anzio, south of Rome. In these and other missions, it used the new Sperry bombsight plus radar, which allowed the lead bomber to pinpoint the target through cloud or smoke cover—or so at least it was hoped. In February, the Fifteenth joined with the Eighth in the first coordinated attack of the U.S. Army Strategic Air Forces in Europe. It was the "Big Week," when the Eighth and Fifteenth targeted German aircraft factories and a ball bearing plant at Steyr, Austria. On the last day of the Big Week, more than 1,000 bombers, a record, from the two air forces struck Regensburg, Augsburg, Fürth, and Stuttgart. The damage done was frightful to behold. So were the losses. On the record-breaking day, sixty-four bombers were lost, thirty-three of them from the Fifteenth. The week's total cost to the Fifteenth was ninety aircraft and their crews.

Through March, April, and May the Fifteenth stayed at it. In that period it received twenty-five sets of the new APS-15 radar, known as "Mickey," complete with operators. On April 5, 1944, 230 bombers from the Fifteenth raided Ploesti—the first time it had been hit in eight months. More Ploesti missions were carried out on April 15 and

24, on the last raid using the Mickey for the first time. On D-Day in Normandy, June 6, 1944, the Fifteenth raided Ploesti again, then again on June 23 and 24, and again on July 9 and 15. Losses mounted—ten B-24s on one mission, fourteen on another, twenty on another, forty-six on the July missions—this out of a force of between 200 and 300 bombers. Missions against other targets in the first half of 1944 were equally costly. Meanwhile the Eighth Air Force, which had spent much of the time before D-Day bombing tactical targets such as bridges and railroads in France in preparation for the assault, did its own strategic bombing and suffered similarly heavy losses.

The campaign in France was called the "Transportation Plan" and was much objected to by General Spaatz, who wanted instead of hitting bridges and trains in France to be conducting strategic missions inside Germany. But Eisenhower, the supreme commander of the Allied Expeditionary Force, had insisted on the Transportation Plan. To him, the closer to the front lines the bombers did their work, the better. After many loud arguments and only after threatening to resign his post if not given temporary command of the AAF in Europe, Eisenhower got what he wanted. But only for the invasion. On June 8 Spaatz issued an order that remained in force until the war ended— the primary aim of the Eighth and Fifteenth Air Forces would be to deny oil to the enemy. Following that order, Ploesti and other oil refineries were the major targets.

How could the Germans take such punishment? How could they defend their country? Where did they get the fighters? The pilots? The antiaircraft guns? Their tanks and trucks? Their ammunition? These questions were difficult for the AAF to answer, especially since the feeling had been that just one more blow—or two, or three—would do it and the Germans would pack it up.

Nothing like that happened. The Germans made vast efforts to disperse their aircraft factories and at the end of 1943 were producing twice the number of fighters estimated by the Allies. At that stage of the war, German fighter pilots were among the best in the world. German technical knowledge and skill were equally outstanding. They were bringing a rocket-propelled fighter, the ME 163, and a jet-propelled fighter, the ME 262, on line. Despite many attacks on aircraft-producing factories, the Germans built 2,177 single-engine (propeller-driven) fighters in June 1944 (compared to 1,016 in February 1943) and more than 3,000 in September. The jet aircraft were the most serious threat and the Fifteenth went after the jet factories in Friederichshafen in a series of July raids. A postwar assessment determined that these missions destroyed 950 jet aircraft, fewer than the estimates at the time but still an impressive result.

The raids on ball bearing plants had caused much physical damage but had hardly interrupted the flow of ball bearings to the factories where they were needed. Indeed, German armaments production increased sharply in early 1944 and threatened to rise even more during the second half of the year. Having France, the Low Countries, Norway, and central and eastern Europe as a source of almost unlimited slave labor helped.[18]

Oil was the critical item. Ploesti remained the principal target. It was attacked by the Fifteenth Air Force, but following the April attacks the Germans began to experiment with a new defensive measure, which for at least a time worked well. Whenever their warning system indicated the approach of the Fifteenth's air fleets over Yugoslavia heading toward Romania, the Germans would use the time available to them before the bombers were over Ploesti—about forty minutes—to light hundreds of smoke pots around the refineries, so that when the bombers were over the target most of the area would be concealed. As a counter, the Fifteenth began using more radar-equipped leading planes and raised its level of accuracy. But the German counter was to move additional antiaircraft batteries into and around Ploesti, along with fighter aircraft, making it the third best defended target on the continent. Second was Vienna, also a crude oil refinery site often struck by the Fifteenth. First was Berlin. The Fifteenth countered with new techniques, most of all the use of diamond-shaped formations that gave some additional security to the bombers and greater precision in its attacks.

In July 1944, the Fifteenth lost 318 heavy bombers in its many missions against refineries scattered across southern Europe. It was the worst month of the war for the Fifteenth, which had a higher ratio of loss than the Eighth. The AAF thought, however, that it was doing great damage to the refineries, especially because of its use of radar to overcome the smoke screens. The results may not have been quite as good as hoped, but still they were spectacular. It was the sustained offensive by the Fifteenth that finally rendered Ploesti all but useless to the Germans. By September 1944, a total force of 59,834 airmen from the Fifteenth had flown against Ploesti, dropped a total of 13,469 tons of bombs, at a cost of 350 heavy bombers. The Fifteenth had flown twenty daylight missions against Ploesti. Later estimates were that these raids denied the Germans 1.8 million tons of crude oil. When the Red Army took Ploesti on August 30, the Russians reported that the Ploesti refineries were idle and ruined. This was the payoff of the Fifteenth's sustained campaign.

———————

On August 30, with the Red Army overrunning the country, Romania abruptly changed sides in the war. That development in turn led to a buoyant episode for the Fifteenth Air Force. There were over 1,000 AAF men who had bailed out over Romania and were being held there as POWs. Those in camps near Bucharest were in danger of being evacuated to Germany or having to spend a long time in Russian hands before they got home. One of the internees, Lt. Col. James A. Gunn III, took matters into his own hands. He climbed into the radio compartment of an ME 109 after painting it with the Stars and Stripes. He had persuaded Captain Cantacuzene, a prince of the royal family of Romania, who was the top Romanian ace against Allied aircraft, to be his pilot. Cantacuzene flew Gunn to Italy and managed to land safely. Gunn talked General Twining into sending a rescue mission. Twining had the Fifteenth hurriedly convert fifty-six of its B-17 bombers into transports and had Cantacuzene fly a P-51 (there was no suitable fuel for the ME 109) to the airport outside Bucharest to see if it was clear of Germans. It was and the B-17s started coming in. The POWs, happy beyond belief, crowded into the bombers, twenty of them in each plane, and flew back to Italy in relays. In all 1,274 of them got out over a three-day period. Deloused, fed, and treated as necessary in hospitals, they were soon on their way to the States.[19]

The losses the Fifteenth inflicted on the German refineries vastly aggravated the fuel crisis faced by the Germans, bringing the enemy's fuel position to the point of catastrophe. In his memoirs *Inside the Third Reich,* the Nazi production czar Albert Speer said: "I could see the omens of the war's end almost every day in the blue southern sky when the bombers of the American Fifteenth Air Force crossed the Alps from their Italian bases to attack German industrial targets."[20] Eighth Air Force attacks on the armaments industry, especially tank, truck, and aircraft factories inside Germany, also led to shortages for the enemy. Strategic bombing was paying off, which helped Spaatz ward off proposals to attempt to terrorize the Germans into capitulation through night bombing of cities.[21]

American losses mounted. In the summer of 1944, out of its 2,100 operational heavy bombers, the Eighth Air Force lost more than 900. The 1,100 operational heavy bombers of the Fifteenth Air Force suffered a still higher ratio of losses. But the German losses were even higher. The *Luftwaffe* had combat losses in personnel that climbed from 31,000 to 44,000 per month between June and October.[22]

The presence of the American P-51 long-range fighters, beginning in mid-1944, provided the American bombers with air cover all the way to the target. They made a critical contribution to the German losses. Indeed, some historians contend that it was the coming of the P-51 that made the continuation of the strategic bombing campaign possible. It surely helped, but the biggest problem for the Germans was fuel. The Ploesti raids, and others, had the enemy down to 20 percent of the fuel needed to continue the war. Training in tank warfare, for example, became for the Germans a luxury beyond reach. The German army had to abandon most of its trucks and other vehicles and revert to being a horse-drawn army.

For the airmen, what mattered most was the cutbacks the *Luftwaffe* was forced to adopt, especially in its training period for pilots, which was reduced to a few insufficient days. Further, along with a severe shortage of good pilots, morale in the *Luftwaffe* was declining or becoming almost nonexistent. German pilots were not rotated out of combat and made into instructors after a certain number of missions—they continued to fly until killed, which a steadily growing number of them were.[23] Increasingly, the Germans had to rely solely on their antiaircraft guns to defend their cities. They had come to realize that it was not possible to stop an Allied bomber from dropping its eggs on a target. Their goal was to cause the casualty rate to be high enough to force the Allies to discontinue the raids, something they could never accomplish.[24]

But if the Germans were having morale problems, so were the Americans. The airmen suffered greatly, from the intensive scale of operations, from high operational losses, sometimes from the lack of sufficient fighters for escort, from the almost unbearable pace of missions on consecutive days. General Arnold had long planned to provide two crews for each bomber so that every man would feel that he had a chance of surviving his tour of thirty-five missions, but trained crews were not being produced fast enough and it was not until December 1944 that the Fifteenth Air Force attained the ratio of two crews for each bomber.

Morale was so low that rumors were widespread in the AAF

about pilots and crews landing in neutral Sweden or Switzerland, not because their bomber was so badly damaged that it could not return to base but just to get out of the war. The stories said the men who had thus opted for safety over risk were enjoying a comfortable sojourn while they were interned. Investigation revealed that such reports were almost wholly inaccurate. The bombers that landed in the neutral countries had indeed been so shot up that the pilots had no choice.[25] That many airmen nevertheless believed the rumors was an indication of how low morale had sunk. This was the situation into which George McGovern and his crew, along with all the other replacements and reinforcements, were headed.

McGovern would be joining the 741st Squadron, 455th Bomb Group in September 1944. The group also included the 740th, 742nd, and 743rd Squadrons. It was based at San Giovanni Field, near Cerignola, Italy, a bit south of Foggia. The 455th shared the base with the 454th Bomb Group, both being part of the 304th Bomb Wing. The 455th's emblem was the "Vulgar Vulture." Walt Disney Studios in Hollywood did the artwork. It was a vulture with a bomb in its talons. The emblem, often called a patch, was worn on the left breast of flight jackets by the crews. The group's tail marking had a black-colored diamond shape on the upper half of both vertical stabilizers and yellow-painted lower stabilizers and rudders. The squadron symbols were on the upper rudders—a black rectangle for the 740th, a black four-leaf clover for the 741st, a black diagonal stripe for the 742nd, and a black horizontal stripe for the 743rd. The aircraft had their numbers painted on both sides of the rear part of the fuselage. These markings were necessary during rendezvous to insure that the plane joined the proper group formation.[26]

The 455th's first commander was Col. Kenneth A. Cool. He was an experienced airman, with over sixteen years of flying experience. He had flown B-24s for the Eighth Air Force over Germany, then flown in North Africa and from the Libyan desert. His sense of humor, along with his competence, endeared him to his men. So did his continual puffing on his pipe. His expression when a piece of information surprised him was, "Well, I'll be dipped in gravy." His group headquarters B-24 was named *Bestwedo*, after another of his common sayings. He often led the group into combat. When it was announced during premission briefings that Colonel Cool would lead the formation, whispers of approval could be heard from the combat crews.[27]

The 455th flew 139 missions before November 1944. May was its busiest month, with 21 missions. The group put 745 B-24s over targets, dropping over 1,630 tons of bombs. Losses were severe, but the group kept at it. At least enemy fighters were, by late August, no longer much of a threat, but accidents and even more German antiaircraft batteries (usually 88s, sometimes including 105s) were more dangerous than ever.

Once at least, in April, the flak that hit one plane brought down two of the B-24s. Lt. Jerome Slater was the pilot of one of them, Lt. Michael Callen had the controls of the other. After completing a bomb run over Porto San Stefano, Italy, flying in a diamond formation, Callen had Slater's B-24 and another bomber tucked up under each of his wings. Slater's plane was hit by a flak burst on its number one engine. It severed the wing and his plane immediately went out of control. It rolled to the left as it flipped over on its back and struck Callen's plane back to back. "Debris was flying everywhere," reported the six-plane flight leader, Lt. Eugene Hudson. "Only one parachute was seen to open." The twenty crewmen were listed as missing in action. Callen's regular navigator, Lt. Guy Kuntz, was flying with Hudson that day. He wept all the way home after witnessing his crew lost.[28]

In August 1944, after the 455th's one hundredth mission, Colonel Cool was transferred to 304th wing headquarters as operations officer. Lt. Col. William L. Snowden of Oakland, California, a graduate of the University of Texas, replaced him. Like Cool, Snowden was immensely popular.

McGovern would become part of a war that, after Rome was liberated on June 5 and after D-Day in Normandy on June 6, every participant in Italy—whether on the ground, at sea, or in the air—would call "the forgotten war." For the men of the Fifteenth, what they resented most was the maximum publicity given to the Eighth Air Force. This was not only because it was bigger, and had more of the glamour bombers—the B-17s—but also because reporters preferred England to the Italian campaign. Movie star Jimmy Stewart flew as a squadron leader in a B-24 for the Eighth (and was generally regarded as an absolute top pilot). Clark Gable also flew with the Eighth, as did many youngsters soon to be famous, including reporters Andy Rooney and Walter Cronkite. This led to even more publicity for the Eighth.

In the little less than a year and a half that the Fifteenth was in operation, it had 3,544 B-24s and 1,407 B-17s. Of these, 1,756 B-24s and 624 B-17s were shot down in combat.[29]

CHAPTER FIVE

Cerignola, Italy

IN 1492 CHRISTOPHER COLUMBUS became the first Italian-born man to set foot in the New World. Over the 450 years that followed, hundreds of thousands of Italians came to America in his wake. From 1943 to 1945, a million and more Americans, many from Italian-American families, others whose parents or grandparents or ancestors had been born elsewhere in Europe or in Asia or Africa, came to Italy. They were mainly young men, overwhelmingly in the armed services of the United States. They came not to settle and start a new life, not to conquer, but to undertake an air offensive against Germany and its satellites, to drive the German occupiers from Italy, to liberate the country and allow it to choose its own government.

They came to the mainland right after the Italians had overthrown Benito Mussolini, but evidence of his two-decade rule was all about them. Italy was in ruins. Mussolini was no Hitler or Stalin, but he was nevertheless a disaster for North Africa and a catastrophe for Italy. He had turned a country of skilled artisans and expert farmers, full of so much life and spirit and art and fine food and wine as to be an object of envy to much of the rest of the world, into a country virtually without young men, a country that made almost nothing, a country on the verge of widespread starvation. He had gathered up nearly all the young men and forced them into his army, which he hoped against all reason would make Italy into a major power. By 1943 it was a country of old men, women, and children, almost all of them hungry, ill-clad, suffering medically and in nearly every other way. The American servicemen had grown up believing that Italy was poor, a place to escape from, but they had no idea until they arrived that Mussolini had made the country destitute.

What Mussolini had not done, the Germans did. In their retreat north after the Allied invasion of the mainland in September 1943, the Germans had taken with them damn near everything—virtually all food, wine, vehicles of every type whether horse-drawn or machine-powered or pushcart, artworks, whatever they could carry.

One afternoon in September 1944, George McGovern and his shipmates arrived in Naples harbor. From the deck they could see dozens of little boys lined up on the wharf, holding out their hands and yelling in broken English, "Babe Ruth," or "Hershey Bars," or "gum." Just as the Americans began to reach into their pockets, the ship's loudspeaker came alive and the captain said, "Now look, nobody throw anything to these children. These kids are starving and a couple of days ago an American ship came in here and the soldiers started throwing candy bars and the kids jumped into the water to get some and several of them drowned. We don't want to repeat that. We came to help these people, not to drown their kids. Don't throw anything. I mean anything." McGovern recalled them as "spindly-legged kids with pale faces," and he admitted, "This was my first exposure to people on the edge of starvation." Outside Naples that night, in an AAF base, he could hear "mothers scrounging around in the garbage cans looking for scraps of food that they could take home to their kids."[1]

The American soldiers had come out of the Depression. Many of them had been deprived. But none of them had ever known anything like this. To the Italians, they were incredibly rich. Their uniforms were far better than those of the Italian army and much superior to those the German army. They had what seemed to be unbelievable quantities of food, gasoline, weapons, trucks, jeeps, airplanes, tents, medical supplies, cameras, money, movies and projectors, and more.

The newly arrived Americans were discovering the vast difference between their country and others, even their closest ally, Great Britain. Lt. Roland Pepin, assigned as navigator to the same 741st Squadron, 455th Bomb Group as McGovern had been, also came to Italy by ship, but Pepin's "rusty old tub" had deposited his crew in Tunis, where they transferred to a British luxury liner for the journey across the Mediterranean to Naples. That sounded nice, and it was—for the officers, not for the enlisted men. Pepin found that "the British have an entirely different approach than us to the separation of officers and enlisted men." As an officer, he was in a stateroom with one other man "with all the luxury usually granted first-class passengers." The enlisted men were in the bowels of the ship packed like sardines, sleeping in hammocks. Sanitary facilities for the enlisted "were a disgrace, causing a stench that was inhumane."[2]

McGovern, Pepin, and the hundreds of other AAF reinforcements and replacements boarded trucks for the drive across Italy, almost straight east to the airfield some five miles outside Cerignola, about twenty miles southwest of Foggia. Cerignola was reputed to have been a center for Mussolini's Fascist party and had become a place of refuge for Italians fleeing the frequent Allied bombing of Foggia. Before the war it had been a town of 25,000 but by 1944 it contained about twice that, none of them young men. The name Cerignola meant land of cereals, and it was thus the origin of the word "Cheerios." It grew hard wheat, the best in Italy and possibly the best in the world for making pasta. The Romans stored the wheat in the ground, silos in reverse. They covered the holes with wood that kept the water out when it rained. There are still 600 such storage places in and around Cerignola today, all with Roman numbers on them. According to local people, this is the only place in the world where hard grain was preserved in this way. Mussolini, however, had sapped Cerignola's resources for his army and in 1944 one could not tell that it once had been a major agriculture center for the Romans. Although it was generally flat and fertile, with plenty of rain, by 1944 almost nothing was cultivated there. The olive trees were neglected. The people were even worse off.

An AAF medical officer wrote a description: "The town was a reservoir of malaria, venereal disease and dysentery with flies and mosquitoes to insure spread. The streets were filled with pot-bellied bambinos openly defecating in emulation of their elders because there was no sewer system or toilets. They ate food when they could get it on the black market obtained from fly-infested fruit stands and vermin-filled butcher shops where rotten meat was the rule. There were no medicines, the death rate among children was appalling, the splenic index was 40 per cent and malaria was a children's disease—all the adults had it long since. Avitaminosis, tuberculosis, and frank starvation were everywhere. The only music to be heard was the sound of a passing funeral, and that band had a full-time job."[3]

Cerignola was an ancient city. On June 29, 1863, its modern cathedral had its first stone placed as the American Civil War was being fought, even as Robert E. Lee's army was marching into Pennsylvania for what would be the battle of Gettysburg. The cathedral's dome stood out. Pilots could see it from ten miles away. "Many times I was reassured that I was on course when that dome loomed up ahead of us," McGovern recalled. It is still there in the twenty-first century, upgraded and active.[4]

Nearby were the ancient ruins of Cannae, site of one of the most famous battles ever fought. In 216 B.C. Hannibal of Carthage set up his base at Cerignola, because of the grain stored there. Eleven miles away, at Cannae, Hannibal's force encircled Roman troops that outnumbered his army by two to one and, in a single afternoon, destroyed them. Most of the Americans had never seen a building as much as a hundred years old nor a battlefield that went back as far as the mid-eighteenth century, much less two millennia. One AAF pilot of the 456th Bomb Group, Lt. Robert S. Capps, was so intrigued by Cannae that he visited the site and later wrote a biography of Hannibal.[5]

When the Germans retreated and the British Eighth Army swept past, the people of Cerignola hoped they were out of the war. They were not. In January 1944, when the AAF arrived to transform the area around Cerignola into a major airfield, an incredible storm of activity began. Massive numbers of ground support vehicles and huge amounts of matériel arrived. There were more than 2,000 young men at the base from the 455th and the 456th Bomb Groups. Army olive-drab tent cities sprang up among the olive groves, along with massive amounts of ground support equipment, fuel, bombs, ammunition, food, medicines, and other supplies, which continued to arrive daily. The people of Cerignola began to learn about the way Americans made war. They had never seen anything to match it.[6]

Lt. Colonel Horace W. Lanford, twenty-five years old, was the first commander of the 741st Bomb Squadron.* He arrived in Cerignola early in 1944. At that time the town was only sixty miles south of the front lines. The airfield, bombed by the Fifteenth Air Force in 1943 and then abandoned by the Germans, was in poor condition. The group had sixty-four B-24s; Lanford had flown in with them. There were no hard stands (parking ramps), so the group had to line up the bombers either wingtip to wingtip or nose to tail on what little runway there was. Still, the pilots managed to take off and land. On their early missions, to help morale on the stalemated beachhead at Anzio on the western coast of Italy, the Cerignola-based bombers formed up with other groups. The B-24s and B-17s flew directly over the beachhead to let the American infantry see their awesome power. Lanford remembered it as "an exciting, unforgettable sight." The

---

* Lanford had been in the AAF for four years. Once in Italy he ran into a West Point graduate who was also a lieutenant colonel. "Horace, how old are you?" Lanford gave his age. The West Pointer smacked his head and said, "I used to think I was a young lieutenant colonel at twenty-seven."

bombers stretched "as far as you could see in front and as far as you could see in back."7

To provide adequate space and runways for the B-24s and B-17s, the Americans brought in bulldozers. They leveled what had once been wheat fields. Engineers laid down steel matting for the 4,800-foot runway, and made taxiways and hard stands. They did not bother to make hangars—all maintenance, repairs, and other work on the bombers was done in the open, from the first and until the end of the war.

The 456th Bomb Group had confiscated an old farm building to use as headquarters. There were two brick buildings used as air crew briefing rooms and navigators' and bombardiers' study rooms.

The 455th Bomb Group had its headquarters on the other side of the runway. It had been part of a nobleman's estate but was sadly neglected. Group headquarters was located in a farm animal stable, which was also used for briefing the crews for the combat missions. The building, made of stone with no windows, had sunk into the ground. The men had to clean out manure that had been accumulating for years, and fight off the fleas as they were working. The briefing room was later also used as a movie theater.

Lanford, commanding the 741st, won the right to a barn in a coin flip with the commander of the 743rd. It had two big bays and an aviary on top. Next to it was a small storage building, which went to the 743rd. For the 741st, Lanford made an officers club in one of the bays and an airmen's club out of the other, "after clearing out tons of junk." In the aviary, Lanford knocked off the bird perches and sealed the holes and cleaned up the interior, painted it, and built a ladder to climb up to it. The aviary thus became the quarters for Lanford and five other officers.

At first, the enlisted men in the 741st slept in the big plywood boxes that lined the bomb bays in which baggage was placed in the B-24s for the flight over to Italy. "You can't imagine those living conditions," Lanford said. The only tent was used as a mess tent. The men had to stand in line to have their mess kit filled, and when it rained, as it often did, they had to run for cover. Lanford hired local labor to put up a mess hall made of stone. In the process, he learned that one of the residents was reporting on what went on at the airfield to the Germans. One night during construction, the German propaganda broadcaster nicknamed Axis Sally by the Americans—who liked to listen to her program because she played American music—said, "We see you down there, 741st Squadron, building your mess hall. You'll never get to use it, we'll bomb it before it's complete." The Germans never did bomb it. (The base was defended by a British antiaircraft gun crew, as Cerignola was in the British Eighth Army area.)[8]

Axis Sally seemed to know everything. Radio operator Sgt. Robert Hammer was in the 742nd Squadron. Once in the spring of 1944 his squadron, nicknamed the "Checkerboards" because of their tail insignia, was on a mission when two ME 109s went after a straggler that had lost an engine. The pilot of the bomber ordered the crew to lower the landing gear as a sign of surrender. The ME 109s came in close to escort the B-24 to a landing field, one off each wing. The pilot told the crew to open fire. They knocked both fighters down and the pilot returned to base safely. That night, Axis Sally declared that the Checkerboard B-24s would thereafter be the top priority of the German fighters. The squadron changed its insignia several times, but the Germans kept after it. Hammer said that the Germans had "fantastic intelligence reports. Berlin radio would tell us where we were going even before we got off the ground."[9]

In early 1944, Lt. Robert Capps arrived to join the 744th Squadron. "We were deposited on bare, damp ground in olive groves. We were instructed to pitch tents on the hard, moist ground like Boy Scouts. The olive groves became muddy quagmires from rain mixed with human activity."[10] The men anchored the pyramidal tents by ropes attached to the olive trees. There was one tent for the three or four officers and another for the six enlisted men, side by side. They slept on fold-up cots with either two wool blankets or a sleeping bag for cover. The men made mattresses by packing straw into cloth mattress covers, but the straw had insects in it, which led to bites.

If a man touched the inside of the tent while it was raining, the tent leaked. It was cold—it snowed more than once in the winter of 1944–1945—so the inhabitants applied a bit of Yankee ingenuity by rigging a stove from a fifty-five-gallon oil drum, cut in half. The fuel was gasoline, fed into the stove through a makeshift plumbing device from another, full drum outside. It was a drip-by-drip method. The men cut a little door at the bottom of the stove for ventilation. If the stove got too hot it burned too high and soot would build up in the smokestack and ignite, sending hot sparks out the chimney, then down onto the tent. The holes caused other leaks.

The floor was mud. To make it livable, the men would build a concrete floor, assisted by hired Italian labor. First they put down crushed rock, then topped it with a layer of concrete. Bill Rounds, who shared a tent with McGovern and Sam Adams, wrote in his diary, "We sleep in tents, no lights or running water." Soon there were lights—a single bulb hanging in the center—and by December 4, 1944, Rounds could write in his diary, "Our tent is now in good shape—good stove—clothes rack and front door."11

McGovern, Rounds, and Adams's tent was located near two of the more elaborate tents that were occupied by veterans who were close to the end of the thirty-five missions required to go home. McGovern met one of the pilots for the first time when he and Rounds went for a joy ride in a "liberated" jeep. Rounds was driving, at high speed. He flew down the "street" between the tents, turned a corner on two wheels, caught one of the ropes from the veterans' tent, and the ensuing rip tore the tent in half. The stove, uniforms on hangers, shelves of books, magazines, and photographs, all flew into the olive grove. Climbing out of the jeep, McGovern saw an aging pilot "with heavy circles under his eyes who had to be at least twenty-five" walking over to the vehicle. His name, McGovern found out later, was Capt. Howard Surbeck. His voice quaking with rage, Surbeck said, "You two sons-of-bitches will never make it through combat. I should kill you right now." Rounds and McGovern spent the rest of the day putting up a new tent for him. "So," McGovern recalled with a laugh, "that's the way I broke into the 741st Squadron area."[12]

Rounds was nonetheless unstoppable in his practical jokes. One night shortly after the incident with the jeep he rolled a fifty-five-gallon drum of fuel oil into the middle of the squadron area, set it on fire, and shouted, "Enemy raid!" There were cries of panic and anguish all around, except from Rounds, who was laughing.

Adams was different, a capable, highly conscientious technician. He wanted only to do his part in winning the war, then get back to Milwaukee as quickly as possible to begin his studies to become a minister. He and McGovern talked, almost always it seemed, about everything. Adams spent what idle hours he had writing long letters home, cleaning his equipment, reading, or simply lying on his cot, thinking. McGovern also did a lot of reading and writing letters to Eleanor. After he began flying in combat, he always put in a number, which seemed innocent enough to the censors, but each one was the number of missions he had flown. Eleanor knew that thirty-five was the magic number—when George had completed thirty-five missions he could come home.

Those who arrived in the summer or fall of 1944 were assigned to tents already in place. This had its good points, but one notable drawback as well. Frequently, the tent had belonged to a crew that had been shot down. When pilot Lt. Donald Kay of the 465th Bomb Group arrived in Cerignola, he heard those who were already there call out, "You'll be sorry!" He and his crew took over the tents that had been those of a Lieutenant Greenwood and his crew, who had been shot down two days before Kay's arrival.[13]

135

The food may have been the envy of the people of Cerignola, but it was never close to the standards the Yanks were accustomed to eating. Powdered eggs were the breakfast staple, served in various forms, often scrambled. But no matter what was done with the eggs, most of them ended up in the garbage can. There were pancakes, made from flour and the powdered eggs. They looked like and had the consistency of a Frisbee. The Army-issued "tropical butter" was treated to prevent spoilage under any imaginable circumstance, so it was too hard to melt, no matter what was tried. The bread was fresh, baked on the site by the cooks, but it was coarse and suitable only for French toast—again made with powdered eggs. Sometimes there was oatmeal, but it was on the rubbery side and Lieutenant Pepin of the 741st was convinced "that what wasn't consumed was used to repair the planes, as it was gooey and sticky enough to be useful."[14]

At noon and in the evening, there was canned food—stewed prunes, hash heated in garbage cans, and meat, which was mostly Spam, called "mystery meat." Like nearly every serviceman in the armed forces of the United States, the AAF men at Cerignola came to hate the sight of Spam. This was true even at the very top. After the war, General Eisenhower met the president of the Hormel company and thanked him for the Spam, then added, with a grin, "But did you have to send us so much of it?" One writer in the 455th—calling himself "Anon"—commented: "For breakfast the cooks will fry it. At dinner it is baked. For supper they have it paddy caked. Next morning it's with flapjacks. Where the hell do they get it all, they must order it by kegs! . . . SPAM in stew. SPAM in pies, and SPAM in boiling grease!"[15]

At Cerignola, the alternative to Spam was canned Vienna sausages. After a month of eating them, one of the men tacked a proposal on the squadron ready-room door, offering to stop bombing Vienna if its people would stop sending their sausages.[16]

Lieutenant Shostack had flown 2,500 cases of K rations in his B-24 to Cerignola, and had discovered that nobody wanted it. So he put the cases into his tent and whenever he could he would take ten boxes of them into town, go to what passed for a restaurant, "and trade them for an Italian spaghetti dinner." The spaghetti sauce had no meat in it "but the Italians had great tomato sauce and a bottle of cheap wine to go with the meal."[17]

Whenever weather prevented a mission, which happened often, some of the men would try to break the monotony at the base by going into town. The AAF sent in a truck every half hour or so, which would then wait at an intersection so guys going back had a ride. There was a Red Cross club across the street from the cathedral, with a movie theater for the Americans, a pool table, books, and cards.[18]

The men had ample money. They were paid in Allied military currency, which at one penny to the lira was the legal tender for occupied Italy. The exchange rate was more than favorable. Skilled Italian laborers, those who helped put in the concrete floors or worked on the runway or elsewhere, were paid 75 lira a day. Unskilled laborers received 50 lira a day. A haircut in town was 7 lira. A shave cost the same. To the initial surprise of the Yanks, there were barbers all along the streets, usually small boys with straight razors. Lt. Donald Currier noted that "as poor as the people were, many of the Italian old men went to the barber for their shave every day. It was a male ritual." For a hot bath—unavailable at the base—the men went to a public bath in Cerignola. They brought their own soap and towel. The cost was 25 lira.[19]

Another surprise to the Yanks: the residents of Cerignola wore, mostly, only black clothes. The poverty of the people precluded bright, colorful clothes. Many of them were starving, or nearly so. "We watched the women standing in long lines with their pieces of cloth," Currier wrote, "waiting for their small allotment of flour." The flour came from the American supplies. Hard to imagine—flour coming from the States to the Romans' land of cereal, where Hannibal had had his supply base. Currier also noted that on the roofs of ancient houses there were bundles of twigs and small branches. "This was the fuel they cooked with." The AAF men would bring their laundry into town, where for a few lira the local women would wash it and hang it out to dry, then fold it.20

Lieutenant Pepin went into Cerignola frequently. There he had met a teenage girl named Maria, "cute and dark-eyed." He overcame his inability to speak Italian by using his high school French. Maria also had learned some French in school. He recalled that "the customary way of the Italians required the meeting of the family as a prerequisite to any form of social contact." Maria lived with her grandmother, mother, and two aunts. All the men of the family had died in the war. "The women accepted me, but I doubt if they ever trusted me. Maria and I were never alone for more than a few moments. A fleeting kiss now and then was permissible, but nothing else."

For Pepin, the friendship of the family and his visiting in their home "became very important to me. It offset the inhumane rigors of war and added gentleness to my life." He wrote his own mother about Maria. She sent him packages of women's clothing. Maria and her family "were overjoyed and honored me with great meals." But, Pepin added regretfully, "I won no free time with Maria."21

Sgarro Ruggiero, a thirty-year-old who had been in and gotten out of the Italian army, worked at the airfield. One day he brought an American pilot to his home for a lunch made by his mother. She served pasta, with no meat, no cheese, no tomato sauce. Still the pasta was homemade and the wheat was homegrown, and the American ate it with gusto. Ruggiero's mother said, "If there were meat, it would be better. It would be ragu." The next day, an American truck pulled up outside her home. The driver unloaded 100 tins of meat—chicken breast, beef, bacon, and the inevitable Spam. Ruggiero said the Americans "brought richness to us."22

Sgt. Joseph Maloney, twenty years old, was a tail gunner on his B-24, in the 415th Squadron, 98th Bomb Group, based near Cerignola. A child of the Depression, Joe knew hard times. He found a nine-year-old Italian boy named Gino who would come every week to clean his tent, and he paid far above the going rate for it just to help out the boy's family. Gino's mother did his laundry in return for a cake of soap. Gino also supplied him with fresh eggs on occasion, for which Joe paid him two packs of American cigarettes.[23]

Sgt. Anthony Picardi of the 742nd Squadron got to visit Volturara Irpina, the village where his mother, father, and oldest sister were born. "As we arrived in the village square, people were pointing and asking questions: '*Sono Americani?*' ['Are you American?'] I answered back yes in Italian. They ran off to seek my relatives to tell them that I had arrived from America. I never knew I had so many relatives in Italy. I met my uncle, aunt, and cousins. Everyone was happy, hugging and kissing. I met my grandmother, who was ninety years old at the time. That was the first and last time I would ever see her. She embraced me and said, '*Figio mio.*' ['My son.'] It was a very emotional moment. I could not for the love of me figure out how she recognized me. She said I had my father's face and she knew immediately who I was." Picardi handed out gifts—candy, sugar, coffee, cigarettes, and more. He had saved the items from his purchases at the PX for the occasion.[24]

Francesco Musto was born in Cerignola in 1928, the oldest of what became a family of nine children. His father was a skilled electrician, but his house had no running water—his mother bought the water in containers brought to her from the town fountain by small boys. After 1939, there was no salt at all, no sugar for months, and often no milk. As a boy, Musto would ride his bike for ten kilometers to a farm to get a bit of milk for his one-year-old sister. In his memory, the townspeople had little or no contact with the German occupiers of Italy and nothing the Germans did impressed them. The Americans, however, "opened our minds in an incredible way." Musto recalls that when the AAF came, "I can remember that for three weeks—three full weeks—on the road outside our house for twenty-four hours a day we had a continuous flow of everything, trucks, jeeps, tanks, amphibious vehicles, everything." Then in just a few days the Americans built their airfield. They put up their tents, made the briefing room and headquarters building, and more. They threw away a lot. Musto managed to salvage a radio and other items. "So I discovered an entire world of new products, technologies, services." On the radio, his listened to "something I never had heard before," the music of Glenn Miller. Like everyone else, he loved it.

There were some romances between American servicemen and the local women, and at least a hundred marriages resulted. But there were many women selling themselves. In Musto's memory, "There were too many girls doing what they should never have been doing. There was a terrible degradation of morality." There were many Italian-Americans in the AAF, most of whom spoke Italian. But not well, at least according to Musto. He said "they spoke some horrible dialects that we couldn't understand. They were dialects used more than a century previous."

As for food, "The first thing that the Americans brought was the very white bread, white, incredibly white, white like milk." The second thing that impressed Musto was "the variety." The people of Cerignola were accustomed to dried fava beans with chicory and a little bit of olive oil, and sometimes fish from the sea. But the Americans brought in Spam, peanut butter, chocolate, and so much more. As far as Musto was concerned, "This was modernity. The new world was this one."

The local residents went to work for the Americans, another miracle. First, the Americans would hire women to clean, wash clothes, prepare food, and so on, and pay them for it. Second, the men could get almost any kind of work, on the airfields, in the barracks, everywhere. Best of all it wasn't day work, as they were accustomed to—one day on, many days off—but steady. Three months. Four months. More. Along with the work for women, this was "an incredible novelty."[25]

According to Gionanna Pistachio Colucci, a twenty-five-year-old married woman and mother in 1944, everything about the Americans was "fantastic, marvelous. When the Americans arrived it was a joyous celebration. The Red Cross was here. The children got covers for their beds. They had clothes, jackets. The Americans also brought medicines." She recalled that the day before the Germans fled and the Americans moved in, a group of Italian soldiers, deserters, unarmed local boys, appeared in Cerignola. The Germans killed them all and put their bodies into one of the Roman granaries. Today, the Cerignola cemetery has a monument to these boys. Many local people can never forgive the Germans for the atrocity. But, Colucci said, "We have a beautiful memory of the Americans."[26]

Michele Bancole, a sixteen-year-old boy who worked at the airfield, recalled that he had keys to the American warehouse. Unbelievable. "But they trusted us." He added that a "typical characteristic" of the Americans was that "they were handsome." He was especially impressed by their physical appearance and the way they played sports, such as softball, or engaged in boxing matches. He and other boys would watch. Bancole was impressed because "the Americans knew first to enjoy life and then after that to go to work."[27]

Mario Carpocefala was a ten-year-old boy when the Americans came. He went to work for them, doing whatever needed doing, sometimes for money, other times for cigarettes. When the German soldiers had occupied Cerignola, Mario remembered seeing a loaf of black bread on a truck. The German driver had stopped to be shaved. Mario had to have that bread. He grabbed it. Just then some other German soldiers came down the street and one of them shouted. Mario tried to hide behind a Roman milestone. A soldier aimed his rifle at him. Mario threw the bread down the street and took off running. Decades later, he would show the spot to his children and comment, "Look, there for a loaf of bread I almost lost my life."

The Americans were different. Once Mario was scrounging around a garbage pit, gathering food. Nearby were some crushed cigarette butts, which Mario was also pocketing. An American sergeant grabbed him. "Kid, what are you doing? You're too young to smoke." With his broken English, Mario said he was taking the cigarettes for his father, the food for his mother.

"Throw that shit away," the sergeant said. "Come with me." He took Mario to the supply tent and gave him some rations and packs of cigarettes.

One of the bombardiers stationed in Cerignola, Major Riccardi, was the child of immigrant parents from Italy. He had four brothers in the service during the war. He took Mario under his wing. Each day he taught Mario English words and after missions would review them with him. Mario learned the language and later said that had it not been for Riccardi's influence and English lessons, "I would have been a bum."[28]

As for politics, there was little discussion by the people of Cerignola. Many who had been Fascists in the 1930s changed their minds. The one topic everyone agreed upon was how crazy Mussolini must have been to get into the war. Look at Spain, people would say. It is a Fascist country. But General Franco keeps Spain out of the war. Why didn't Mussolini? According to Musto, "Italy made two mistakes. First, entering the war. Second, entering on the wrong side."[29]

The Americans were not in Italy to sightsee or romance or drink or otherwise have fun. They were there to engage the Germans in combat. Not on the ground or at sea, but in the air. That gave them some privileges, such as cots to sleep on, hot—if not very good—food prepared by cooks, time off, faster promotions, and more. They were grateful that they were not in the infantry, sleeping in foxholes and being shot at, or in the Navy, cooped up on a ship for interminable voyages, going wherever the captain directed, almost never seeing the enemy except in the air yet still taking great risks that, when a ship got destroyed, led to the death by wounds or drowning of almost every one of their mates. (Except for a tiny number of volunteers no one wanted to be in a submarine.) But it was the case in World War II that the U.S. servicemen in the Navy were glad they were where they were, instead of in a foxhole or a bomber, while those in the infantry wanted no part of flying—they liked keeping their feet on the ground. Virtually every sailor or soldier shuddered at the thought of being in an airplane when it got hit by enemy fighters or flak.

McGovern met two infantry officers after the war and said to them, "Whenever I'd fly over you guys I thought it must be terrible to be down there in the mud, hand-to-hand fighting, all that shelling." And the infantrymen told him, "Seeing you guys overhead and the Germans shooting away at you, we thought you didn't have a chance if you take a direct hit." To McGovern's surprise, "They were feeling sorry for us." For himself, McGovern said, "I always knew that it would take infantry to win the war, but I also thought that the bombers and the fighter planes were essential too, that without those planes the infantry could not prevail against the Germans."[30]

For the men of the AAF flying the planes, death was a constant threat. Lieutenant Capps of the 456th Bomb Group arrived in Cerignola in January 1944. That month he celebrated his twenty-first birthday. There were three other young officers with him, Lts. Douglas S. Morgan, Gail J. Scritchfield, and Edward J. Heffner. Morgan and Scritchfield were fellow pilots, Heffner was a bombardier. They shared a camaraderie. "We were all very young, eager, patriotic, and anxious to begin the great adventure of flying combat missions."

At first they were fed by the 301st Bomb Group mess kitchens. Capps never forgot the faces of the 301st crew members when they arrived in the mess tent where he was eating, after returning from a mission into Germany. "They all looked stunned, strained, emotionally drained, and very fatigued. They talked amongst themselves about how their buddies had been shot down on the mission, the number of parachutes they had seen coming from the falling planes, and planes that had blown up without any chance of men bailing out."

The looks and talk of the returned crew brought a sense of reality to Capps, but still "I didn't believe that I was going to be one that was shot down and I couldn't wait to get into combat."

Within four months of his arrival at Cerignola, all three of Capps's friends—Morgan, Scritchfield, and Heffner—were gone. Each had a violent death in crashes in their B-24s. Later a tent mate of Capps's, Lt. Nicholas Colletti, a bombardier, was shot down and killed. When Capps completed his missions—fifty-one of them!—on July 7, 1944, his co-pilot, Lt. Sydney Brooks, became the B-24's pilot. Two weeks after he took command of the plane, Brooks had a wing knocked off by enemy fire and his plane collided with another B-24 in the formation. Brooks spun violently to the ground and was killed. The other plane exploded.[31]

As with the other squadrons, the 741st was taking heavy casualties and losses. Commander Lanford was one of them. He had been awarded a Distinguished Flying Cross for leading a mission over Vienna on March 17, 1944, but on July 21 his plane was shot down on a mission against Brux, Czechoslovakia. The flak bursts severed the control cables. Lanford attempted a hard right turn, but "the control wheel spun like a roulette wheel." The plane was losing altitude fast. He ordered everyone to bail out. Lanford landed safely, got in contact with Tito's partisans, and managed to return to base, where he went into the mess hall to be greeted by the operations officer, who exclaimed, "My God, I thought you were dead!" Lanford went back to flying in combat and completed his tour. But the squadron historical diary noted the destruction of his and other B-24s and declared, "Replacements are sorely needed as our status at the moment could aptly be called quasi-operational."[32]

Beyond the many B-24s shot down there was sudden death from accidents. Shortly after arriving in Italy, Sgt. Kenneth Higgins, McGovern's radio operator, saw one. Right after taking off, the pilot was supposed to hit the brake pedals to keep the landing gear's wheels from spinning as they retracted. But on this occasion, the Liberator was not yet airborne when the pilot hit the brakes and the plane

1. Cadet George McGovern in 1943. His cadet pay was $125 per month. He was twenty years old, had flown only a few hours in a small single-engine civilian plane, and had no military experience. But he had embarked on learning how to be a pilot of a four-engine bomber.

2. McGovern poses on a primary trainer—PT 109—on the dirt airstrip at Hatbox Field, Muskogee, Oklahoma, in October 1943. The instructor rode in the rear seat, the trainee in front. The plane had no canopy—thus the goggles and heavy flight gear.

3. The pilot and his crew beside the *Dakota Queen*. Standing (*left to right*): Lt. George McGovern, co-pilot Lt. Ralph "Bill" Rounds, and navigator Lt. Sam Adams. Kneeling (*left to right*): flight engineer Sgt. Mike Valko, ball turret gunner Sgt. Bill McAfee, waist gunner Sgt. Bill Ashlock, radio operator Sgt. Ken Higgins, nose gunner Sgt. Robert O'Connell, and tail gunner Sgt. Isador Irving Seigal.

4. The enlisted men lived in this tent in an olive grove outside Cerignola, Italy. It was cold and damp through the winter of 1944–1945, with cots, naked electric lightbulbs, a gasoline-fed drip stove, and no toilets. But it was home.

5. The desolate street scene of Cerignola, circa spring 1945, contrasted with the bustle of the Air Force base.

6. Lt. Bill Rounds, the co-pilot from Wichita, Kansas; Lt. George McGovern, the pilot from Mitchell, South Dakota; and Lt. Sam Adams, the navigator from Milwaukee, Wisconsin, pose in front of the tent in which they lived. They were a long way from the American Midwest. Rounds and McGovern were together in the tent for almost a year. After Adams was killed on a bombing mission in 1945, Lt. Carroll Cooper took his place.

7. The mechanics of the ground crew at work on a B-24 in Cerignola. Ask any bomber pilot or his crew of the Fifteenth Air Force and they will tell you how superb these men were. Sometimes it seemed that they never slept. It was always apparent that they knew engines, they knew the plane, and that they had the training and the tools and the skill to keep 'em flying.

8 and 9. (*Above*) Two armorers prepare to load a 1,000-pound bomb in a B-24 for its next mission, Cerignola. (*Below*) Armorers load 500-pound bombs into the B-24s in the winter of 1944–1945 at Cerignola. These bombs were the reason for everything—designing and building the bombers, training the pilots and crews, establishing and maintaining the base in Italy, flying missions through enemy flak and fighters. Their purpose was to destroy Germany's ability to make war.

10. A salute to the magnificent men in their Liberator machines. Over 18,000 were built—more than any other American airplane. The bomber was big, heavy, terribly cramped, with no creature comforts. But the B-24 could deliver bombs that could destroy German refineries, marshalling yards, factories, and airfields.

11. A B-24 from the 461st Bomb Group drops 1000-pound bombs. They did not always hit the target, but they did so enough times to cripple the German war machine.

12. B-24 over Ploesti, August 1, 1943. There were 177 bombers on the mission. They came in low, at 100 to 300 feet, to achieve surprise. But 54 of the bombers were lost, along with 532 airmen. The oil refinery was badly damaged but not destroyed.

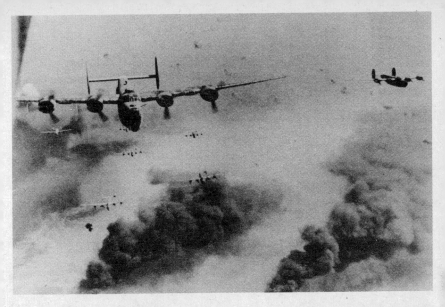

13 and 14. B-24s return to Ploesti on May 31, 1944. They avoided the mistake of coming in low, but the Germans used smoke pots to obscure the targets and sent up flak. They returned again to Ploesti, August 10, 1944. The missions to this and other refineries were critical to the war effort. By this time the Germans were suffering badly from their lack of fuel; by the spring of 1945 they had virtually none left.

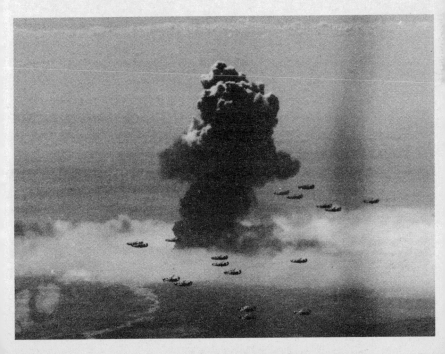

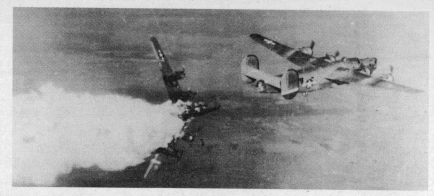

15. November 20, 1944, Belchhamer, Germany. A B-24 of the 781st Bomb Squadron, 465th Bomb Group, is hit by flak and starts to go down. The pilot, Lt. Col. Clarence Lokkar (who was the squadron commander) and five of his eleven crewmen aboard parachuted out and were captured. Lokkar escaped but was killed that same day.

16. August 1944: B-24s hit the marshalling yards at Linz, Austria. It was Hitler's hometown and a major transportation target. For those reasons it was heavily defended. "I hated Linz as a target," McGovern declared. He went on a mission there in December 1944 and again on his last mission in April 1945.

nosed over and plowed into the ground. All the men in the front of the aircraft were killed. Another time, a B-24 came in to land. It had a bomb hung up in the bomb bay but the pilot, who should have checked to make sure all the bombs had dropped, had not. The bomb fell out when he landed, went off, and blew the whole plane into pieces. "The whole crew burned," Higgins recalled. "I mean they were just charred ashes."[33]

Pilot Lt. Guyon Phillips saw a similar accident. Just before liftoff, the pilot hit the brakes. "A B-24 with a full load of gas and bombs just won't get in the air without full power," Phillips commented. This time the plane was at the end of the runway. The nose gear sheared off and the nose of the plane ground into the earth with such force that it chewed off the front of the plane, right up to the engines. All the men in the front were instantly killed.[34]

Once a bomber gained altitude, the crew had some chance of survival when things went wrong. Some managed to get out of a doomed Liberator, pull the rip cord on their parachute, and land safely. Some of them managed to bail out over neutral Switzerland or Yugoslavia, where if they were lucky enough to join with Tito's partisans they could return to Italy. But many, perhaps most, became prisoners of war. Until the Battle of the Bulge, in December 1944, the Germans held far more AAF men as prisoners than they did American infantry.

The AAF knew that the capture of men who had bailed out was always a possibility. To prevent this, it gave each member of a crew an escape kit, consisting of some candy bars, a shot of morphine, a silk map of Europe, and a compass. That wasn't much. The men were also instructed that the only information they had to give their captors was their name, rank, and serial number. Generally, they gave out more than that, not necessarily willingly but sometimes to avoid torture, more often in what they regarded as casual conversation. The German interrogators were young men, good in English, usually former fliers themselves, now without an arm or otherwise injured, and they would get the POWs to chatting, almost like shoptalk. Like most people their age, the prisoners were willing to brag about such matters as "How fast does your plane go?" or "Can you do a roll in it?" and so on. Further, the Germans already had excellent information, such as the base of the squadron or the name of its commander. A vast majority of POWs insisted, after the war, that they had never told the Germans anything of value. The Germans, however, said they got everything they wanted from the prisoners. The men on both sides were stretching the truth pretty considerably.

Once a man was captured he was out of the control of the AAF, but he was still in the military and subject to military discipline. The POWs hated the experience, but most of them managed to live through it without compromise. Pilot Lt. Walter Shostack of the 741st Squadron was one of them. He was on his fourth mission, over a refinery in Austria, when the plane he was flying took a direct hit from a flak shell that exploded on the B-24's nose, killing the bombardier and nose gunner instantly. The plane began to lose altitude so badly that it was about to crash into a mountain. Shostack ordered the crew to bail out. They were now over Yugoslavia and all of them, including Shostack, parachuted down safely, but three of them were shot on the ground by SS troops who claimed they were terrorists. "They didn't give them a chance."

Alone, Shostack managed to hide for a week. He hooked up with some of Tito's partisans and they were helping him to escape, but unfortunately they stopped at a farmhouse and a boy ran to tell partisans fighting for the Germans. They found Shostack in the attic. When they discovered that he was an American, they gave him an apple. Shostack had grown up speaking Russian, which is similar to Serbian. The Serbians said they were not fighting the Americans, they were fighting the communists. That was a bit ironic to Shostack, whose family had left Russia to get away from the communists. As he noted, "You really couldn't tell who was who in that war without a program."

Eventually Shostack was taken to Frankfurt, where he underwent interrogation. The German asking the questions was, of all things, a former used car salesman from Detroit. It was mid-1944 and, as Shostack put it, "He knew by then that the war was lost so he gave me some tea and cookies." The German really was hoping to loosen Shostack's tongue, "but unfortunately for him having been shot down on our fourth mission I didn't know anything." Shostack was sent to Stalag Luft 3. It was a large camp. Prisoners in it before Shostack arrived had dug a tunnel and some sixty of them managed to wiggle through it and escape, but unfortunately for them, the Germans rounded up most of them, brought them back, and shot them in front of the other POWs. So they stopped digging tunnels, and for Shostack there was nothing to do except play cards, wonder when the next meal was coming, and wait for the end of the war.

Because of the German respect for rank, Lieutenant Shostack and the other officers had "a little easier time of it" as compared to the enlisted men. Officers were not made to work. The prison barracks were divided into twelve tiers, each tier had twelve beds, four beds three layers high. There were 144 men in Shostack's barracks, one stove at one end and one faucet with cold water at the other. That faucet was the sanitary facility. There was a latrine outside, but the POWs had to get permission from a guard to use it.

Rations were miserable. The bread was made, apparently, from sawdust and there was only one piece of it per man. The guards would set the ration down outside the door. The Germans did hand out coffee, but as far as Shostack could tell it was made from ground-up acorns. Once a week, if he was lucky, he got a piece of horse meat. Occasionally the American POWs received Red Cross parcels with food, but there was a contingent of Russian prisoners next to Stalag Luft 3 and if the Americans thought they had it bad, all they had to do was look at the Russians to know what true misery was. So they would divide their Red Cross parcels and throw half of the food over the fence to the Russians.

The Red Cross also sent cigarettes, which "did a world of good when it came to trading for food." The Germans would barter anything they had for American cigarettes. The POWs had a radio hidden in a tin can, which allowed them to keep aware of what was going on. The main thing they wanted to know was, How close are the Allies to our camp? On April 29, 1945, just as they were being liberated, they got the American Armed Forces Network on the radio. The first thing they heard was a popular song, "Don't Fence Me In." Given where he had been for almost a year, Shostack thought the words were "kind of comical."

Shostack's final judgment was, "War is a terrible thing and anybody that tells you otherwise was probably a supply sergeant somewhere in the middle of Kansas who had no idea what combat is about." As far as he was concerned, "It was just something we had to go do." In the end, "I loved my crew and that's about all I loved. War is not a joyful experience." Decades later, he enjoyed watching war movies. His wife asked him how come he did, as he hated war so much. "I explained that while watching a war movie there is no danger of getting shot and you can concentrate on the story line and not worry about a piece of flak coming through the windshield."[35]

In the 741st Squadron there were twelve B-24s and twenty-three crews. That meant forty-six pilots and co-pilots, plus more than fifty other officers. When McGovern arrived, many had been in combat, while others like himself were waiting to go. Whatever their status, every one of them knew the dangers of getting shot down or being forced to bail out or how likely it was that they would have a fatal accident. Death or the possibility of captivity was all around these young men.

Whether in the officers club or the airmen's club for enlisted men, the newcomers would sit quietly and listen to the talk of the veterans who had just returned from a mission. McGovern listened hard and thereby picked up tips on flying a B-24 in combat. The talk was about what had happened, how the plane performed, what the German flak was like, and other details. Always they discussed how many parachutes they had counted coming from a plane going down, but not about who had made it out of the doomed craft and who had not. They assumed that a parachute meant the man had landed safely, but they had no idea whether he had escaped and was on his way back to Italy or had been made a POW or had been killed on the ground. Shostack's name never came up.

Sgt. Mel TenHaken, a radio operator in the 455th Bomb Group, remembered the talk as both enlightening and frightening. It was unlike the talk one usually heard from young men after an examination or a football or basketball game. "There was no pride of individual accomplishment here, or boasting about comparative achievements." Further, "There was no jesting about those [like TenHaken, McGovern, and the other recent arrivals] who hadn't been up yet because everyone knew that would happen tomorrow or a day after." TenHaken also noted that "there was no overt elation by those who had completed thirty-four missions," because everyone remembered "the one who got his on his thirty-fifth." No one talked to impress. Experiences were shared only because better understanding of techniques and tactics would improve the odds for survival.[36]

Sergeant TenHaken had arrived at Cerignola with two other crews. One of those crews was the first to go on a mission. It was a long one. Their plane returned safely, but with holes caused by flak in its wings and fuselage. That evening, after they had finished their postmission interrogation, they were withdrawn and did not want to talk. "They felt it might be better if we discussed feelings later, maybe after we had all completed some combat missions." As for TenHaken and his crew, "We wondered if they'd ever again have the optimistic, cheerful, normal personalities we had known."

A day later the second crew flew its initial mission. The plane was two hours late getting back to base. Suddenly, in the darkness along the row of tents, one of the gunners appeared, panting, with some of his parachute gathered over his arm and the rest of it dragging behind. He was frightened. He demanded to know where the rest of his crew was. Told that no one knew, he explained that his B-24 had been hit over the target. He could not assess the effect of the damage but related that his pilot had gotten the plane to the airfield, where he circled to test the controls and to burn the remaining fuel— crash-landing a B-24 was always hazardous, but especially so when there was fuel in the wings. The pilot was unsure of whether or not the landing gear would operate, as his hydraulic power was gone. He told the crew to bail out. He would stay with the plane and try to bring it down.

A messenger came running in from the flight line. He said the pilot had made it safely but the plane had broken up on landing. Had the crew still been on board, many of the men would have been injured or killed. Over the next two hours the rest of the crew straggled in, dragging their parachutes. There was no celebration and precious little discussion, but the men sure were grateful for the pilot's action.[37]

The AAF had a rule that enlisted men and officers were not allowed to fraternize, which was why the officers had their own club at Cerignola, the enlisted men another. But their tents were next to each other. They ate together. Most of the time, they went into each other's clubs. The clubs had beer, usually warm, and soft drinks. The vast majority of the men did not indulge in even the beer on the night they were listed for a mission in the morning. Most officers and the sergeants considered the nonfraternization rule absurd. "Our crew was one family," Lieutenant Shostack said, "and we fraternized all the time."[38]

The crew went wherever the pilot took them, and he went wherever the bomb group commander told him to go. It was the same with an infantry platoon or a naval crew on a destroyer or other ship of war. They had the need for togetherness to bind them. On the ground as in the air, they shared. Whatever the pilot's age or number of missions, they all looked up to him, trusted him, would do whatever he told them to do. As with the pilot who had his crew bail out over Cerignola, then landed the plane himself. That was, after all, his first mission.

On the fiftieth anniversary of V-E Day, I was with Joe Heller, a bombardier with the Twelfth Air Force, and the author of *Catch-22*. Heller told me, "I never had a bad officer." Astonished, I said, "Joe, you created Major Major Major, Colonel Cathcart, General Dreedle, Lieutenant Minderbinder, and so many others. Everybody in the world knows about them. How can you tell me you never had a bad officer?"

"They are all invention," he replied. "Every single officer from when I went into the service to going over to Italy to flying the missions to when I got discharged, every one of them was good."

In the course of interviewing George McGovern for this book, I told him what Heller had told me. McGovern agreed. "That's my experience," he said. "I was impressed by the pilots, the bombardiers, the navigators, right across the board and with the operations officers and our group commander. I thought they were a superior bunch of men and I can honestly say I don't recall a bad officer. All through combat I had confidence that our officers were doing the very best they knew how—if they made mistakes they weren't foolish mistakes. Our officers were superb."[39]

Obviously there were some weak, some poor, some inefficient or ignorant, and some absolutely terrible officers in the U.S. armed services in World War II. But if such men ever got into combat positions, the AAF, the Army, the Navy, or the Marines got them out. At once. Men's lives depended on them, after all. The combat officers knew it and acted accordingly. Ask the Germans who opposed them how good they were. Or the Japanese.

The American officers were superb. And that is the way it was in the 741st Squadron, 455th Bomb Group, in Cerignola, Italy.

CHAPTER SIX

Learning to Fly in Combat

THE AAF POLICY IN THE FALL OF 1944 was to have the pilots fly their first five combat missions as co-pilots with a veteran and an experienced crew. McGovern was, in his words, "lucky," because his pilot was Capt. Howard Surbeck of Washington state. He was older, twenty-four years old to McGovern's twenty-two, "and he had circles under his eyes and he was obviously feeling the strain of combat." He had flown twenty-five missions when McGovern flew with him. It was his tent that Rounds, with McGovern on board, had torn in half with his jeep, but Surbeck never mentioned it to McGovern.

Surbeck let McGovern do quite a bit of the flying from his co-pilot's seat, sometimes half the mission. The experience taught McGovern "more about what it's like to have all that gear on and to go to 25,000 feet in subzero temperatures and stay in formation and get shot at and all the other things that go with combat missions." Surbeck "brought me along."

McGovern's first mission was November 11, 1944—Armistice Day. The night before he checked and saw his name on the assignment sheet. The morning began for him when the operations sergeant came into his tent at 4:00 A.M. to wake him. On his first five missions, Rounds and Adams could stay in the sack, as they were not going. McGovern went to the mess hall for a powdered egg breakfast. Then he climbed into a truck for the drive to the group's operations room for the briefing. At the door, an MP examined his identification and checked his name on the assignment sheet, then opened the door so McGovern and those from his truck could enter.

Inside, the 300 or so crew sat on planks placed over cinder blocks. When a staff officer announced that they were all present and accounted for, the door was locked. The group commander by the fall of 1944 was Col. William Snowden. He was in his mid-forties, a "grandfather" figure to the pilots and crews. He had gray hair but a commanding presence. McGovern said he had "the total confidence of everyone in our group. A good man and a good leader. Just the way he moved around, he was reassuring without being condescending."

When Colonel Snowden strode in, everyone stood at attention. Snowden climbed onto the platform, put the men at ease, and after saying good morning motioned to a member of his staff to pull a drawstring. Behind the curtain was a large map of southern and central Europe. The pilots and crew members saw their route and the target drawn on the map with erasable marks. When it was Vienna, or Munich, or any other target known to be well defended by antiaircraft guns, or if it was four or more hours flying time from Cerignola, a dismal groan slowly became audible, but on this occasion there were murmurs of approval because the target was Linz, Austria, not so terribly far away, without any known antiaircraft batteries to fly over, and not so well protected itself. It could be what the men called a "milk run." Later in the war Linz would become one of the most heavily defended targets in Europe.

Colonel Snowden got the men to quiet down and gave way to the weather officer, who described what the cloud cover and winds were likely to be like over Linz. Then he went over conditions on the route and what to expect on the way home and what it would be like over Cerignola when they got back. Next the operations officer described the nature of the marshaling yards they were going after and explained that the mission was important because the Germans were moving men and matériel through Linz on their way to the Italian front. He warned the pilots and bombardiers to make every possible effort to avoid hitting the cultural sites and educational buildings. By this stage of the war, the bombardiers in the squadron would toggle their switches when they saw the lead plane, with the best navigator and bombardier, drop its bombs.

Next the men were told who would be the pilot of the lead plane. He was always a good pilot. Sometimes he was a major, but often Colonel Snowden would lead the missions—when that happened, the men would again murmur their approval. The briefing would conclude with the group chaplain leading them in a prayer.[1]

Dismissal came from Snowden, but only after he had the men "hack" their watches. They would pull the stems of their watches when the second hand reached 12. Snowden would have them set the minute and hour hands to correspond to his, then count to ten and call "hack," and they would push the stems back in. They filed out of the briefing room, to go to another briefing—one for pilots and co-pilots, another for radio operators, another for navigators and bombardiers, still another for gunners.

The men climbed into trucks for the ride to the storage sheds just off the runway where their flying equipment and parachutes were located. Each crew got out and dressed for the mission. They were going up to 20,000 feet or even higher and it was going to be cold up there, between 20 and 50 degrees below zero Fahrenheit. McGovern and the others pulled on heavy winter underwear. Next they put on long wool socks and a wool military uniform, slacks and shirts—olive drab. Then a leather jacket and leather trousers, both lined with sheepskin, then sheepskin-lined heavy boots. Big, heavy silk-lined leather gloves followed. The sheepskin-lined helmet came down over the ears. Surbeck and McGovern wore Colt .45 automatics in a shoulder holster, then put on backpacks containing their parachutes. The other crew members picked up their parachutes in chest packs, which they carried into the plane by hand. They could snap them on if needed. The parachute packers made their standard joke when giving them out, "If it doesn't work, bring it back and I'll give you another."[2]

Dressed, they walked to their plane on its hard stand. Surbeck, accompanied by the chief of the ground crew, walked around the B-24, checking it out visually. The navigator, bombardier, radioman, and gunners would check out their equipment.

Later, when the plane had gotten up to 10,000 feet, the pilots and crew put on their oxygen masks. It covered the nose. They plugged cords from their electrically heated flight suits into an outlet on the plane—the four engines created the power for the electricity. They could adjust the heat, turning it down a little or up a bit as needed. Below 15,000 feet the crew took off their oxygen masks. Surbeck and McGovern kept theirs on until they were down to 10,000 feet. At that altitude, all the smokers lit their cigarettes. The smoke was so thick it looked like there was a fire.[3]

The bombs had been loaded during the night into the bomb bay by the ground crew led by an ordnance officer. They assembled the bombs by taking the stabilizing fins, stored in a separate box, and screwing them on the bombs. Using winches and tractors, the ground crews had hoisted the unwieldy, blunt-nosed 500-pound bombs into their racks. They were inserted into the B-24's womb in a horizontal position and attached to the metal racks. They had a cardboard tag between the bomb and the nose fuse, and at the back end a wire arming pin. The tail gunner would crawl out on the catwalk over the bomb bay door to pull the tag and then the pin.

Climbing into the B-24 with those big heavy boots and the layers of clothing was always cumbersome, as the men waddled ponderously. They carried flak jackets, mandatory since Ploesti. The crew members had difficulty getting themselves into and then adjusted in their cramped positions, especially the nose turret and the tail gunner. The belly turret gunner waited until they were in the air before squeezing—with the help of the waist gunner—into his bubble. Surbeck and McGovern settled into their seats, with their parachutes serving as a sort of back rest. The seats were encased in cast iron. The iron came up to the knees, then under the seat and up the back. It was there in the event that flak hit the plane on the bottom side so that, in McGovern's words, "the pilot and co-pilot would have some chance of survival because somebody has to fly the airplane. It wasn't that they were worth more than anybody else on the crew, but if both got killed or badly injured, that plane is going to go down."[4]

The moment Surbeck got into the plane, went to his seat, and put on his earphones and mike—attached to his helmet—he was, in McGovern's words, "totally in command, of the officers and sergeants." McGovern already knew that, but watching Captain Surbeck go through his routine reinforced the point. McGovern explained, "It had to be that way because the pilot was the only one with his hands on the controls that determined where the plane was going to go and how it was going to be flown." Of course he had help, especially from the navigator and bombardier, the radio operator and the flight engineers, "but the request for their help came from Surbeck." It was his job to check on the crew, frequently. He needed to make sure that nobody's oxygen hose had come unhooked; if a tail gunner or someone else failed to answer when the pilot called to him on the intercom, he might well have passed out from a lack of oxygen or frozen because his electric plug had come out, without ever noticing that his hose or wire was unhooked. These and other things Surbeck did as a matter of routine, McGovern noted.[5]

To get the engines started, Surbeck would signal to the flight engineer, who would start the single-cylinder gasoline-powered unit on the B-24. It was called the "putt-putt" and gave a boost to the batteries. Engine number three, the one nearest McGovern, started first. It powered the generators, which helped start the other engines. When all were operating, Surbeck did a "run-up," checking on each engine's performance, magnetos, temperature and pressure checks of fuel, oil, and hydraulic systems. When a flare went up planes began to move out of their hard stands over the taxiway and onto the runway, looking like elephants getting ready for a circus parade. Surbeck called out the final checklist to McGovern:

"Booster pumps"—"On"

"Mixture"—"Auto rich"

"Props"—"Full high"

"Superchargers"—"Set"

"Half flaps"—"Set"

and so on.6

Surbeck lined his plane up on the taxi strip, behind some planes and ahead of others—there were twenty-eight in the group, seven in each squadron. The 454th Bomb Group was on the other side of the runway, parallel to the 455th, so that the planes from each group could take off side by side. Setting the brakes, Surbeck pushed the throttle to get the engines running at maximum. When his turn to take off arrived, the roar was almost deafening. The plane vibrated as every nut and bolt, every rivet and tube rattled and shook.

Twenty or at most thirty seconds after the plane ahead of him began to roll down the runway, Surbeck released the brakes. A modern air traffic controller, or a pilot of a commercial airliner, would be appalled at the sight, but for the bomber pilots of World War II that was how close to each other they were. Down the strip Surbeck started rolling, picking up speed until he reached 160 miles per hour. He had his flaps set at 20 degrees, brought the engines to maximum power, and at the end of the runway he pulled the nose off the ground and became airborne. With the bomb load, the full tanks of fuel, the weight of the crew and their equipment, including the .50 caliber machine guns and ammunition for them, Surbeck had to fight to gain altitude. It seemed to McGovern that he would not get the plane above treetop altitude, but he did. Barely, but he did. Once the plane was in the air, even if only just, McGovern as co-pilot had the task of raising the landing gear and bringing up the flaps.7

Surbeck circled, as did all the other pilots, their planes looking rather like hawks over a marsh. And he climbed. The gunners tested their guns. They were Browning M-2 .50 caliber machine guns. Each gun had about 150 working parts and the men had been required to strip and reassemble it blindfolded wearing gloves. The guns weighed sixty-four pounds and fired 800 rounds of ammunition per minute to a range of 600 yards. Sgt. Louie Hansen, a tail gunner in the 743rd Squadron, once discovered that both his guns were jammed—the cocking levers had been put in backward after the guns had been cleaned after the previous mission. He described what he did. "There was only space in the turret to get one hand through to a gun. I did one with my right hand, the other with my left. Sweat started to trickle down my back, my goggles steamed over which made no difference as there was no way to see what I was doing. The intense cold made me afraid to remove my gloves. But I got the job done and, as most combat crew members know, one can sweat at 50 degrees below."[8] Fortunately for Surbeck and McGovern, the guns on their Liberator tested okay.

After an hour or so, Surbeck's plane had become a part of the formation. It was a squadron box of seven aircraft. There were two three-plane echelons. The lead plane had a wingman just behind and on either side. Surbeck was one of those on the wing of the leader. The second echelon was forty feet below and forty feet back of the lead echelon. The seventh aircraft, known as "Tail End Charlie," was behind the second echelon. Flying the wing, even for Surbeck, was more difficult than being in the lead, but easier than flying Tail End Charlie. As the last plane in the squadron, Tail End Charlie was the most vulnerable if German fighters attacked, and it was the hardest position to hold. Usually new pilots and crews got that assignment. On the wing, Surbeck wanted to stay close to the plane he was flying on so as to make as small and infrequent power changes as possible, to save the engines and save fuel. Pilot Lt. John Smith said that "in due course flying formation became a reflex like driving a car." The group consisted of four squadrons, the lead box, the high box, the low box, and the middle box.[9]

More climbing, to 20,000 and eventually 25,000 feet over the

Adriatic. Then off for the target. When the group got to the initial point it turned. But clouds had moved in over Linz and the lead pilot decided to abort. He turned, so did the others, and returned to base, still fully loaded with the bombs.

———————

McGovern's first mission went better than that of Lt. David Gandin, a navigator in a B-24. In his war diary, Gandin reported that when his Liberator, called the *Snafu,* was over the target a piece of flak came through the cockpit window. The pilot, Lt. Bill Marsh, lost the top of his head. The co-pilot, Lt. Hilary Bevins, was on his first mission. He called to his radioman, who came to the cockpit wearing a walka-round oxygen bottle "and removed Marsh from the pilot's seat. Bevins couldn't stand it with Marsh in the seat and all the blood flowing around.

"Bevins moved over to the pilot's seat and kept in the formation until it headed off. All the compasses were out, so Bevins flew the opposite direction of the setting sun. All the men were freezing because of the hole in the top of the cockpit. The engineer was sick to his stomach from all the blood. Bevins's eyeball was scratched and Marsh's blood was frozen on his hands."

When darkness descended, Bevins flew opposite the North Star. Finally *Snafu* got back to base—but Bevins had never made a night landing before. "As he came in, he banked too far to the left and knocked off the left landing gear, bounced over and did the same to the right one; the ship crash-landed and caught on fire.

"Thank God all got out okay, though Bevins wouldn't leave till they took Marsh's body out also. The plane burned to a crisp."[10]

———————

On November 17, McGovern flew his second mission as Surbeck's co-pilot. The target was the marshaling yards in Győr, Hungary. Over the target the flak began. It was heavy and accurate. Sticking tight to the formation, his plane and the others could achieve a better bomb pattern but it also made a concentrated target for the flak gunners. "It was just solid black except for flashes of red where shells were exploding," McGovern remembered. The Germans were using a box-type defense. Each of the 88s fired into an area as the bombers approached, the shells traveling faster than the speed of sound and set to explode at the group's altitude. "They just boxed it." The boxes were 2,000 feet deep and 2,000 feet wide, sometimes more. The German antiaircraft units employed almost a million personnel and operated over 50,000 guns, most of them the dreaded 88s. The shells were time-fused to explode at 20,000 feet, or above or below that altitude according to the flight pattern. As the shells exploded, sending out hundreds of pieces of steel shrapnel that had a killing zone radius of some thirty feet, the bombers flew into them. "Well they had filled that box," McGovern said. A standard expression from Surbeck or crew members was that "the flak was so thick you could walk on it." McGovern "often wondered if that's the way hell looks."[11]

Another pilot, Lt. Robert Reichard, recalled that "the barrage was so intense that the daylight disappeared and it was as if someone had cut out the sun." The B-24s had nowhere to hide and with the ground 25,000 feet below, there was no place to dig in. The bursts around them posed a threat to the airplane, as it had ten 500-pound bombs and over 2,000 gallons of 100 octane gas on board.[12]

When the bombs dropped the plane jumped a few feet. "Everything improved when they went away," Lt. Vincent Fagan remembered. "The plane was 5,000 or 6,000 pounds lighter, we were leaving the flak instead of going into it and we could take evasive action—usually a diving turn towards the shortest escape route from the flak area."[13]

One didn't always get out of the flak. On his first mission, October 7, 1944, B-24 pilot J. I. Merritt, in *Liberty Belle,* flew over Vienna to hit an oil refinery. After dropping the bombs, he banked steeply to the left and headed toward the rally point and home. Sgt. Art Johnson, a waist gunner and assistant engineer, was on his twenty-sixth mission. He recalled, "We had flown through the worst of the flak. I sighed a bit, for this was my third time in the vicinity of Vienna and I knew about where the flak began and ended." Just then, there were four explosions in quick succession.

Johnson's oxygen hose pulled apart, his gun was knocked out of his hand, and he hit the floor, hard. Luckily his headset stayed connected and he heard Merritt ask, "Is everyone okay?" Johnson checked the tail gunner and the ball turret gunner, then pressed his mike. "Pilot from left waist—everyone okay back here." But he added, "Number three engine throwing oil and smoke, number four dead, holes in flaps and wings. Over."

Johnson later found out that the first burst had exploded directly in front of the plane and the force of it took the top off the nose turret. The second burst came through and cut the nose wheel and tire in two, cut the interphone lines to the nose and also the oxygen lines. The third burst ripped up the underside of the right wing and exploded in number four engine. The gunner in the top turret, Sgt. Nick Corbo, had just breathed easy and said to himself, "We've made this one," when the bursts came. One piece of shrapnel exploded through the flight deck.

Johnson and the other crew members began throwing everything that was loose out of the plane. Ammunition, guns, flak suits, anything and everything that was loose except themselves. Merritt fought the wheel as the plane heaved and slowed to the brink of stalling. Then it began dropping. Gasoline streamed from the riddled wing tanks, filling the plane with the reek of the fuel. Only one engine was still working, and that one hardly was. The plane had dropped from 25,000 feet to 12,000 and was still going down. Merritt managed to get up some speed and cross into Yugoslavia. Down to 2,000 feet and almost out of fuel, he called out over the intercom, "Bail out and good luck!"

Johnson recalled that the right waist gunner was the first out, followed by the tail gunner and the ball turret gunner. "I was alone in back. I faced the front of the ship and put my head between my knees and out I went. The slipstream caught me and I went end for end. By the time I had slowed down a bit I had pulled my rip cord. One long pull. I was jerked straight up and down as the silk billowed open and I breathed a prayer of thanks."

Johnson and the others, including Merritt and the co-pilot, landed more or less intact. They were picked up by partisans who managed to get them back to Italy, but not until November 26.[14]

Lt. Glenn Rendahl, a co-pilot from Hollywood, California, with the 514th Squadron, said that on his first mission, the flak "exceeded whatever we expected." On McGovern's second mission one bomber of the group was lost. Again there were clouds, but the lead bomber had the Mickey radar and used it to find the railroad and dropped his bombs. The twenty-seven planes following did also. But because of the clouds, no observation of results could be made.[15]

On his first mission, navigator Pepin of the 741st saw a lot of flak, saw some B-24s get hit, but his plane managed to drop its bombs successfully. He felt a sense of joy as the plane headed home. The bomb bay doors were closing and the aircraft's speed was increasing. "The going-home sight of the Alps in the early afternoon was far more beautiful than the morning one." The radiomen tuned to the Armed Services Radio station in Foggia and over the intercom the crew listened to the latest hit records. Both danger and the crew's stamina diminished on the homebound run and "our elation and silliness increased." Everyone was "tired, hungry, and thirsty," as their breakfast and coffee had been hours ago. Finally Pepin could see Cerignola and his plane circled the field. Then, and on later missions, "My favorite sight and sound was hearing the tires touch the steel mat on landing and seeing the props come to a halt." After nine hours of "grueling, horrendous, nerve-racking flying, the mission was over."16

For Sgt. Robert Hammer, now a radio operator with the 742nd Squadron, his first mission was in late September: target, the airfield outside Munich. Two of the men in his crew, a bombardier and a flight engineer, were on their last missions before going home. A fighter escort joined them "and we were bouncing gaily along in the blue" when dead ahead a thick, coal-black cloud appeared. "Take a good look at it, fellows," the veteran bombardier called over the intercom, "because it's flak and you'll be seeing plenty of it from now on." Hammer was appalled to see the squadron of B-24s ahead fly directly into the stuff. Fools, he thought. Why don't they just fly around it? He saw two planes get hit and start down. Shortly after, "we were heading for that same suicidal cloud."

The plane started "bucking like a rodeo bronco." There was a crack. Hammer looked quizzically at the veteran engineer, who pointed to a hole an inch long and a quarter-inch wide made by shrapnel. After what seemed an eternity that in fact had lasted for less than ten minutes, the bombs were away and Hammer's plane turned for home. "We were combat veterans now."17

Radio operator Sgt. Howard Goodner flew his first mission in October 1944. His plane was a B-24 flown by Lt. Richard Farrington, his squadron was the 787th, a part of the 466th Bomb Group, Eighth Air Force. Low clouds covered the airfield and when Farrington got his craft off the ground, he could not see. Flying blind as he climbed, relying on his instruments, following his heading, Farrington was quickly covered with sweat. "Up, up, up he went, until he got above the clouds." As Thomas Childers describes it, "no amount of practice could have prepared the pilot and crew for what they encountered—B-24s, glittering like mica, were popping up out of the clouds" over here, over there, everywhere.

They formed up and straightened out for the target. Farrington called out over the intercom, "This is it, boys. We're on our way to the war."

Ahead shells were bursting all over the sky, sending out shards of shrapnel. The lead squadron of B-24s penetrated the flak. "Mary, Mother of God," one crew member mumbled into the intercom. "Mary, Mother of God, get me out of this." Farrington took them right into it. Jarring detonations erupted around them. The plane bumped and shuddered. But it kept flying straight and level, until the bombs were released. Farrington banked, got away from the flak, and headed home. Sergeant Goodner reached into his jacket pocket for the Tootsie Roll he carried with him. It was frozen solid. When the plane landed, Goodner had his first mission behind him.[18]

———————

On November 18, McGovern was Surbeck's co-pilot on another milk run. The target was the German airfield near Vicenza, Italy. The weather was fair and the bombing was visual. Over 50 percent of the bombs fell in the target area causing extensive damage to the installation. Flak was light and generally inaccurate. No German fighters were seen. The group returned to Cerignola without casualties.

McGovern flew again the next day and it was no milk run. The target was a refinery near Vienna. Because of cloud cover, the lead plane used its Mickey and no results were seen, but dropping bombs by radar instead of visually meant few of them hit what they wanted them to hit and the damage was minimal. Flak was intense but inaccurate and all planes returned to base.

On November 20, on McGovern's final mission as a co-pilot, the target was factories at Zlin, Czechoslovakia. It was a secondary, or alternative, target, but the original objective had been obscured by clouds, so the lead pilot took the group to Zlin. There the weather was clear and the bombing was done visually, with excellent results. Best of all, there was no flak over Zlin. All planes returned safely.[19]

After debriefing, McGovern would meet with Rounds, Adams,

and his crew. They fired questions at him about what it was like, most of all the flak. "They were filled with questions every day," McGovern recalled, "waiting for me when I came back."

Once the session was over, McGovern would steer his way into the officers club for a Coca-Cola or a beer. There he would listen to the veteran pilots talk and ask his own questions. It was shoptalk. From almost every one of the discussions he would absorb information. The topics were the B-24s, the crews, the Germans. What rpm at what altitude? Why was this gauge or that instrument malfunctioning? Is there any way to stay straight and level over the target and still avoid the flak? How long can an engine be on fire before it detonates the gas tank? What can you do when a bomb gets stuck in the bomb bay? How does the plane fly with only three engines operating? With two? When the hydraulic system has leaked or been shot out, how do you get the wheels down?

McGovern had flown four missions in four days. These consecutive missions were about the absolute limit. They left the pilot and his crew haggard, worn, jumpy, frazzled, and spent. But each one counted toward the thirty-five missions that, when completed, would allow McGovern to return to the States. When he had time to write to Eleanor, McGovern noted the number in his letter—number five after the mission to Zlin.

"I worried, as any wife would," Eleanor said three decades later. "I would feel a stab of fear whenever someone knocked at the door or the telephone rang. The first thing I would do when I got a letter from George was to scan through it for a number—the number of missions completed. That was the first thing I wanted to know. Then I'd go back to read the letter."[20]

On December 16, radio operator Sgt. Mel TenHaken flew his first mission, against a refinery at Brux, Czechoslovakia. Because the crew were new, the pilot, Lieutenant Cord, was a veteran of thirty-one missions. TenHaken's regular pilot flew as co-pilot that day. There was another newcomer, a photographer on his seventeenth mission. Theirs would be one of the last two planes on the bomb run and his photos would be among the official records of the raid's effect.

When the group formed up and headed toward the target, Ten-Haken saw "a seemingly endless line of planes. I had never seen this many in one place at one time." He thought that "obviously Rosie the riveter back home had been very busy." The bombers were at 25,000 feet, just below the 26,000-foot ceiling for the craft.

On his B-24, TenHaken was in charge of the chaff, what he had called "Christmas tree tinsel" back home. Its purpose was to confuse German radar, which otherwise would lock on to the group and know what altitude to set the fuses for the shells to explode. The chaff was in packets, each one wrapped and tied with a plain brown band, each one crimped to open in the wind and allow the foil to drift down in individual pieces. Most veterans thought the chaff didn't do much if any good, but they tossed it out of the plane with great gusto anyway.

When his plane got to the initial point and turned, then straightened for the bomb run, TenHaken saw "numerous little puffs ahead forming a black cloud shaped like an elongated shoe box." The leader of his squadron was flying through it. Those behind were about to enter the German box. It was time to pull the flak jackets on. These were for the crew, whose members did not have the cast iron protection the pilot and co-pilot did. The jackets consisted of irregularly shaped metal plates stitched between two sheets of canvas to form a vest. To TenHaken, "their purpose seemed primitive, identical to that of suits of armor." They weighed about twenty pounds each. Most veterans decided early on not to wear them, but to put them between their seats and their butts, thus protecting the most important part.

Over the target, with flak bursting from the shells all around his plane, TenHaken started dropping the chaff packets through one of the waist windows. After dropping one, he tried to count to ten as he had been told before letting the next one go, but in the midst of the flak he seldom got past two or three. Then the plane to his right got hit. "A flak explosion at its number three engine had blown the right wing from the body. The scene was incomprehensible—the wing tumbled over and down, and the fuselage was nosing into a dive." There were no parachutes. "The bam-bam-bams and poof-poof-poofs were exploding everywhere; it was inconceivable to fly through this unscathed."

The bomber lurched. Have we been hit? TenHaken wondered. Through the intercom, he heard the bombardier say, "Bombs away." ("The most beautiful words in the English language," according to one pilot.) Then the bombardier continued, "Now let's get the hell out of here." After a pause, he came on the intercom again to say, "I wasn't supposed to add that last part."

Lieutenant Cord banked the plane into a steep dive to the right. TenHaken thought, Thank you, God. Cord came on the intercom to ask each crew member to report any damage. None. When they were out of the flak, TenHaken lifted his oxygen mask and shouted above the engine noise to the photographer, "You've been through seventeen of these now. Was this flak typical, lighter, worse, or what?" The photographer grinned and shouted back, "It wasn't light. Each mission seems to get worse, but I can't believe they could get more up here than they did."

Over the intercom, Cord asked, "Flight engineer back there?" He wanted to know what the trouble was with the gas gauges. Number three engine sputtered and quit. "Get something to three," Cord ordered.

"I'm trying," the engineer answered. "I'm trying."

Cord realized what had happened. On the intercom he said, "The bastards hit our gas lines over the target. They've just vibrated loose."

The number two engine quit. The engineer repeated that he was trying to transfer the gasoline flow. He could not.

"We're losing altitude and control," Cord yelled. "We're at sixteen thousand; a couple seconds back, we were at eighteen." He added, "Stand by to bail if necessary."

Then number four engine quit. Then number one. There was a long moment of quiet, only the sound of the wind that buffeted the plane about in the glide. Then "the terrible clanging of the bail-out bell crashed the quiet."

Everyone got out okay, landed safely, and became POWs.[21] For TenHaken, the co-pilot, and the rest of the crew, it was their first mission. It was number thirty-two for Lieutenant Cord. For the photographer, number seventeen. For all of them, it was the last.

"Anon" made up words to sing to the tune of "As Time Goes By":

> You must remember this
> The flak can't always miss
> Somebody's gotta die.
> The odds are always too damned high
> As flak goes by . . .
> It's still the same old story
> The Eighth gets all the glory
> While we're the ones who die.
> The odds are always too damned high
> As flak goes by. [22]

Once in the fall of 1944 McGovern went up in a practice run, with only his co-pilot, Bill Rounds, and his navigator, Sam Adams, along. McGovern was upset with Rounds because while McGovern was flying co-pilot with Surbeck, Rounds used his free time to go into Cerignola to find a girl. He contracted VD and had to be treated with sulfa powder. McGovern was about ready to kick him off the plane. But on this practice mission, which was done primarily to give the co-pilots who had not yet been flying some experience, Rounds did most of the flying. "He took that plane as if he'd been doing this all his life,"

McGovern said. "I think I could've done as well, but I couldn't have done any better and I had a lot of practice." Rounds just tucked into position and held it there. That night, the pilot of the lead plane, a captain, came to McGovern in the officers club to say, "You know, George, you've got one hell of a valuable co-pilot. He flies the best formation of any co-pilot I've seen. That guy is tremendous—you better hold on to him with both hands." Right then, McGovern decided to forget about Rounds's VD. He figured he had better let the man do what he wanted on his off hours.

Lt. Donald Currier was a part of one of the first B-24 squadrons of the Fifteenth Air Force to arrive in Italy and thus flew his first mission in January 1944, one of the first of his group. It was two days after his squadron had arrived in Italy. The target was the railroad yards in Perugia, just off the Tiber River, in support of the ground troops. But when the bombers arrived, it was snowing. Landmarks were obscured. The lead navigator, having no radar (which only came nine months later), was unable to see anything but clouds. Currier was the navigator flying in the B-24 on the wing of the lead plane. "I looked desperately for something I could see and recognize," he recalled, but he saw nothing.

The lead plane opened its bomb bays. The bombardier in Currier's plane followed the leader. He put his finger on the toggle switch. When the leader dropped his bombs, he and the other bombardiers did the same. Currier saw the bombs fall in open countryside. He saw some bursts of flak on one side and far away and thought, I don't know why the Germans bothered. We certainly didn't do them any harm. He and the pilot and crew resolved "we would go again and again until we got it right."

Currier would go on to make a career in the Air Force. Looking back four decades, he said that in his experience "it seems incredible that we would be flying a combat mission with so little training or experience." But that was how badly the Fifteenth needed pilots and crews in January 1944.[23] It was because of that need that the AAF instituted the policy of requiring just-arrived pilots to fly as co-pilots for five missions before taking up their own plane and crew, since the men had gone through the speeded-up training program in 1944. In 1945 the commanders changed policy again, putting new pilots and their crews into action as soon as they arrived in Italy. And it was the casualty list that forced the commanders of the bomb groups to keep demanding more replacements.

Bombardier Lt. Donald Kay arrived in Italy in May 1944 and was assigned to the 783rd Squadron, 465th Bomb Group. Of the three classmates in bombardier school who came over with Kay and were close friends, two were killed in the air and the other became a POW. Overall, Kay recalled that of the seventeen original crews that started the war with him, only six finished.[24]

Sgt. Anthony Picardi of the 455th Bomb Group's 742nd Squadron (who had visited his family's village and met his grandmother) saw a B-24 crash on the runway while trying to take off for a mission. It blew up on impact. Nine of the ten crew members were blown to bits. But one had "his arms blown off from the elbow down and his legs blown off from the knees down. He was actually crawling away from the inferno. He was digging into the dirt with the stubs of his elbows, trying to survive. Right then and there, I realized just how precious life is. He crawled right up to us, looked us straight in the eyes, and then closed his eyes forever."[25]

For McGovern, on his first five missions as Surbeck's co-pilot, things were not so rough. He saw some flak, went through it, and got out of it safely. The B-24 did not take one hit. "I felt rather secure after flying those missions," McGovern said. He summed up what he had learned from observing Surbeck: "I heard through the earphones how he handled the radio transmissions to the tower and to the lead plane. I saw how he brought the plane into formation, how slowly or swiftly he got that done, I watched him to see what he was looking at and listened to the way he was handling the crew—everything he said, I could hear through my earphones. . . . I saw how he flew formation in various positions, on the left side one day and the next he might be in the middle, the next day on the right wing. I could observe all those things without having the responsibility of handling the plane myself. I picked up a lot of touches." This was not practice flying in Idaho. This was Europe and the formation was much bigger—sometimes 500 or 600 planes. After completing his five missions as Surbeck's co-pilot, McGovern said, "I felt comfortable to take that plane up with my own crew and get it into formation and get off on a combat mission."26

CHAPTER SEVEN

December 1944

THE LIBERATORS IN ITALY had a distinctive name, usually assigned by the pilot, often after consultation with the crew, painted below and slightly to the front of the flight deck. Many had nose art, some of it quite good, much of it showing scantily dressed, buxom, and gorgeous girls. Frequently, however, the name was the pilot's hometown or home state or the name of his mother or wife. When the pilot and crew completed their missions and went home, the men who inherited the aircraft would sometimes change the name, but that was generally considered to bring on bad luck.

McGovern and his crew came over by ship and were assigned planes on a "ready-to-go" basis, usually a different plane for almost each mission. Most of them already had a name and nose art. McGovern dubbed any plane he flew the *Dakota Queen,* but never painted it on the side. He picked the name to honor Eleanor. That way, he said, "we got double good luck—the name of the plane that was painted on there and a plane named for Eleanor." He had a picture of her he would put on the console. The plane's painted name might be *Yo-Yo,* or whatever, but to McGovern and his crew it was *Dakota Queen.*

The idea may have come from a saying popular with the pilots and crew at the airfield. Planes that had been in combat, as nearly all of them had, often had to be patched up by the ground crews. The B-24s that had been badly mauled and repaired and then pronounced ready to fly were called, derisively, "hangar queens."[1]

The ground crews that did the repairs were superb. Sometimes they would work right through the night, if necessary, using a crane to put in a new engine, patching up the flak holes in the wings and fuselage, adjusting the instruments, loading in the bombs, fresh oxygen tanks, .50 caliber ammunition boxes, and other equipment. Each plane had its own ground crew. Most of the members had been mechanics before they joined the AAF. They loved the plane they worked on and watched for it as the group returned to base. It wasn't only the pilot and crew they were concerned about; it was the plane as well. Those ground crews, in McGovern's words, "were well trained and well motivated. We couldn't have kept anything as complicated as a Liberator functioning very long without their superb attention."[2]

Lt. Henry Burkle, in command of the ground crews, recalled that they would line up beside the runway "waiting for their airplane to come in and hoping that it came back and be there to meet the flight crew and ask them all about the flight in order to find out what maintenance had to be done." Burkle had a crew chief for each plane. Each crew chief had three mechanics under him. "Then I had three flight chiefs, they were master sergeants, each with three flights under him. Then I had a line chief, big old fellow from Campbell, Nebraska, named Al Haggaman. He was a dandy. A big old slow farm boy, but he was sincere and he knew his work, knew his business." Each evening, Burkle would find out "how many airplanes the commanders wanted the next day. And about ten out of every ten days they wanted every airplane that could fly put in the air. It was always maximum effort. We didn't know what sleep was."[3]

B-24 pilot Vincent Fagan of the 450th Bomb Group recalled that he "never went out to the flight line at any hour of the day or night that the mechanics were not out there working. These mechanics were the most dedicated people I ever saw. They'd break down and cry when their plane went down. It always seemed they thought there was something else they could have done to make the plane more airworthy."[4]

There was one other thing that many ground crews did. They could purchase six or seven bottles of beer a week, but there was no ice or refrigeration available. So some of the crews would slip their beer aboard the B-24s just before they took off on a combat mission. Flying at 20,000 feet of elevation for six to eight hours would cool the beer. The crews were always anxious for the safe arrival of their planes to Cerignola. The pilots would accuse them of being more anxious to see that their beer was safe than that the pilot and his crew were.

Pilots were called aircraft commanders. Like captains on a ship, their word was law. The sergeants called McGovern "lieutenant" or "sir" whether on the ground or in the air. But not Rounds, who was called "Bill." Lieutenants Rounds and Adams called their pilot "Mac," but just as the enlisted men they knew perfectly well who was the captain. McGovern called everyone by his first name. On the assignment sheet, the crew was referred to by the pilot's name; thus it would state, "McGovern's going to be flying number three today." Never "McGovern's crew."

On December 6, McGovern prepared to fly his first mission as pilot with his own crew. The target was the marshaling yards at Graz, Austria. He was "desperately eager to do everything right the first time out alone." He confessed that "I was probably more nervous on that takeoff than any other missions that I flew during the war." He was thinking about how he was going to get that big bird off the ground without Howard Surbeck there. It was by far the heaviest B-24 he had flown, what with the bomb load, a full crew, all that gasoline, the machine gun belts, the oxygen tanks, and more. This was not a stateside aircraft—it weighed 70,000 pounds, thirty-five tons. McGovern later said, "I don't think any pilot in World War II ever made a takeoff in a B-24 that didn't scare him."[5]

On his first mission Lieutenant Fagan talked to his crew chief about the load. The chief said, "As far as the total weight is concerned, you may as well know that these 24's are overloaded about eight thousand pounds. Consolidated Aircraft says maximum takeoff weight is 63,000 pounds.

"If you don't like it, what do you want to leave behind? Machine gun ammunition? The flak suits? Take less gasoline? Or what? You're going to have to take the bombs or there is no point in going."[6]

McGovern found taxiing a B-24 a challenge. The taxi strips were just packed clay and dirt. He could not steer the B-24 with the nose wheel, over which he had no control. He would steer with the propellers—if he wanted to turn right he would cut back on the props on that side, speed them up on the left. The taxi strip was narrow and had a ditch on each side. The engineer, Sgt. Mike Valko, would stand behind the flight deck, open the overhead hatch, and put part of his body out of the plane to see if McGovern was getting too close on one side or the other (the pilot could not see the ditches from the cockpit). Valko would call out, "Too close on the right." Or he would say, "A little bit left," or "Right, right, right I said."

Once on the runway, with three or four aircraft ahead of him waiting to take off, McGovern set the brakes and revved up the engines. Rounds went through the checklist with him. When that was complete and the plane in front had started down the runway, McGovern released the brakes. Beside him, he could hear Rounds praying. "Every takeoff I made in World War II was an adventure," McGovern later admitted. A B-24 did not take off like a fighter. It started rolling slowly, only reluctantly picking up speed. He felt "this thing is never going to get enough speed to get off the ground—there's just no way I'm going to make it."

The runway was too short—by later standards it was unsafe—but just at the end of it, now up to 160 mph, McGovern pulled his plane up into the air. He was just skimming the ground. He told Rounds, "Wheels up." Rounds hit the switch and up they came, making for more speed and climbing ability. But McGovern didn't dare pull it up any faster for fear of stalling and crashing, something that happened on occasion. "It seemed forever before I could climb." For over a mile he was at treetop height. He did not dare keep the engines on full throttle because that would use up too much fuel, which would be needed later. "Wing flaps up," he told Rounds, and when that was done the plane had more speed and less drag. Finally, mercifully, he started to climb.

The rallying point was over the Adriatic. Once over the water, McGovern had the gunners test their machine guns. He got the plane up, spotted the lead plane, slid into formation, wingtip to wingtip, almost touching, close enough so that a fighter plane couldn't dive between them. That took almost an hour. Then the formation headed on to Graz (in southeastern Austria), over the Alps. On the way up to 20,000 feet the *Dakota Queen* passed through clouds. For McGovern, on this and later missions, the weather gave him more worry than the possibility of heavy flak. If there had been a contest between weather and flak, "in the amount of shear sweat and fear that it produced, the weather won." Once over the continent, the clouds gave way to blue sky. "You could look right down into those little villages."

Rounds checked the instruments. So did McGovern. Every five minutes or so, he would press the button on his intercom and ask each crew member if everything was okay. When he needed specific information, he would ask. "Sam," he would say to the navigator, "what is that formation off our right wing?" Or, "Tell me our location, Sam." Or, to Sergeant Higgins, the radioman, "Have you picked up anything on the weather ahead?"

Rounds was all business. No jokes, no naps, no pranks. He was coordinated and an athlete and wanted to be flying his own fighter aircraft, but he was, in McGovern's view, almost a perfect co-pilot. Not that he had a lot to do. McGovern said he was there as a "standby. It was like being vice president of the United States. He was there in case of trouble only." They had no conversation other than "watch engine number one" or something about the other planes in the formation or the readings on various instruments. On this first flight,

McGovern did all the flying. Rounds, then and later, when he was free from concern, would read a Bible. McGovern thought that a bit much, given Rounds's proclivities, but sometimes would be startled when Rounds would say, "Mac, listen to this" and read something from one of the Psalms. "Damn, that's good," he would exclaim.

When the formation got to Graz the weather had closed in. Nothing but clouds. The lead plane turned away. The lead pilot did not get on the radio to say he was taking the others back—they simply turned when he did. Over the Adriatic on the way home he jettisoned his bomb load, as did the other planes. For everyone involved it was a milk run—no fighters, no flak. Because they had crossed into enemy territory, however, everyone got a mission to his credit. Back at Cerignola the weather was clear. McGovern told Rounds to put the wheels down. A light came on to tell him the wheels were down and fully locked. He checked to make sure his ball turret gunner was inside the airplane and his turret pulled up. He put the wing flaps down to 40 degrees. Rounds called out the airspeed—"We're at 170 . . . 160 . . . 150 . . . 140." McGovern eased back on the throttles. The plane was almost gliding. It was a good landing. When he pulled the plane onto its hard stand, the crew got out all singing and whistling. McGovern walked around the plane, something he did before and after every mission. Everything was fine.[7]

For this mission, McGovern was paid $9.70. He was earning $290 per month, including his overseas pay and flying pay.[8] He sent $200 of that home to Eleanor each month.

After debriefing, on his way to the officers club, he stopped by the enlisted men's tent to see how they were doing. They were already celebrating. McGovern and Rounds had a beer or two in the club to celebrate their first mission. No holes in the plane, no wounded crew, no danger, but credit for a full mission. Wonderful.

Sgt. Eddie Picardo, a tail gunner on a B-24, later said that he did not know how to explain "the enormous feeling of relief that accompanies returning safe from a bombing mission. . . . Once on the ground, you started to live for the future again and plan what you might do once the war was finally over. . . . I've never had a feeling to compare with it."9

After the mission on December 6, the weather closed in. Most days the assignment sheet had McGovern flying in the morning, but in the morning the clouds were too thick over the base, over the Alps, over the targets, and the mission was scratched. The tension and anxiety, the tossing and turning on the cots, had been for nothing. This was typical. One B-24 pilot, Lt. Walter Hughes, was wakened and briefed eighty-six times to achieve his thirty-five missions.10

None of these pilots or their crews were ever ordered to go on a mission. When they saw their names on the assignment sheet, they knew that they could back off by just saying no, I won't do that. They were always asked. McGovern never said no, "and I don't know anybody that turned one down."

On December 4, McGovern's father died of a heart attack while he was pheasant hunting. Cables took what seemed forever in World War II, and it was not until December 14 that one reporting on the death arrived at the base. The intelligence officer took it to McGovern. The chaplain prayed with him, then said he could be exempted from flying the next day. McGovern said no, he would not take that excuse.

On December 15, the target was the railroad yards in Linz, Austria. At the briefing, the pilots and crews were told that the Red Army was on the move, that the Germans were going through Linz as they ran equipment to the eastern front, that they were also moving other troops and weapons to the western front through Linz, and thus the target was critical. So off they went.

It was at Linz on this, their second mission, that McGovern said "we got introduced to combat." The flak was heavy. Up to that point, McGovern had thought that exploding flak "looked like firecrackers and rockets going off." He learned better when a big slug of flak "came through the windshield, high and to my right. It hit just above my right shoulder and to the right of my head, and then fell down onto the floor between Rounds and me." They looked down at it. Rounds looked over to McGovern and just shook his head. McGovern did the same. The shrapnel was "the angriest-looking piece of metal, just jagged on every edge and big enough to tear your head off if it had hit a few inches to the left or maybe a few more inches on Bill Rounds's side."

It was freezing at 25,000 feet, probably 50 degrees below zero Fahrenheit, and the cold rush of wind—despite all the sheepskin-lined jackets and pants they had on, and despite their electrically heated suits—was ferocious. McGovern managed to keep his plane in formation, but barely. "All I could do was just sit there and do my job," he said. He hoped no more shrapnel would hit the *Dakota Queen*. Two or three other pieces did, but no one was hurt.

McGovern got back to the base and made his landing "smooth as glass." The men did not jump out and kiss the ground, but they were happy and reassured. He had done it twice. That night they talked about their lieutenant and how good he was. Other crews said their pilots "just bang us in." From then on, McGovern said, "They treated me around that airplane almost with reverence." They had developed, already, total confidence in their pilot. "Their lives were in my hands," McGovern explained. "It wasn't just that they thought they were. A mistake on my part and we're all dead."

December 16 was a cloudy, cold day all across Europe, but the 741st and the rest of the Fifteenth Air Force flew anyway. It was the day the Germans took advantage of the weather to counterattack in the Ardennes, launching the Battle of the Bulge. The target for McGovern and the others was the oil refineries in Brux, Czechoslovakia.

One B-24 broke its landing gear on takeoff. It jettisoned its bombs in the Adriatic, then crash-landed at the Gioia, Italy, airfield.

Another bomber had engine trouble and had to return to Cerignola.

McGovern got the *Dakota Queen* into formation in a broken cloud cover, but "all of a sudden everything just goes blank." The formation had flown into complete cloud cover. McGovern held his position, number three, but when they got above the clouds he discovered that they were flying at the same altitude but the plane that was number two had crossed him and was on his left side. "I was just petrified with fear at the sight." The lead pilot saw the situation and called on his radio, "What's going on here?" McGovern motioned to the other pilot that he should go up while the *Dakota Queen* went down, and they crossed again until they got into their proper position. "That's as close as I ever came to being killed and getting my crew killed and losing our bomber," McGovern said. He was shaking with fear and the "knowledge of how little control we had over our fate when the weather took over. There was nothing you could do when you flew into a cloud except pray because you couldn't see anything."

On this occasion, Rounds said to McGovern, "God took care of us."

Over Brux the flak was intense. "They'd lay that stuff up there," according to McGovern, "and it was almost as if an artist had drawn it." To McGovern, it seemed that the German gunners were getting better after each raid. "They were laying that shell in there closer to you." He "uttered many a prayer going down that bomb run, sort of an instinctive thing you would do."

There was a bizarre array of color, ranging from blue sky overhead to white clouds below to solid black from the flak directly in front, then the huge, angry flashes of red when another shell exploded. "Hell can't be any worse than that," McGovern said later. The pilot and crew had heart rates that almost went through the roof, yet unless shrapnel hit the plane there was no sound other than the engines. Mike Valko stood between and slightly behind McGovern and Rounds, watching the instruments. McGovern glanced at Valko. His face was white. Everyone else was scared too, but except for Rounds and Valko, McGovern couldn't see them.[11]

The lead bomber for the 741st was using a Mickey radar, so although Brux was covered by clouds he made his drop and the others followed. In another squadron, however, the lead bomber's bomb bay door was stuck, so it dropped no bombs. Since the pilot did not break radio silence to explain, none of the planes in the squadron dropped their bombs. In all the B-24s dropped sixty tons of bombs on the target, while those in the squadron that did not release their bombs dropped them on targets of opportunity on the way back.

Except for McGovern's squadron. Two or three other squadrons had completed their run and it was the 741st's turn. Ahead, it was solid black except for flashes of red where shells were exploding. McGovern was flying number three, off the right wing of the lead bomber. He thought, Nobody's going to get through this flak. But just then, the leader began making a gentle turn. He bypassed the target "and we threw our bombs into the field." McGovern guessed that the leader's thinking was, I've got this whole squadron up here following my tail—there's no way we're going to get through this and the damage they're going to do to us is greater than we're going to do to them. We may not even hit the target, can't see it, for sure. I'm not going to take these guys into a place where I know none of them are coming out.

Whatever the leader thought, not one of the men following his plane ever said a word about it. Every pilot and co-pilot, every nose gunner and bombardier and navigator knew exactly what happened. None of them uttered a word of criticism. McGovern said his own thinking was, "I'm not sure to this day that he wasn't right in avoiding that almost suicidal bomb run."12

There were other mishaps. On another mission, Lt. Donald Currier reached the bomb release point when a B-24 drifted right over his squadron. Over Currier's head, the plane dropped its stick of 500-pound bombs. Currier was looking out his window at the time and saw the first bomb strike his wingman at the top turret. There was a tremendous explosion and the plane disintegrated into flaming pieces. It happened in an instant. Currier found it hard to believe that the guys who had trained with him and occupied the tent next to him were gone. Just gone.

The concussion was stunning. The plane that dropped the bomb had its bomb bay doors open when the blast took place. The explosion came straight up and into the plane. The pilot, Lt. Vincent Isgrigg, lost control and slipped out of formation, narrowly missing the plane on his wing and plunging toward the earth. Isgrigg punched the bailout button and some of the crew got out. But Isgrigg regained control and sent his co-pilot back to assess the damage. The co-pilot took one look at the broken hydraulic lines and bailed out himself. Isgrigg and his one remaining crew member, the engineer, somehow managed to nurse the airplane back across the Adriatic to the AAF airfield at Grottaglie and crash-landed. For that feat, he received the Distinguished Flying Cross.

Currier thought no one could have escaped from the plane that had disintegrated, but forty-one years later he discovered that two guys did get out. They were the tail gunner, Sgt. Robert Hansen, and a photographer who had come on the mission. Hansen explained to Currier that the whole tail section of the B-24 broke off at the waist windows and began floating down like a leaf. The two men had time to jump. They were captured when they hit the ground and spent the remainder of the war in a POW camp.[13]

From Brux it was a long way back to Cerignola. The mission took eight hours, plus an hour to get into formation. When he turned for home, McGovern used the intercom to check on the crew. He recalled that each man responded with something like, "I'm here. Thank the good Lord!" Sgt. William McAfee was the ball turret gunner. "We never thought enough of him just sitting down there," McGovern confessed. "Nothing to hang on to, hunched over, cramped." But he was the one who was cheerful when McGovern asked how he was doing. McAfee was always upbeat, with a smile on his big red face. McAfee, who could barely move in the turret, had "nothing to do, no one to talk to, nothing." And he could see more than anyone else, all of it. On clear days he would watch the bombs dropping until they hit. "It was awful," he said, seeing the explosion and the fires. But he was eighteen years old, and in his words "not smart enough to be afraid."14

Everyone on board the *Dakota Queen* was exhausted emotionally. "You can't go on indefinitely being terrified," however, and the crew recovered somewhat. McGovern helped. He had been "sweating blood," but during the bomb run he did not have to think about morale or anything else; he worried about doing his job. But, as he said, "the crew would sit back there and bite their fingernails." If he could he would give them something to do so that "they felt caught up in the action and had less time to quiver in their boots." For the gunners, there was nothing except to watch for enemy fighters, but there were none—only flak.

McGovern was also exhausted physically. "It just seemed to me that it was too much." But the bomb run had been successful, the German transportation system disrupted. The men of the AAF took some satisfaction from that, hoping that what they had done would take some of the pressure off the Russians and help the Americans fighting the first day of the Battle of the Bulge.

On his way to the officers club after the debriefing, McGovern stopped by the enlisted men's tent. He thought, I hardly knew they were along on the mission, but they knew it. He got "quite sad and emotional looking at them sitting on their bunks drinking a can of beer. I just had a real sense of compassion for them." Valko was having a "terrible battle emotionally." He was throwing back the beer and reaching for another can. He was drinking himself drunk. McGovern concluded that all of them, but most of all the gunners, "were entitled to every dollar they got in pay and every decoration they got and they were entitled to more praise than they got from me."15

The officers club provided some relaxation. The pilots were young*— the average age was twenty-one or twenty-two—and had been through a gruesome experience. Like almost any young men who had experienced what they had, they needed a chance to relax. Officers in the infantry, or on warships engaged in combat, seldom had the opportunity, but those in the AAF did. There was little, maybe even no, chickenshit on an airfield. No saluting. Casual dress—sweatshirts from their high school or college days. Nearly everyone answered to his first name, or nickname. This was not Gen. George Patton's Third Army.

McGovern loved the club, not so much for the drinking opportunities as for the chance to sit in a real chair and do some reading and even more to have a serious conversation. The man he developed the closest relationship with was the flight surgeon, Dr. Harold Schuknecht.† "He was terrific," McGovern recalled. "If Hollywood was trying to design the most handsome Air Force officer they could, they would have copied him. He was as good-looking as Robert Taylor or Clark Gable." He was smart and had a constant, slight smile. When McGovern entered the club, exhausted, "he was the best guy in the world you could talk to." McGovern never got sick, never missed a mission, but had he done so he would have gone straight to Schuknecht for treatment. "He could turn you around better than any other doctor." McGovern called him, as did everyone else, "Doc."

Doc took to McGovern as much as McGovern took to him. Partly, that was because Doc also came from South Dakota, near Sioux Falls.

---

* So were the Germans shooting at them. Manfred Rommel, son of the field marshal, was an antiaircraft gunner at age fourteen. The others in his battery were about the same age. Rommel after the war became the mayor of Stuttgart, a post he held for many years. When I would bring in veterans to meet him in his office, he would always assure them, "We always missed." That reassured them, but it wasn't true.

† After the war, Dr. Schuknecht joined the Harvard faculty and became one of America's leading ear specialists.

Mainly it was because their personalities were compatible. When Mc-Govern came into the club, Doc would go right over to ask how things were going. "We'd sit there and talk," McGovern recalled.

They would talk for hours. About Italy, about Germany, about the origins of the war, how it might have been averted, how well President Roosevelt was handling it, what the Russians were doing. "We talked about things you wouldn't expect GIs to talk about." As a consequence of the conversations, and as a result of the reading McGovern was doing in books he had brought along and from the AAF library at Cerignola, he made a decision: "If I survived the war I would become a history professor. I knew that I wanted to be a teacher and history was the field."

Doc wanted to go on missions, and did, a number of times. He asked to go with McGovern, but was refused. The commanding officer decided he did not want one of his surgeons taking such risks and ordered him to cease and desist. For his part, McGovern thought Doc was crazy for wanting to go.[16]

Ball turret gunner Sgt. Henry Paris related that when his B-24 landed at Cerignola, all shot up, most of the crew managed to make their way through the hatch, but the cockpit began to flame. Ammunition was exploding, adding the danger of the gasoline tank blowing up. The pilot, Lieutenant Cook, had his hand pinned around the control wheel. His clothes caught fire. He jerked free his hand, but his feet were trapped. At this point Dr. Schuknecht, who had been waiting with an ambulance, climbed up to remove the pilot. The fuselage was enveloped in flames and fire was spurting out the waist windows and the cockpit. Schuknecht grabbed Cook and yanked him out.[17]

In 1972, when McGovern was running for president and the far-right press charged that he had been a coward during World War II, Schuknecht—himself a Republican—told an inquiring reporter, "McGovern showed great skill and sensitivity and concern toward his crew. They felt safe with him. He instilled confidence."[18]

McGovern was on the assignment sheet for the following morning, December 17. At the predawn briefing he learned the target was an oil refinery at Odertal, Germany. McGovern taxied out to the runway, called the tower, got his clearance, opened the throttles, and began speeding down the runway. Suddenly, just like that, *bang*. The right-hand wheel had blown.

"I had to make an almost instantaneous decision," McGovern said, "whether to cut the throttles and try to get stopped before the end of the runway or whether to hold them wide open and pull that plane off the ground. I made one quick look and decided I couldn't stop."

He kept the throttles wide open and just did get up. "We had a full bomb load," McGovern recalled. "We skimmed not just the treetops but the fence post tops." He glanced at Rounds, whose "face was as white as that chair." As for McGovern, "it certainly scared me more than any enemy fighters ever did."

The question became, abort or continue the mission? Whichever alternative was chosen, the plane would be landing on one wheel, or crash-landing with no wheels. McGovern called the tower to explain his predicament. The tower said, "Lieutenant, it's up to you. You're the pilot. We're not going to tell you what to do . . . but there have been B-24s that landed on one wheel and it's not going to be easy, but if you want to do it we'll have the emergency vehicles out there." Or, a third alternative, have the crew bail out and bring the plane in by himself. McGovern flew a couple of circles around the airfield to give himself time to decide.

McGovern thought, We can fly this mission just as well on one wheel as we can on two and we'll get rid of the gasoline that way and we'll get rid of the bombs over the target, which is what we're supposed to do. He turned on the intercom and told the crew what he had decided and then added that anyone who wanted to bail out could do so right now. None did.

McGovern got his plane into formation. Catching up had been

an effort, but there was a substitute navigator that day, a man from Wichita, Kansas, Lt. Marion Colvert. McGovern said flatly of him, "He was the best navigator I ever flew with." He was an old man, twenty-seven years of age, a big guy who had played football at Kansas State. He had been Howard Surbeck's navigator. He gave McGovern a course that worked.

The mission took seven hours, thirty minutes, not counting the hour to form up. Flak was heavy but the Germans only shot down one B-24, while inflicting damage, not crippling, on many others. McGovern came through unhit.

Coming home was the time of worry. He was going to do what he had not done before, land a B-24 on one main wheel plus the nose wheel. He thought, I just can't screw this up in front of Marion Colvert. Colvert was standing up on the flight deck between Rounds and McGovern.

Because McGovern had plenty of gas after the relatively short mission, the tower decided to have him circle the field and then land last. Now, McGovern thought, I have to land this plane with all these other pilots watching. The pilots were hovering around the runway. So, McGovern said, "We came down and I made the best landing I'd ever made in my life. I never made a landing like that before or since."

He brought the airplane in "just barely floating." He could hardly tell when the left wheel touched down. He advanced the throttles on the right side, cut them on the left side, "and that bomber went right straight down the runway. It never wavered." As the plane lost airflow, the right wing settled down. McGovern had her slowed down enough by then that he just turned her off the runway.

Lieutenant Colvert said, "Lieutenant McGovern, that's the best landing I have ever seen in a B-24." McGovern said that was "a compliment I'll take to my grave." At the officers club that night, the other pilots cheered. "That particular incident elevated my status for good in that group," McGovern recalled.19

In his diary, Rounds recorded that McGovern was recommended

for the Distinguished Flying Cross on that mission. For the 455th Bomb Group, the losses weighed heavily, but there was some pride in what had been accomplished. Thirty-four B-24s dropped sixty-six tons of bombs on the refinery.[20]

Hearing praise from Lts. Charles Painter or Ed Soderstrom, both pilots in the 741st Squadron, was good for McGovern's emotions. He thought Painter was the best of all the pilots; big and muscular, he was to McGovern "one of my heroes." Another was Soderstrom, a slender guy about six foot one, "who did something that the rest of us didn't do," according to McGovern. He was given an assignment of going out at night, alone, and bombing carefully selected targets, such as a bridge. One bomber at night would be a surprise to the Germans, it was thought, and Soderstrom was the pilot for the job. So McGovern was glad to receive their praise.

Encounters in the club were not always pleasant. Once McGovern started talking to two fighter pilots. The two pilots got to talking about strafing two Italians fishing on a bridge. The pilots machine-gunned them and they had dropped into the water. "Did you see those I-ties drop," one pilot enthused. "Yeah!" the other answered. He grinned and declared, "They won't fish again."

That chilled McGovern. "My blood just ran cold. How could they do that to two innocent guys who were just fishing. . . . I was embarrassed. . . . They seemed to me like a disgrace to the country, disgrace to their humanity." He thought that was what Hitler and his gang did.

Yet he was a bomber pilot. Almost certainly he was responsible for more civilian deaths than the two fighter pilots. But he was bombing Austrians, Germans, Germany's allies, from high up, and couldn't see the effects of the explosions, not at all like the pilots who had shot the Italian fishermen. He felt that as the casualties were Hitler's followers he did not need to exercise his conscience about bombing them. In a sense he thought they needed it, because of what they had done throughout Europe. He wanted to show them, "You can't get away with this kind of conduct."

At the base, he had a lot of time to think. Sometimes he would go for days without flying because planes could not get off the ground. There was little, or even nothing, to do—no planned recreation, no physical training exercise, occasionally a softball game, depending on the rain— and yet he and his crew had to be there every day, available to fly.

After the Odertal mission, McGovern saw on the assignment sheet that he was flying again the next day, December 18. It turned out to be almost a milk run. The target was in Germany, but weather forced the lead pilot to turn away and set off for the alternative target, the marshaling yards at Sopron, Hungary. There was no flak, none at all. All planes returned to base safely.

Three consecutive missions surely required at least a day of rest, but that night on the assignment sheet there was McGovern's name again, along with many others. At the briefing in the morning, Mc-Govern noted that most of the pilots looked "like old men, with deep circles under the eyes." He thought they were ready for a rest camp, or being sent home, not another mission. Instead, they were flying. The officer on the platform pulled the drawstring. The target was Mu-nich, one of the two or three most heavily defended German cities.

One of the men in the audience gave out a sort of scream: "AHH-HHHH!" For some that broke the tension and they managed to laugh. But McGovern looked at the pilot beside him. "I thought when he saw Munich on there that he was going to collapse." The briefing officer assured the men about the importance of Munich, a major in-dustrial site that had been bombed repeatedly but still needed more. It had been raining all night. It still was. Off they went anyway, to get into their planes. McGovern could almost see some of the pilots thinking, This is the last one, we'll never make it home.

McGovern was in the number three position for the 741st. He put on his earphones and heard the tower telling him to taxi. He pulled onto the taxi strip. The strip was slippery due to the mud and rain. McGovern listened for directions from Valko, standing in the top hatch, but none came. McGovern felt a slight tug on the right. Before he could correct the plane, its right wheel had slipped into the ditch beside the taxi strip. McGovern increased the power to the right engines, eased off on the left side, and tried to get the wheel to climb back onto the strip. Instead, it just dug deeper into the ditch. No matter what he tried, nothing worked.

Behind the *Dakota Queen* there were four other B-24s, waiting for their chance to get to the runway and take off. But McGovern blocked them. He talked to the tower, explained the problem, and then heard an order to him and the other four pilots—scratch the mission. The others shut down their engines and got out of their planes. So did McGovern (whose bomber was pulled out by a tractor).

McGovern was chagrined. Those four pilots were close to their thirty-fifth mission, the Going Home Mission. He thought, he later said, that they were "just going to shoot my ass." But instead they came over "and practically kissed me." They couldn't thank him enough. No Munich!

For McGovern, "that was the first time that it occurred to me that people had any motives other than just defeating the enemy. These guys wanted to survive." At the officers club that evening, they talked. They didn't blame McGovern, they said it was the engineer's fault. But they did tell him that he was taking an unnecessary risk in gunning his engines, that he should never try to power his way out when stuck in mud. Beside the wear on the engines, they told him that his actions had caused a dangerous situation because of the possibility of fuel spilling on the ground and catching fire.

McGovern learned. But though the people who knew the best told him it wasn't his fault, he never forgot the incident. He had wanted to go, to get another mission under his belt. "But I tied up the other planes so I didn't have any feeling of exhilaration at all. I was embarrassed—my crew and I had screwed up in front of the whole squadron. I found it enormously embarrassing. It still pains me after all these years [more than a half century] to think about it."21

━━━━━━━━

That night, McGovern's name was on the assignment sheet. In the morning, December 20, he learned that the target was the Skoda works at Pilsen, Czechoslovakia. It too was heavily defended because it was a principal manufacturer of arms for the Germans.

An hour away from the Skoda works, *Dakota Queen*'s number two engine (inboard on the left wing) quit. McGovern feathered the prop, that is, used a flight deck button to turn the propeller into a perpendicular position to keep it from windmilling and acting as a drag or brake on the plane. With only three engines functioning, McGovern had to struggle to keep up with the formation.

"Any time you lost an engine up there," Rounds said, "there was no trouble back at base if you dropped out and returned. A lot of guys did it." McGovern could have done it, but instead he told Rounds, "So we're minus an engine. Let's keep going." They did. But after turning at the initial point and heading over Pilsen, when they were only thirty seconds or so away from the drop point, flak hit the plane.

In his diary, Rounds described what happened. "All at once No. 3 [engine] began throwing oil and smoking badly." The engine lost oil pressure so rapidly that McGovern was unable to feather the propeller. It became a windmill, creating enormous drag and reducing the effective power of the plane to about one and a half engines. McGovern ordered the bombs dropped and turned away. But, Rounds wrote, "One minute later, she began vibrating fiercely. We tried to feather it again but it wouldn't and just kept windmilling. We lost altitude rapidly and No. 3 burst into flame." Radio operator Ken Higgins recalled that "oil streamed out of the runaway engine and flame was belching out of the thing. It looked real bad."22

McGovern had read in the B-24 manual for pilots that in five minutes the flame would break through the wall and explode the gas tanks. He began descending rapidly and the increased speed put out the fire. But the prop continued to windmill. McGovern tried the feather button once more. No response. He tried again. Still nothing. "Prepare to bail out," he called over the intercom. Waist gunner Tex Ashlock was ready to leave. "I sat with my legs dangling out the escape hatch," he said, "waiting for the word to parachute out."23

Neither Ashlock nor any other man in the plane had ever used a parachute. Or been trained on how to do it. McGovern had said to a veteran pilot at Mountain Home, Idaho, "Colonel, we're about through with our training and none of us have had a parachute jump. Shouldn't we be trained in that?"

The colonel replied, "Son, let me tell you something—when you get into combat you don't need any training on how to get out of that plane. What you need is good judgment on how long you can stay in. You're going to want to get out if it's on fire, if half the wing is broken off, if it's in a spin. What you need is the discipline to stay with it as long as it's safe. We don't have to teach you when to jump. You'll find a hole that a cat couldn't jump through if you have to get out of that plane."

McGovern came to agree. "There were lots of times I thought it'd be a lot safer to jump out," he recalled.

On the flight deck, McGovern tried yet again to bring the prop under control. He pushed the button and this time it worked. "Resume your stations," he ordered over the intercom. "We're going to try to bring her home."

He looked at his map, however, and decided they would not get home. The airplane "just couldn't go that far, it wouldn't stay in the air that long." The gas supply was low and the fuel was leaking. McGovern got on the intercom to his navigator, Sam Adams, to ask if Adams knew of any landing strips between where they were and Cerignola. "I'll call you right back," Adams replied. "The best bet is a little fighter strip on the isle of Vis out on the Adriatic," Adams told him, "but it's only got a 2,200-foot runway and we need 5,000 feet to land. Do you think you can bring it in on a 2,200-foot runway?"

Well, McGovern thought, that's better than our being up here with two engines out and one windmilling. "How far is it?" he asked Adams.

On such and such a heading, Adams replied, "we can make it in less than an hour."

The *Dakota Queen* was losing altitude. The alternative to Vis was to crash-land in the sea. That had no appeal. The B-24s were not built for crash-landing in the sea. Only about 25 percent of those who tried made it. The others broke up on impact, killing everyone. Besides, it was winter and that water was cold. "I didn't think we'd survive," McGovern explained later, "and bailing out didn't appeal to me."

He ordered everything loose thrown out of the plane to lighten it up. So most everything went—not the radio, but the machine guns, the oxygen tanks, all the ammunition, flak jackets, chart table, and more. That helped, some. McGovern said on the intercom that anyone who wanted to bail out could do so. None did.

Vis was a fifty-eight-square-mile mountainous island some forty miles off the Dalmatian coast. Marshal Tito's partisans had taken it from the Italian army in September 1943, and the British RAF had built a runway there for their Spitfires. It was also Tito's headquarters. A number of B-24s and B-17s had used it as an emergency strip. For the morale of the B-24 crews, knowing that Vis was there was important. "It was an unsinkable island in the Adriatic with a landing strip and medical attention," said Ed Brendza, a technical representative for the Fifteenth Air Force sent to the island to work on the planes that landed there. "For them it was another chance at Mother Earth."[24]

The island came into view. The approach required coming in over a mountain and dropping suddenly down to sea level. The number three engine caught fire, again. McGovern cut back on the gasoline to make the final approach, which had the benefit of putting out the fire.

"Both of us were on the controls," Rounds recalled. "I was helping

Mac hold it. The two good engines throbbed a little but they were being overtaxed. But when we saw that strip we weren't worried." Rounds raised the Vis tower by radio—its call sign was Sand Sail—and said that a B-24 with one engine afire and another dead was coming in for an emergency landing.

McGovern was worried. At the far end of the runway a mountain rose up and he could see "carcasses of half a dozen bombers beyond the field." He figured he had only one shot at the thing. If he came in too high and tried to pull up, he doubted he could do it on two engines. If he failed to bring the *Dakota Queen* in on the first pass, "we would have all had it."

He brought the plane in as slow as he could without stalling. He couldn't land short of the runway because of the mud. He had to hit it exactly. He told Rounds, "When you hear those wheels touch that runway get on those brakes just as hard as you can and I'll do the same." He sat it down on the far end so as to have all those 2,200 feet of runway.

McGovern and Rounds pressed the brakes in just as hard as possible. "They were on the brakes all the way down the strip," waist gunner Ashlock recalled. The tires screeched and smoked. "We just kind of wheeled off at the very end of the runway, going pretty fast. We bogged down in the wet clay and stopped." From where he sat, McGovern could see the mountain just ahead of him. A British foam truck was already spraying the smoldering engine.

The men piled out of the plane. Half of them threw themselves on the ground and kissed it. That was the only time McGovern ever saw them do that. McGovern and Rounds hugged each other.

McGovern shook hands with a man named Anton Sever, who had been on the ground giving signals to McGovern telling him to stay in the center of the runway. McGovern embraced him and thanked him for his assistance. Then he noticed that Sever had on English overalls with RAF insignia on it, plus a cap with a red star. "What are you doing here?" McGovern asked.

"I'm a partisan squadron aircraft mechanic, Section B," Sever answered.

"Good boy," McGovern replied, shaking his hand once again.25

A truck picked them up. As they were driving to headquarters, another stricken B-24 came in to land. Ashlock watched. It "went right into the mountain and everyone was killed."26

McGovern did not know that Tito was on the island and never got to meet him, but more than three decades later, President Jimmy Carter had a reception for Tito in the White House. McGovern, who was a senator at the time, was there. In his remarks, Tito expressed his appreciation for the American people and then added, "At least one of you, Senator McGovern, came to see me in World War II and now I'm returning the favor."

At the time McGovern hoped the British could repair his plane and he could fly it out the next day, but the ground crew said no, this runway is not long enough. They added that every four-engine bomber that had come to Vis was still there, and would be forever. The next day Cerignola sent a DC-3 to pick up McGovern and his crew.27

Some months later, the AAF awarded McGovern the Distinguished Flying Cross for his actions that day at Vis. The citation praised him for his "high degree of courage and piloting skill."

———

McGovern got back to Cerignola on December 21. On Christmas afternoon, he saw his name on the assignment board. The target was a refinery in Oswiecim, eastern Poland. Twenty-six B-24s of the 455th Bomb Group dropped fifty tons of bombs. Flak was intense and accurate. One B-24 was seen with a feathered engine heading toward an emergency landing field in Russia, then another was seen jettisoning equipment and heading east. A third bomber landed at Vis.28

On the way out, McGovern asked Rounds to fly the plane for a while. Rounds was so good at it that McGovern began increasing his time in control. The mission took the bombers very near Auschwitz. Later, McGovern wondered why the concentration camp had not been the target. Neither he nor anyone else at Cerignola knew much about Auschwitz, but by that stage of the war rumors circulated about the mass killing going on there.

President Roosevelt had been urged by Jewish leaders to bomb the place, but he refused. He said the United States had not built those bombers in order to hit concentration camps, that they were built for a strategic function. Besides, bombing Auschwitz would have killed many Jews as well as Germans. His attitude was that the best thing America could do for Europe's Jews was to win the war sooner, that the quicker it was won the fewer Jews would be killed.

Over the next four days, weather prevented any missions. Thus did 1944 come to an end. In December, the 455th had flown a total of sixteen missions with 359 aircraft deployed over target. They had dropped a total of 650 tons of bombs. The losses were fifteen aircraft, 111 crewmen reported missing in action, and thirty-two reported killed. It had not been a good month. The men at Cerignola looked forward to the new year, the one that they hoped would end the war.

CHAPTER EIGHT

The Isle of Capri

"TONIGHT IS NEW YEAR'S EVE," McGovern opened a letter to his co-pilot's parents. Their son had been hospitalized with pneumonia and McGovern wanted to reassure them. Lieutenant Rounds was recovering, McGovern wrote, then promised to "get him back to his usual top form in a few days."

"We are experiencing our first Italian snowfall," he noted. "I'm finding it pretty easy to get homesick tonight for those old snow-covered plains of Dakota." He added, "We haven't been doing a whole lot of flying lately" because of the weather. It "promises to be even worse." Another promise: "We're expecting to see you next spring, regardless of mud, rain, flak or what have you."[1]

Although there had been that mission on the day after Christmas to Oswiecim, Poland, that the *Dakota Queen* had participated in, because of the weather on New Year's Day there was no mission to fly. On New Year's Eve and again on the first of January, 1945, there were parties in the officers and enlisted men's clubs, where records were set for sales. The dispensaries had the fewest number of men on sick call for more than three months.

Rounds was one of those out of the hospital and he was in high spirits. Defying the miserable weather—rain, sleet, fog—he told Bill Ashlock to help him spill a fifty-five-gallon drum of white gasoline on the field next to the cooking area. He wanted to spill the fuel and set it afire as a form of fireworks to celebrate the new year.

"Rounds, you don't have any idea what you're about to do," Ashlock said. "If that stuff gets in the air while you're pouring it, it will create an explosion and the flames are liable to cover a huge area. You don't want to do it."

Rounds did want to do it. Ashlock recalled that "he did it anyway by himself." Ashlock retired to his tent. A half-hour later he heard a "big whoomp sound." Rounds came running to the tent, "his eyebrows singed off, his face black. And he says, 'You know, you were right. That thing blew me about thirty feet through the air.'"[2]

It was an inauspicious start to the new year. And the weather through January was even worse than predicted. Only an occasional mission was attempted, and McGovern did not go on them. His tentmate and close companion, navigator Lt. Sam Adams, did go on two missions. Because McGovern had flown as a co-pilot for five missions, he was five missions ahead of his crew in reaching the magic number, thirty-five. Adams hated to fly with any pilot other than McGovern, but he wanted to get home as soon as possible to take up his studies to become a Presbyterian minister. So he volunteered for missions as a substitute navigator. On his second substitute service, in the second week of January, Adams's plane was blown apart by German flak. There were reports, unconfirmed, that two or three parachutes had been seen after the plane exploded.

McGovern and Rounds held on to the hope that Sam had made it out of the plane and came down by parachute. They depended on substitute navigators on their missions, but for a few weeks they lived with Sam's empty bunk, his photographs, and his neatly hung clothing, waiting for word that he had made it. The word never came.[3]

"I had seen other men killed before," McGovern said, "but never anything like that. When there are just three of you living together so closely in a tent in an olive grove in Italy, a helluva long way from home, you really got to know one another. And then all of a sudden you see the empty bunk and it really gets to you."[4]

There were many empty bunks. Lt. Victor McWilliams was a pilot in the 741st Squadron. Once that January he was watching as other pilots and crew from the squadron took off for a mission that was ultimately aborted. One B-24 got into the sky but then turned around to come back to base. Suddenly, for no reason McWilliams could ever find out, the ten bombs in the plane exploded. "You looked up and all you saw was dust." Everyone on the plane was killed.

Another plane was headed down the runway. The pilot got the nose up and the tail went down and "you knew he wouldn't make it. At the end of the runway he cut the throttle and the plane nosed over and caught fire." McWilliams and four others dashed to the plane, picked up a piece of drill pipe and knocked the windows off around the cockpit. The tail gunner meanwhile jumped out, as did a waist gunner, who broke his arm. "But the cockpit was on fire and the plane was burning. We hauled out the pilot. He was burned almost beyond recognition. We laid him on the ground. All the time he was saying, 'Just leave me in the plane, leave me here, leave me here,' because he knew he was gone." McWilliams and the others got him into the ambulance "and he didn't even last to get to the hospital. That was the first time I ever saw anybody burned up that way. His hands were just burnt down to nothing." Somehow the co-pilot got out. "I don't know how. Just one of these unexplained things."[5]

Lt. Francis Hosimer was a B-24 pilot in the 741st Squadron. He flew his first five missions as a co-pilot. On one of them, going over Vienna, his squadron was part of a four-squadron group. There was another group ahead of his. The flak came up, heavy. "Just while we were watching the group in front, three of the planes started burning. They just kept flying on level, they didn't go down but then just burst into real bright flames almost like a flashgun going off. Very intense fire and there were no chutes coming out so that meant that thirty men died right there. The pilot looked over to me and said that is where we're going to be in a minute. I wondered what in the world I had gotten myself into." His plane was shot up but got through.6

The men of the 741st Squadron badly needed some rest.

In mid-January, McGovern and Rounds learned that they were entitled to ten days off duty, in Rome, the Isle of Capri, or Naples. General Eisenhower, commander of the Allied forces, ordered the U.S. Army and Army Air Forces to provide ten days leave for combat veterans. That was easier to do with AAF personnel than infantry, but still the attempt was made. Eisenhower also got involved in picking the hotels for his boys. On a cruise around the Isle of Capri, he spotted a large villa. "Whose is that?" he asked.

"Yours, sir," was the reply. His aides had arranged it.

"And that?" Eisenhower asked, nodding at another large villa. "That one belongs to General Spaatz."

"Damn it, that's *not* my villa!" Eisenhower thundered. "And that's not General Spaatz's villa! None of these will belong to any general as long as I'm boss around here. This is supposed to be a rest center— for combat men—not a playground for the brass!"

He meant it. When he returned to shore, he wired Spaatz, "This is directly contrary to my policies and must cease at once."7

As a consequence of Eisenhower's orders, the Isle of Capri, Naples, and Rome were hosts to thousands of GIs in late 1944 and 1945. It was like a dream, or could be anyway. "'Twas on the Isle of Capri that I found her," Lt. Roland Pepin remembered of his trip to the famous island. "She told me she was a contessa and that her name was Monica." Pepin didn't care what she chose to call herself. He had a "torrid ten-day romance." Monica lived in a villa and Pepin stayed with her. She spoke English, French, and Italian, and took Pepin on sightseeing tours. They rented a boat and explored the caverns of the Blue Grotto. Pepin's conclusion, after ten days of living on a near-paradise, was that Eisenhower and his fellow generals were right to assign weary men to a rest and recreation interlude. For Pepin, "The salt, sun, sea, and Monica rejuvenated me into my former self, and I was ready to get on with the war."[8]

McGovern and Rounds took off for Capri, along with some of the crew. Radio operator Kenneth Higgins was one of them. Like everyone, Higgins had been bored at Cerignola. "When we didn't fly a mission there wasn't a lot to do," he recalled. The weather precluded any softball games or other outdoor exercise. Occasionally the crew would go to the target range and practice with their .45s, but there wasn't much fun in that. So, "we would sit around and argue with each other and play cards or dice. One time we said no more cussing. Everybody cusses all the time so the first guy that does cuss has to put some money in the pot. Well that lasted about ten minutes." Being a Texan, Higgins always wore a pair of cowboy boots, whether he was in the plane, on the ground, or on leave. When he got to Capri, he kissed the ground and had a big glass of fresh milk. Italian kids came up to him to ask if he was a girl with those long boots and big heels and leather jacket. No, Higgins replied. He said he was just a cool cat.

He too rested and rejuvenated. He got ready to return to the war. Fifty-five years later, when he was being interviewed, Higgins said that whenever things were going bad at work or home in his postwar career, he would settle down by thinking of the guy at the airfield who woke him up in the morning at four o'clock to say get dressed and go fly a mission. "There's nothing worse than that." So they could call him whatever names they wished in Capri, Higgins decided; he was going to enjoy himself.[9]

Everyone did. Lt. Ted Withington, a prewar Harvard student who was by late 1944 a B-24 pilot in the 780th Squadron, wrote his parents about his experience. "Talk about wonderful vacations!" he declared.

"Nothing to do we *don't* want to and lots of interesting things to do if we care to." It was a "week of luxury with no worries." He stayed in the AAF villa on "one of Europe's most beautiful Isles." He had taken a steamer from Naples, out into the Bay of Naples, past Pompeii and Vesuvius and out to Capri at the mouth of the bay. He had a "lovely room" overlooking the sea, complete with balcony. Most blessed of all, "You sleep as late as you want to, in real large beds with *pillows & sheets!* Maid and waiter service all the time. This *ain't* the Army!"[10]

Radio operator Bob Hammer of the 742nd Squadron got to Capri right after New Year's. He loved it, especially that except for booze everything was free. There was a dance each night, alternating officers and enlisted men. Sergeant Hammer and his pilot went to all of them by wearing each other's uniforms. In the morning, they overslept and missed the ferry going back to the mainland. Again the next day they slept late. After missing the ferry three times, they finally caught it and then lucked out by catching a B-24 back to Cerignola. Fearing a court-martial, they were, on the contrary, not even reprimanded, as the 742nd had flown no missions due to weather while they were gone.[11] As Lieutenant Withington put it, this wasn't the Army!

McGovern and Rounds stayed on Capri for three days. They rode the funicular, took a tour of the Blue Grotto, and examined the ruins of Roman emperor Tiberius's castle. The second night one of his enlisted crew got drunk and into a brawl. McAfee, the ball turret gunner who was present, recalled that the culprit "wound up in the pokey on Capri, and McGovern had to get him out."[12]

McGovern and Rounds decided there was not enough action on Capri, so they hopped on a boat that was just crossing to Naples, where they caught a train to Rome. They registered at the Regina Hotel, which had been taken over by the AAF and is still in operation in a grand style in the twenty-first century. In 1945, every night starting at 6:00 P.M. the whole ground floor of the lobby was turned into a dance area. Girls from Rome were there, after passing through a screening by the AAF authorities, designed to keep teenagers away. Most of the women were in their mid-twenties.

They were beautiful but they were caught up in the desperation that comes to many civilians in a war zone. Many were educated, spoke at least some English, had lost husbands, fathers. Beer, vodka, scotch, gin, and more was flowing. There were free bedrooms upstairs. The fee for the women was $30, but they would take payment in cigarettes or mattress covers. The covers were very popular because the women could make clothing for all the family from them.

Rounds had a great time, of course, but he also got up with McGovern each morning to go on foot for ten or twelve hours of sightseeing. Looking at every art gallery, every church, every statue, using their guidebook, every day for seven days. Rounds accounted for his interest in the city by explaining to McGovern that his father had told him if he ever got to Rome he must see this or that. So, Rounds said, "I don't dare go home without seeing this or that, my old man will kill me." With that much motivation, Rounds started reading up on the great artists.

McGovern meanwhile learned of a special audience for American servicemen in the Vatican with the Pope. He persuaded Rounds to go with him. After standing around waiting for an hour, Rounds stage-whispered to McGovern, "I"m getting the hell out of here."

McGovern replied, "Look, this man is the head of state and he's the symbol of the Catholic world, and you will feel very silly if you go back to the States and you haven't met the Pope." He talked Rounds into waiting fifteen minutes. When that time was up, he asked him to stay for just fifteen more minutes.

"I wouldn't wait another fifteen minutes for Jesus Christ," Rounds shot back. But he said it too loud and "it stirred up quite a commotion among the devout Catholic troops." There were 500 or so at the audience. The Pope did soon arrive and shook hands with every one. He spoke English and blessed each of them. Rounds said,

"For the rest of my life I'll tell people I saw and shook hands with the Pope."13 To McGovern, Rounds's desire to see all he could in Rome was "an indication, a tiny one, that ours was the best educated army ever put into the field. And the best paid. We were paid way better than the British and enormously better than the Germans. I don't know if the Italian army ever got paid at all or the Red Army either."14

———

In the U.S. Army infantry, there was a certain amount of resentment of the AAF officers and men. How could there not be? No ground trooper ever wore cowboy boots, not even on leave, certainly not when up on the line. No one in the infantry ever reported back from a leave three days late without being severely reprimanded or possibly subjected to a court-martial. And the ages of the lieutenants, even the ages of the captains and majors in the AAF were astonishing to foot soldiers.

At a bar in Rome, two infantry officers from the U.S. Fifth Army, which was doing the fighting on the ground in Italy under the command of Gen. Mark Clark, approached McGovern. One of them sat down on the stool next to McGovern, reached out, and flicked the wings on McGovern's jacket with his finger.

"You fly boys think you're pretty hot stuff, don't ya."

"No, not really," McGovern replied. "I think the Fifth Army is doing a heck of a job and I hope we can help."

"Bull," the infantry officer responded. "You fly boys are just too good for us, aren't you." McGovern resisted the temptation to hit the man.

———

When the leave was over it was back to Cerignola. For Lieutenant Pepin, a navigator, his first mission after returning was almost a disaster. It was on January 20. The target was the main marshaling yards at Linz, Austria. The flak was heavy. Shrapnel punctured some of his plane's hydraulic lines and the pilot was unable to close the bomb bay doors or lower the landing gear and could barely keep the Liberator in the air. He had managed to get back over Italy and close to Cerignola. He ordered the men to bail out. The plane was at 3,000 feet. "Petrified," Pepin related, "I was sitting with my feet hanging out of the bomb bay afraid to jump when the pilot pushed me into the wild blue yonder. Stark fear gripped me until my chute opened. The ground appeared to rush toward me and fear came again. My landing was the same as taking a wicked body check from a big hockey player." He rolled over several times, got up, and discovered that he was unhurt. Ambulances from the base came around to pick him up. "Every member of my crew survived and without injuries."[15]

On January 31, McGovern and his crew went up on a mission, to bomb the oil refinery at Moosbierbaum, Austria. There were nineteen B-24s on the mission, each carrying 500-pound bombs. They encountered moderate, but accurate, flak, and dropped on target.

On this mission, as on all the others, the ground crew noted that Lieutenant McGovern brought back the *Dakota Queen* with more gasoline in his tanks than all the other pilots. In the ground crew's opinion, this was the mark of his flying ability. Ken Higgins remarked, "I don't know how you describe a good pilot. I do know George, though, and as far as I was concerned, he was the best. Because he always got us back on the ground." Another member of McGovern's crew said, "If he ever panicked, I never knew about it. Whatever happened, that sort of nasal twang of his came over the intercom as clear and flat as it was on the ground."[16]

Valko disliked Seigal. He went to McGovern to ask him to get Seigal transferred out. McGovern put it up to the other enlisted men. "I decided they had to live with him," McGovern said, "so it was up to them to decide." The vote was four to one to drop Seigal. McGovern had him replaced with a tail gunner from another crew, Sgt. John B. Mills. Mills was tall and he had to hunch up a bit to get into position, but he liked being back there in the tail. In February and March, McGovern would sometimes tell him to get out of the cramped quarters when the *Dakota Queen* was halfway back to base. "We're not going to see any fighter planes today," McGovern said, "so come on up and stretch out a bit." But Mills would be asleep. One good thing, according to McGovern: "He didn't get sick."

On one mission, with Sam Adams gone, McGovern had a substitute navigator-bombardier. Weather forced his squadron to abort. The lead pilot said to jettison the bomb load. The standard procedure was to drop the bombs either over the Adriatic or an unpopulated area. Sgt. Tex Ashlock was watching the ground through the camera hatch when the bombardier let the bombs drop. They fell on a farmhouse. It disappeared in a rolling cloud of smoke. In Ashlock's mind it was murder, pure and simple.

When the *Dakota Queen* got back on the ground, Ashlock grabbed the bombardier. "Listen, you son of a bitch," he yelled. "I saw what you did. I'm not going to have anything to do with you again. As far as I'm concerned, you're a disgrace to humanity."

When McGovern got out of the plane, Ashlock went to him to report on what had happened. McGovern asked, "There isn't any doubt in your mind it was deliberate?"

"How could it not have been?" Ashlock replied.

McGovern thought for a few minutes, then said, "You know, if we bring charges, it's going to be your word against his—an enlisted man against an officer. It's going to be hard to make it stick without any other evidence of witnesses." McGovern let that hang, then added, "I'll tell you one thing, though. We aren't going to fly with that guy again." And they didn't.[17]

For the 455th Group, according to its historical account, *Flight of the Vulgar Vultures,* "January was our least productive month to date." Fewest missions flown—seven in all—putting 168 bombers over targets, dropping a total of 200,035 tons of bombs. That was the lowest total since February 1944. The group could only hope for an improvement in the weather.[18]

CHAPTER NINE

The Tuskegee Airmen Fly Cover

February 1945

FEBRUARY BEGAN WITH MARGINAL WEATHER. Then it got worse. The first mission for the 741st Squadron, on the first of the month, had as its target the oil refinery at Moosbierbaum, Austria, but the weather was so bad en route and at the target that the group leader decided not to bomb. All planes returned to base.

Oil refineries and the marshaling yards in Austria and Germany were the primary targets that month. On February 5, McGovern flew to bomb the oil storage facilities at Regensburg, Germany. Clouds covered the target but the squadron dropped its bombs, using the pathfinder method of following the actions of the lead plane. The results were unobserved because of the clouds. No one in the squadron was lost. Two days later, on another mission to Moosbierbaum, the flight leader's bombsight was inoperative so no bombs were dropped. The bombardiers dropped the bombs over water, then the planes returned safely.

On February 8, twenty-four B-24s hit the Matzleindorf marshaling yards at Vienna. The clouds covered the target, but the Americans dropped fifty-four tons of 500-pound bombs, again using the pathfinder method. The flak was intense but all the bombers made it through. However, one B-24 with the group's markings took a position off the number two man in one of the boxes. It was a plane that had been forced down, then repaired by the Germans. It shadowed the squadron, radioing down to the gunners on the 88s the altitude, direction, and speed of the squadron, which was a practice, that while not frequent, was used whenever the Germans had the opportunity. The lead pilot realized what was happening and told every gunner in the squadron to train on the German-manned B-24. As the gunners did so, the aircraft's pilot saw what was happening. He made a 180-degree turn and got out of there.[1]

By February 1945, the defensive capabilities of the *Luftwaffe* were almost nonexistent. The Germans had little or no fuel left for training pilots, and their ME 109s had just about been blown out of the air. What fighters were left had few runways available. For his part, McGovern never saw a German fighter attack the *Dakota Queen.* Flak, of course, was another matter altogether. Following the Battle of the Bulge, as the Allies moved up to the Rhine and prepared to cross the river, the Red Army was headed toward Berlin and Vienna. The shrinkage of the front lines forced the Germans to pull back. The American, British, and Russian air assaults on Germany were increasing in number of bombers flown and damage done. So the Germans concentrated their 88s around their cities, to defend their few remaining oil refineries and most of all their marshaling yards. That meant that even as the Allies were winning, their bombers were flying through ever heavier flak concentrations.

And the Germans had developed a jet-propelled fighter, the ME 262, the fastest fighter in the world. Their problem was a shortage of fuel and trained pilots and airfields. Had the ME 262 been developed earlier it could have been a war-winning weapon, but it was not. When a group of the jets attacked an Eighth Air Force formation, it was havoc for the Americans, as the jets were three times faster than the American bombers. But that didn't happen very often. There were not enough of them.

One reason for the shortage was the sustained Fifteenth Air Force attack against factories making jets and against the airfields where

THE TUSKEGEE AIRMEN FLY COVER

they underwent final assembly. Altogether the Germans built 1,400 jets, but only a small percentage of them got into the air. The Regensburg airfield was one of their bases. A photo reconnaissance by the Fifteenth Air Force on February 8, 1945, showed 48 ME 262s on the ground. The Fifteenth mounted missions to hit them on the field. The 455th, and its 741st Squadron, participated in the February attacks. The group destroyed twelve ME 262s and damaged four others. Other participants put more jets out of action. This proved to be a knockout blow. Individuals or small groups of jets continued to be seen, but no squadron-sized formations.[2] Indeed, as the official Army Air Forces history put it, "The few prize jet aircraft that appeared . . . offered little opposition but hopped almost comically from one airfield to another or to the empty *Autobahnen* behind German lines."[3]

Pilot Lt. Glenn Rendahl, in the 514th Squadron, 376th Bomb Group, flying out of San Pancrazio, Italy, near Taranto Bay, was attacked by ME 262s. In February 1945, he was on a mission to Austria when he had "runaway turbo" problems. He was over the Adriatic. "The cure for the turbos," he related, "was to move a good amplifier, after locking in its setting, from the slot for that engine into a slot in need of boost, then set and lock the desired setting there." He did so, but by the time he had fixed the problem he had lost 5,000 feet of altitude and some speed. His formation was out of sight. "We could never catch them, so we would just have to look for and join with another formation."

As Rendahl gained enough power to start climbing again, "I took a look back over my left shoulder—just as you would before you pull a car out of a parking place." As he did, "Oops!" He saw "two German jet fighters with black swastikas on their sides sweeping in from our left and I saw their tracer bullets already coming into our plane."

It was a favorite strategy for the German fighter pilots to catch stragglers flying alone. It was often an easy kill. Rendahl called over the intercom, "Jerry's at seven o'clock level, when are you guys going to start shooting back?" The upper turret gunner called back, "Hold

211

your fire, here comes three of our P-51 escorts from high overhead."
With the P-51s coming at them, the Germans turned and ran, then
dove for the ground of northern Yugoslavia just to the east. The three
P-51 escorts stayed right on their tails until they all went out of sight.
Rendahl managed to hook up with another formation "and added
our bombing strength to their mission in what we regarded as a very
useful contribution."

Later, Rendahl praised the P-51 pilots: "If we had not had an escort trio watching us from above, and timely enough to be there quite
soon after the shooting started, we would have surely been subdued
by two of the Nazis' latest jet fighters doing what they specialized in.
Without the intervention of our escorts and their willingness to risk
their lives for those of us whom they had never met, we would have
been most fortunate to end up in the Adriatic Sea below us. Or we
might have stretched it to Trieste, which was then German-occupied.
Most likely, some of our crew would be lost either way."4

The P-51 pilots were African-Americans of the 99th Fighter
Squadron, Fifteenth Air Force, flying out of Terni, north of Rome.
They were called the Tuskegee Airmen and they were justly famous.
The men of the bombers seldom saw them, because they stayed up
high to watch over the formations. As Rendahl put it, "When you
needed them they came, and with a full head of steam." He called the
performance of the Tuskegee Airmen "exemplary." He felt that "their
vigilant watch over us that day saved ten of us from a potential
tragedy. We, plus all our families, will forever be grateful to them." He
added, "The important thing is that when our nation goes to war, real
patriotism has only one race. You are either American or you are not.
There are those who want to kill you, and then there are those who
want to save your life. It is that simple, and undeniable."5

Pepin of the 741st Squadron spoke for many. "It was a favorable
day for us when we caught escort protection from the men from the

99th Fighter Squadron. Because of the P-51's long-range capabilities, they were able to escort us to and from most of the targets. It was quite a vision to observe these great pilots engage the German jets and prevent them from attacking us. We would watch them as they dispersed the enemy with their superior skills. They never let the Germans get close enough for our gunners to fire at the enemy." Unfortunately, Pepin added, "they could give us no protection from the flak; we just had to plow through and pray a good deal."

The U.S. Army in World War II was a segregated force. In Pepin's words it was "still practicing discrimination. But those P-51 Negro fighter pilots did not discriminate." Once late that winter Pepin was in Foggia when he and his buddies met some of the 99th Fighter Squadron pilots. "We showered them with our thanks and respect. The drinks were on us."6

The men of Tuskegee admired the B-24 pilots and crews without stint. Lieutenant Edward Gleed said, "We didn't want any part of that flak" the bombers flew through. "It was a horrendous sight to see six B-24 Liberators with all that flak starting to come up and—bang—there's only five airplanes left and one big ball of smoke." Lieutenant Herb Sheppard said his most vivid memory of the war was "the sight of bombers being hit by an 88 and the bombs going off—a big red eruption with black smoke going by you." Lieutenant Jefferson recalled, "Planes fell in flames, planes fell not in flames, an occasional one pulled out and crash-landed, sometimes successfully, sometimes they blew up. Men fell in flames, men fell in parachutes, some candle-sticked [when their parachutes didn't open]. Pieces of men dropped through the hole, pieces of planes." The Tuskegee Airmen prayed and wept. "Have you any idea of what it's like to vomit in an oxygen mask?" According to Jefferson, "These bomber guys had seen the inside of hell."

The African-American pilots loved their P-51s. Lt. Woody Crockett called the plane "a dream. It could climb, turn, and fight at low level and at high altitude." The Mustang carried six .50-caliber machine guns, three in each wing. Lt. Lou Purnell said, "If that plane had been a girl, I'd have married it right on the spot. Damn right! It was like dancing with a good partner." They painted their tails bright red. Lt. Herbert Carter explained, "We wanted the American bombers to know we were escorting them. The red tails would also let the German interceptors know who was escorting those bombers."

Their task was to protect. Their orders were to stay with the bombers, whatever happened. "Protect them with your life" was the saying. They flew about 5,000 feet above the bombers, meaning they flew at 30,000 feet or even above. Lieutenant Sheppard felt "the extra five thousand feet gave us an edge if we had to ward off attack. If you have speed, you can get altitude, and if you have altitude, you can get speed. That P-51 really accelerated when you put its nose down. Man, altitude just disappeared like smoke in the wind."[7]

On a February mission, McGovern heard in his briefing that the 99th would fly as escorts. After dropping the bombs and turning for home, he looked out the window and saw German jets looming in the distance. "Our group leader tried to establish radio contact with our fighter escorts," McGovern said, "but couldn't. There was some pretty harsh language on the air, questions about where the 'blasted niggers' were. Just then, the squadron commander of the black pilots broke in and said, 'Why don't you all shut up, white boys? We're all going to take you home.' And they did. They drove off the enemy fighters."[8]

Ken Higgins looked out and saw the P-51s flying at the side of the Dakota Queen. The black pilot saw the camera in the camera hatch and called up on the radio, "Is that a camera in there?" Higgins said yes, and the pilot said, "How about taking my picture?" Higgins did.

Over the radio, he heard some fighter pilots talking: "Red Tail One to Red Tail Two. Is that you behind me?" Another voice: "Who that?" And the first voice: "Who that? Who say that?"

The colonel in the lead B-24 cut in: "Get off the radio. No speaking on the radio. Get off."

The fighter pilot came back on: "Who that?" he asked. In Higgins's view, "That would keep you going, you know. A little levity here and there didn't hurt."

Like Pepin and everyone else in one of the bombers, Higgins had the deepest respect for the men of the 99th. He pointed out that, among many other things, "they made it a point when they were in a town, they were dressed immaculately. I mean their brass was polished and their clothes were pressed. They were really sharp. They made it a point to be that way." Higgins added, "There was a lot of talk during the war about blacks being cowards and stuff like that. I never saw any of that. Never did I see any cowardliness."9

Neither did anyone else. Sgt. Erling Kindem of the 742nd Squadron was on a February mission against Vienna. He later wrote in his war diary, "Before reaching the target, a 'phantom' B-24 joined our formation." It was a downed bomber the Germans had restored and were flying to radio back to base the formation's altitude, speed, and direction. Fortunately, the Tuskegee Airmen were flying as escort. Kindem's pilot reported to the black pilots in their P-51s the information. The leader responded, "I'll go scare him out but you tell your boys not to point their guns at us."

Kindem's diary went on: "The P-51s came in and over the radio the German phantom pilot said he was from the 55th Wing and got lost. But the 55th Wing wasn't flying that day and the plane had no tail markings. The fighter pilot squadron leader gave him some bursts from his guns and warned the phantom to turn back. He added, 'You will be escorted.' The German pilot replied that he could make it alone. The P-51 pilot said: 'You are going to be escorted whether you want it or not. You're going to have two men on your tail all the way back and don't try to land in Yugoslavia.' The phantom protested and said he wanted to drop his bombs. The response from the fighter pilot was: 'You ain't gonna drop no bombs.' The phantom left with his escort and we heard nothing further from the event."10

Back in October 1944, Lt. C. W. Cooper—the "old" infantry officer (he was twenty-eight years old) who had after some time with the troops volunteered for the Army Air Forces and trained as a navigator—shipped over to join the 741st Squadron at Cerignola. It was a long trip by a leaky cargo ship. He was in command of fifty-five replacements, all soon-to-be crew members of the B-24s. "They were hell to take care of," he recalled, not like the infantry enlisted men he was accustomed to leading. After disembarking at Naples, Cooper and his men traveled by truck to a staging base in southernmost Italy. They arrived in November. The first officer he saw was "a big, raw-boned second lieutenant, with red hair and a red beard. I said, 'Golly, that guy's still a second lieutenant, he must be thirty-five years old.'" Cooper and his crew boarded the lieutenant's B-24 and flew toward Cerignola. As they were landing, Cooper heard the lieutenant say to his co-pilot, "Have you got runway on your side?" The co-pilot said, "Yeah." The pilot said, "I've got some over here too," so he set the plane down. Later when the pilot had completed his missions he shaved and to Cooper's astonishment, "He was an eighteen-year-old kid!"

Cooper and the crew lined up for their first meal at Cerignola. The man in front of Cooper asked, "You haven't eaten here before, have you?"

"No," Cooper replied.

"Well, we've been eating here quite a while," the man said. "Tell you what you're supposed to do. If you have a bug in your food when you get it first, you throw the food out. After about a week though, if you have a bug in your food, you go ahead and eat the food. And then the third week, you look and there's a bug in you food, you make him stay and don't let it get away because it's good, it's got nutrients."

On an early mission Cooper's plane climbed well above freezing altitude. "I think our bombardier may have been reading a comic book or sleeping back there. Anyway when you go through the level where things will freeze, you keep working the bomb bay doors so that they won't jam on you, they won't ice up." Cooper's plane got to the target "and the bombardier hadn't done what he should have done going to that level, and the bomb bay doors had frozen. He couldn't get them open. So he dropped the bombs through the bomb bay doors." In other words he hit the toggle switch and the bombs just broke through the aluminum. The wheels, when let down, were below the now broken bomb bay doors flapping in the breeze. "We didn't know whether it would be enough room or not. If those things hit the runway, they may cause a spark and there may be a buildup of gas in the bomber and bloody, we would've had it." Fortunately the plane landed safely.

Cooper was so good as a navigator that he soon was flying on the lead plane on his missions. He did so on six missions. "The pressure was really on then, because you had to be absolutely right where you were supposed to be at all times. I was *the* navigator." He was struck by the difference between being an infantry officer and a pilot. "The pilot didn't exercise command like an infantry platoon leader," he felt. "In the infantry, you're under pressure all the time. For us, we were only under pressure when going on a mission." In the infantry, a lieutenant told his platoon what to do and how to go about it. But "the pilot had to recognize the role of each air crew member and not get in the way." Cooper thought the biggest difference between the infantry and the Army Air Forces was that "you are individuals when you're on a crew. The pilot's not going to tell me how to navigate, he's not going to tell Ken Higgins how to run his radio. Those were our specialties and we did our job." Cooper added, "It was a whole different situation than it was in the infantry." B-24 crews socialized together, mixing regardless of rank. Never had Cooper seen such a thing in the infantry.

Cooper had eleven missions behind him. Compounding the tension of navigating the lead plane, with six other navigators watching in their following planes, was the reality of flak. On nearly every mission, his plane took various hits, losing power on one or two engines, and in other ways making what he was doing in the most dangerous place in the world even more fearful. So was the possibility of accidents. One time Cooper saw a B-24 drop its bombs right on top of a plane flying below, setting off a flashing explosion that destroyed everything except the engines. Cooper watched as they fell.

A few days later, Cooper flew a mission, got back to Cerignola, and was told to make up a route for the mission the next day. "I noticed that one of the turning points they gave us was right over a flak-up area in northern Yugoslavia. So I thought, That's no good." He called Wing Headquarters: "Say, you gave us a wrong turning point—"

"Don't say any more," the officer at Wing shot out. "Don't say any more. Our telephone lines are bugged all the time so no more. We will get you a correction." The men at Wing Headquarters had already spotted the error, which had come about because two towns in Yugoslavia had the same name. One had heavy flak, the other nothing. The turning point was changed.

Radiomen on the B-24s kept changing their frequencies so that the Germans would have a hard time listening. Occasionally, they could pick up and get on the German frequency. On one of Cooper's missions, a German-speaking radioman came along. Cooper listened as he went to work: "He got on the radio, on their frequency, and he heard a German commander talking to his fighter planes, directing them toward our formation. So the American, identifying himself in German as their ground control officer, ordered them, 'Return to base, immediately.' So these fighter planes took off to go back to base, and before their real commander could get it corrected, they were already gone, and couldn't get back up there to us." Cooper added to the story that he knew of at least one other native German speaker in the 455th Group who used that technique.

One of the pilots Cooper flew with was, in his view, wishing he were up in the sky in fighter planes, not B-24s. He took chances, in turns, wagging his wings, climbing or diving. One February day, when Cooper was not on the plane, that pilot took it up for a practice run. As a stunt, he began buzzing Wing Headquarters. Wing called Group Headquarters on the radio to say, "There's a plane buzzing us and it's your plane. Get this damn plane out of here." The group commander, furious, ordered, "Ground that pilot when he gets back to base. Nobody in his right mind would do that." Even before the B-24 landed, there was a jeep waiting for the pilot. Cooper recalled that "they took him into headquarters and grounded him right there on the spot. And they kept him grounded for quite a while and then when they did let him fly again on a combat mission, they gave him a plane that was doubtful whether it'd get up there or not."[11]

The day the pilot was grounded, Cooper was moved out of his tent and out of his crew and sent to George McGovern's tent. From now on he would take Adams's place permanently, as McGovern's navigator. The next night, February 19, he wrote his buddy, Lt. Joe Prendergast with the 4th Infantry in Germany. He told Prendergast, "My new pilot is a honey—very sincere, a mature man, and a good pilot. He's married and expecting a baby in three weeks so he'll add a thousand feet for safety." As Cooper signed off on the letter, McGovern came into the tent. He had just been promoted to first lieutenant. Cooper added a postscript: "Mac, my new pilot, just came in and let me pin his thirty-minute-old silver bars on him. I'm sure glad 'cause he rates." Sometime after sending the letter, Cooper got the V-Mail back. Scribbled on the front beside Prendergast's name was a note: "Killed in action. J. A. Wesolowski, Capt., 4th Inf."[12]

When Cooper met McGovern and Rounds, he knew he had joined an experienced pilot and co-pilot. He went through details of what he had done up to that point, then listened. He was impressed by McGovern, "serious without being obnoxious." Rounds had more of a wait-and-see quality to him. Cooper later said that Rounds "would go in all directions at once. I quickly called him 'Rounds the Rounder.'"[13]

On February 20, McGovern and his crew stood down. The next morning, at 4:00 A.M. they were up, getting ready. The briefing officer informed them the target that day was the marshaling yards in Vienna. He was answered with groans. Vienna still had one of the heaviest flak concentrations in Europe.

Among the bomber crews in the formation was one with Lieutenant Hammer as radioman. He had had a dream the previous night, which he related to his crew as they were waiting to take off. He had dreamed that the target would be Vienna. And it turned out to be true. The other crew members, Hammer confessed, were "amused—in a sickly sort of way."[14]

Off they went anyway, along with twenty-six other B-24s. The *Dakota Queen* was in the middle of the 741st Squadron's box. The flak over Vienna was, according to the 455th Group's account, "intense and accurate."[15] Some fourteen of the bombers were hit out of the twenty-one that got over the target.

Hammer was in one of them. As the plane pulled away from Vienna, number three engine quit. Lt. Ray Grooms, the pilot, and Lt. Jim Connelly, the co-pilot, tried unsuccessfully to feather the propeller. The windmilling prop cost the plane altitude and speed and it dropped behind the remainder of the squadron. Grooms ordered the crew to jettison everything possible, but still the plane lost altitude and just did get over the Yugoslavian mountains. Grooms decided not to try to cross the Adriatic; his navigator told him there was an emergency landing field under American control at Zara, just ahead. He headed for it, but as he checked his systems he discovered that the hydraulic system had been damaged. He had no brakes.

He snapped out orders to his waist gunners. Remove the waist windows. Tie a parachute to each waist gun. Be ready to toss it out and pull the rip cords on my word. They acknowledged. In Hammer's words, "Shortly after the wheels made contact with the ground we got the word and threw them out and pulled rip cords. The one on my side opened first and we veered crazily in that direction until the pintle holding the waist gun to its mounting was sheared cleanly in half. The pintle, made of solid steel, measured two inches in diameter at the point of breakage. The other parachute finally opened and braked us down."*

---

* According to Francis Hosimer, "It was a standard procedure to fasten parachutes to the waist guns and throw them out after landing whenever your hydraulic fluid was gone."

Once out of the plane, the crew members told Hammer "that I could, in the future, keep my dreams to myself." GIs in trucks and jeeps picked them up and took them immediately to a C-47, which was soon in the air. Hammer and his buddies got to sleep in their own bunks that night, back in Cerignola.[16] The *Dakota Queen* had taken only a few hits from shrapnel, which made holes in the wings, but McGovern was on the ground to welcome Hammer back.

On February 24, McGovern, Rounds, Cooper, and the crew flew a mission headed toward the marshaling yards in Vienna, but bad weather forced them and the other planes to abort. On the twenty-eighth it was back into the air, with the target the marshaling yards in Isarco Albes, in northern Italy. The flak was not as heavy as over Vienna, but it was there. They returned to Cerignola safely.

In the winter of 1944–1945, the 741st improved its living conditions. By then every tent had either a wooden or a concrete floor. The food was better and had come to include steak, fresh chicken, real eggs, and ice cream. Squadron officers started to give classes in algebra, business administration, aircraft maintenance, history, and the Italian languages. The ground crews flocked to the Italian instructions, as they had come to the conclusion that since there was no hope in their going home before war's end, they might as well understand what the natives were talking about.

Still the rain came down. It created much mud, especially around the new mess hall. Two GIs were heard discussing the mud. One said he had stumbled into it and had sunk in ankle deep. The other GI said he had gone in as well, but the mud was up to his knees. The first GI said, "Yeah, but I went in head first."

The men put out a group newspaper, called the *Journal*, and each squadron also had one. The 740th Squadron's was called *Il Castoro Ardente*, meaning *Eager Beaver*. The 741st called its paper *Stagrag*. The papers were typed and run off on hand-cranked mimeograph machines. The January 1945 issue of the *Journal* carried an article written by Maj. Al Coons, the group intelligence officer. One year had passed, he opened, "a year that most of us would rather not have lived as we did, had the world we inherited been one in which free choices were possible. At the same time, it is a year most of us would not have spent otherwise, given the world as it was in February 1944." He then wrote of all the territory liberated in Russia, France, Belgium, and elsewhere, and noted that the Fifteenth Air Force had made its contribution to the victories. He gave credit for this accomplishment to the pilots and their crews, to the ground crews, to the clerks, cooks, communications personnel, "and all the rest."

But, Coons went on, "all of us have a responsibility for the failures—the briefings that were inadequate, the truck drivers who were late in getting the crews to their briefings, the crew members who stayed in the pad when they should have been familiarizing themselves with their planes or their guns or their targets, the cooks who didn't have breakfast on time and the linemen who failed to check the plane carefully. These failures have softened the blows against the enemy, they have cost the lives of Americans and our Allies."

Coons concluded, "All that we have learned in one year of combat can be used to insure that the second year will be a short one."

The *Journal* carried one article about Demo, who was the first mascot of the 742nd Squadron. Demo had flown from Africa when he was just a puppy. "Demo refused to leave the empty tent when his masters failed to return from their mission . . . brokenhearted . . . waiting. Demo never went hungry. Someone always remembered and carried food to the little soldier on guard."17

McGovern wrote an article called "This Thing Called Spirit" for the second issue of *Stagrag*. He gave various tips on how to keep morale high. "First of all," he wrote, "we can make sure that we don't go stale on life. We can keep alive and interested in what is going on around us. The army already has plenty of Joes who exist just to eat, sleep and bitch." He urged his readers to keep posted on the war fronts and on developments in the States, to read best-sellers, "of which the squadron is well supplied," try to improve personalities by "using a little tact and thought in our relations with others," plan postwar careers, and even write for *Stagrag*.

"A second aid to good spirit is to refuse to let our bitches and troubles get us down." He concluded that "our primary source of satisfaction comes from being true to ourselves and the best that is in us. The finest praise any man can receive is to be satisfied himself with what he has accomplished. . . . Combat may be rough, but it won't be half as rough if we go through it in the right spirit. Let's make it easy on ourselves!"[18]

February 12, 1945, was the first anniversary for the 455th Group flying out of Italy. On February 22, it flew its 200th mission. It came at the end of thirteen consecutive days of combat flying—the *Dakota Queen* had gone out on five of them. Group commander Col. William Snowden led the wing over Linz. It was a common practice in the 455th for a major or a colonel, sometimes even a general, to fly the lead. *Ole Tepee Time Gal* flew her 100th mission over Linz. By early 1945, she plus *Glamour Gal* and *Bestwedo* were the only B-24s left out of the original twenty-four.

Despite the losses, in its second 100 missions the 455th dropped 4,412 tons of bombs in 2,521 sorties. Bombing accuracy was improving. In the period from December 1944 through February 1945, the group greatly exceeded the average performance of the Fifteenth Air Force as a whole. But a total of forty-seven bombers had been lost, mostly to flak. Considering that the group put up sixty B-24s for its 101st mission, those losses were high.

Shortly after the 200th mission, the group had a party to celebrate. Italian laborers put up tents and bandstands. Entertainers were hired to perform. The airmen pitched in to do their specialities. There were shows of all types, contortionists, muscle acts, rifle ranges, ring games, and variety shows. Four different movies were shown in the wine cellar used for the mission briefing room. There was plenty of beer. It was a chance to relax, eagerly seized by these airmen far from home and living dangerous lives. For that day, at least, they could be the boys they were.

February was over. The 455th Group had flown twenty-six missions, seven aborted. It had put 505 aircraft over the targets and dropped 840 tons of bombs. It lost five B-24s that month and had forty-one men missing in action, one man killed in action in a plane that got back to base, and sixteen severely wounded. The history of the group comments, "With weather conditions as they were, it speaks highly of the support given by the ground echelon as well as the effort put forth by the crews. With better weather on the horizon, things would only get better."[19]

CHAPTER TEN

Missions over Austria

March 1945

BUT THE APPROACHING END OF WINTER brought little improvement in the weather. In the first two weeks of March, the 455th flew thirteen missions, five of them aborted due to weather. On another three, the bombers went after alternate targets when the primary was socked in. Marshaling yards were generally the target; occasionally the bombers went after refineries. The *Dakota Queen* was part of the force on March 4, when the target was marshaling yards at Wiener Neustadt, Austria. On this mission, McGovern saw a B-24 flying on his wing "just peel off in flames. The plane took a hit right near the fuselage and the number three engine broke off. The plane just went into a spinning fall. Didn't see any chutes."[1]

On that mission, ball turret gunner Sgt. William McAfee, who had just turned twenty-one, got unplugged from his electric suit. McGovern called on the intercom to check on the crew and McAfee informed him that he had no heat. He told McAfee to come up to the cockpit because "you'll freeze to death back there." Hesitant to get into the cockpit, McAfee instead changed shoes with waist gunner Ashlock and radioman Higgins. "I'd just stick my foot in their shoes long enough to get it thawed out a little bit, then I'd give it back to them."

McGovern kept checking on him until assured that he was okay. In a 1999 interview, McAfee recalled the incident, then commented, "McGovern took good care of me. That was one thing he did. He was like an old mother. He was supposed to bring us back in one piece and he did."

McGovern, at age twenty-two, was a year or more older than everyone on the crew except Cooper and Valko. But he was responsible and he knew and had learned to respond to that. As McAfee said, "We were much, much too young to even know anything about what was going on or anything. We did what McGovern told us to do and that's all."2 McGovern, in his autobiography, *Grassroots,* wrote: "The members of my crew were boys when we entered combat. They emerged as serious men." He felt that they, "like hundreds of others, were welded into a highly competent team by their common yearning to survive."3

McGovern had his own special reason to survive. On March 5, Cooper wrote a letter home. "My new crew and I get along swell," he said. "Mac is still sweating out a cable telling of a new son or daughter. Still sweating out his missions so's to get home."4

About this time, McGovern had a snapshot taken of himself standing outside his tent. C. W. Cooper sent a copy back to his fiancée. On the back of the picture, he wrote, "The best B-24 pilot in the world." McGovern never would accept such a judgment. He knew there were better pilots than he in the 741st, starting with Lt. Charles Painter, and certainly in the 455th. Painter, McGovern said, was a "big guy. One thing I remember about those pilots is that most of them were big and had been athletes. I was one of the few skinny debaters who had never been an athlete." Still, it was good to have the approval of one of the old men of the crew, especially when Cooper was a former infantry officer and now one of the top navigators in the Army Air Forces.

After the March 4 mission, McGovern stayed on the ground for nine days. There was little to do but wait, "and yet you had to be available to fly every day even though you didn't get off the ground. You had a lot of time to think." For one thing, he wondered why the Germans didn't surrender. He knew they had been beaten, if only because "they did not have sufficient fuel to keep their fighter planes in the air."

When you were on missions you had no time to think. "You're so busy handling that plane and staying in formation and watching the fuel supply—making sure the gauges are not giving any trouble—that it really kept you occupied. You had to keep all four of those engines working, synchronized, proper oil pressure, temperature, and keeping that big bomber in formation at all times—you had about all you could handle. In a sense the pilot was insulated from the war. You had a perfect view of the flak—you could see the puffs out in front of you, the flashes of red and black. You could feel the plane shudder better than anyone else. So you knew there was a war going on but you had only an indirect relationship to what was being done by the bomber—you couldn't see the target and you were 25,000 feet away from the action on the ground. There was the explosion of the flak shells all around you, but you had no weapon to shoot back with and you didn't have the toggle switch. You didn't have the navigator's view of where you were going."

Recalling his mission over Vienna on February 21, McGovern said that until then he had felt "a sort of nagging and anxiety on take-offs and turbulent air and hoping that all the mechanics were working right. But on that day everything seemed to go smoothly—and it just dawned on me that I had largely overcome any fear that I had previously had about flying."[5]

As Cooper had remarked, and as every crew member of the *Dakota Queen* later testified, McGovern was a serious, mature officer. The responsibilities he carried on every mission—for that big, expensive plane, for getting it over the target tightly packed into the formation, for the lives of his crew—were much bigger and more serious than twenty-two-year-old men ever carry in civilian life. But there was a war on, and those were his responsibilities.

Lt. Cmdr. Edgar D. Hoagland, USNR, a PT boat skipper and later commander of a squadron of PT boats at an age when he should have been going to college, spoke for all pilots, infantry company and platoon leaders, and naval skippers when he wrote in his war memoir, "A destroyer of anxiety and fear is the fierce, overwhelming desire to take care of your men. The more responsibility you have in a combat situation, the easier it is to remain cool and resolute. . . . Fear is more than balanced out by the exhilaration of danger, which puts every sense on full alert and makes you feel supremely alive. Then, after conquering a dangerous situation, you are left fulfilled and confident beyond description."6

Eleanor was due to have her baby in mid-March. McGovern wrote her, and she him, every day. But it took more than a week for the letters to be delivered.

On March 14, McGovern and his crew were awakened at 4:00 A.M. The stars were out. It promised to be a clear, bright day. After breakfast, they walked over to the briefing room and joined about 300 other airmen to sit on the planks laid across cinder blocks. The target that was marked this time was Vienna. The alternate target, also marked, was Wiener Neustadt. If Vienna was clear, the bombs should be dropped on an oil refinery. If it was not and Wiener Neustadt became the choice, the target was marshaling yards.

The weather officer took over. He described the likely conditions between Cerignola and Vienna and what to expect over the target. He said there could be a storm over the city or on the way to it, and the clouds might build too high for the formation to fly over them. If that proved to be the case, the alternate would be bombed. He thought the weather conditions over Wiener Neustadt might be better. He described the weather conditions to expect on the way home.

Another officer mounted the platform to tell the airmen what they were going after and why. He explained the need to hit the refineries or, if necessary, the marshaling yards. If it was Vienna, he told them to stay well away from St. Steven's Cathedral, the Opera House, the Palace and other historic buildings, and schools.* At Wiener Neustadt, the marshaling yards carried north-south rail traffic moving to Munich, Vienna, or elsewhere. Group commander Col. William Snowden would lead the mission, which was about the first piece of news that morning that pleased everyone. The last briefing was on how to form up.

At the hard stand, McGovern inspected his plane as his crew got in. Then he pulled himself up and climbed into the pilot's seat. The *Dakota Queen* taxied, took off, began to climb and circle over the Adriatic, and after an hour of flying, having reached 20,000 feet, got into formation. There were forty-two B-24s, twenty-one from the 455th Bomb Group, twenty-one from the 454th. They flew as squadrons, seven planes in each, in a diamond formation. They set off for Vienna, still gaining altitude, to 25,000 feet.

The day was clear until the formation started to approach Vienna, but over the city the weather had built up into a storm and Colonel Snowden decided it was too dangerous to risk losing his bombers when he couldn't see the target, which also added the additional hazard of possibly hitting the monuments in the city, or schools and hospitals. He began a slow, 180-degree turn toward the alternate. That made every pilot and his crew following Snowden happy—Vienna, as usual, meant heavy and accurate flak, while there would be none at Wiener Neustadt.

There was some cloud cover at Wiener Neustadt but Snowden's radar could pick up the marshaling yards. Everyone dropped their bombs right after he did, and the formation turned for home. It would be a milk run.

---

*A few decades later, McGovern was in Vienna and visited St. Steven's. It had taken some damage from high explosives. But he was certain that no American bombs had hit it and was relieved when he discovered that it had been hit by Russian artillery.

But in the middle of the turn, Sergeant Higgins called up to Lieutenant McGovern on the intercom. The last of the ten 500-pound bombs they were carrying had lodged in the bomb rack. McGovern thought about it for a minute. Landing the *Dakota Queen* in that situation would be suicide. "Well look, we can't land this way with a live bomb in the rack. Either you guys gotta get rid of the bomb or we're going to have to bail out when we get back within reasonable distance of Cerignola. I'm not going to take this bomber down with a bomb in the rack."

The crew left the bomb bay doors open and Sergeant McAfee and Lieutenant Cooper went to work, trying to trigger the little steel catches on each end of the bomb, hoping to pry them open so the bomb would drop. McGovern remembered: "It was scary as hell. If the plane suddenly made a lunge when the 500-pound bomb dropped . . ."

McAfee and Cooper were doing their work standing on the catwalk, less than a foot wide, hanging in the center of the bomb bay. McGovern looked behind him to see how they were doing, "but about all I could see was the top of their heads and their backs."[7]

The danger was acute. McGovern had heard the story told by Sgt. Art Applin, a tail gunner on a B-24. Once after turning away from a mission over Munich, Applin had seen a Liberator on his wing. The bomb bay doors were open. As Applin related, "One of the crew was standing right at the end of the catwalk relieving himself out of the bomb bay and an 88 shell exploded below him and it cracked the catwalk and he fell out. When he did, the heel of his foot got caught in this crack and I saw him dangling there and I called the pilot on the intercom. I couldn't communicate with the plane on the wing but our pilot could. I told him about the situation and he called the pilot on the other plane and his crew pulled the fellow in. Naturally he didn't have his parachute on. He was lucky he made it that day."[8]

As McAfee and Cooper labored, McGovern throttled back to slow down the *Dakota Queen* and they began to lose altitude. "I didn't want to drop a bomb in front of other airplanes," he explained. "Also, I wanted to give McAfee and Cooper undivided time. I didn't know how long it would take to get rid of the bomb. Keep in mind that I had to know all this stuff to survive. Whereas the other guys, their feeling was, 'George will take care of us.'"

The *Dakota Queen* descended to 12,000 feet, several thousand feet below the formation, which was pulling ahead in any case. Then Cooper yelled something "and all of a sudden the plane jumped and I knew the bomb had been cut loose." They were approaching the Austrian-Italian border. McGovern watched the bomb descend, "a luxury you didn't have at 25,000 feet. It went down and hit right on a farm in that beautiful, green part of Austria. It was almost like a mushroom, a big, gigantic mushroom. It just withered the house, the barn, the chicken house, the water tank. *Everything* was just leveled. It couldn't have come in more perfectly. If we had been trying to hit it we couldn't have hit it as square. You could see stuff flying through the air and a cloud of black smoke."9

Sergeant Higgins watched the bomb descend. He commented, "It just blew that farm to smithereens. We didn't mean to do that, we certainly didn't try to do that."10

McGovern glanced at his watch. It was high noon. He came from South Dakota. He knew what time farmers eat. "I got a sickening feeling. Here was this peaceful area. They thought they were safely out of the war zone. Nothing there, no city, no railyard, nothing. Just a peaceful farmyard. Had nothing to do with the war, just a family eating a noon meal. It made me sick to my stomach."11

Navigator Lt. Roland Pepin had a similar experience. On a bombing run over Munich, the last bomb in his plane got stuck. "We were on our return, flying over the Alps. The crew chief and the bombardier were successful in releasing the bomb. I viewed it descending and watched in horror as it landed in the center of a small village and destroyed it. It was a Sunday, midmorning, and I could not help but feel the deepest remorse and shameful guilt for the people of the village. Following this mishap, I couldn't sleep. I was in a stupor and couldn't get these innocent people out of my mind. I was cracking up and didn't know it. My pilot, Lieutenant Barnhill, ordered me to drink about half a bottle of whiskey. I passed out and slept for eighteen hours. Other members of the crew felt as I did. We were all getting jumpy and tired. The surgeon ordered us to take ten days off on the Isle of Capri."[12]

After the bomb fell, McGovern closed the bomb bay doors and headed home. On the intercom, he and Cooper talked. McGovern asked, "What's the highest elevation between here and where we are going?"

Cooper looked at his map, did his calculations, and replied, "Eight thousand feet, George. Eight thousand feet." In an interview, he admitted, "Actually it was only 7,000 feet, but I added another 1,000 feet because I was engaged to get married." Cooper grinned, then added, "As George was expecting his first child, he added another 1,000 feet on top of that."[13]

Back at Cerignola, it was an easy landing. There had been no flak on the milk run over Wiener Neustadt. There was not even a scratch on the *Dakota Queen*. No one had been hurt. McGovern jumped into a truck and rode over to the debriefing area, where the Red Cross women gave him coffee and a doughnut. An intelligence officer came running up to him—the same officer who had handed him a cable back in December that told him his father had died. This time, however, the officer was grinning from ear to ear. As he handed a cable to McGovern, he said, "Congratulations, Daddy, you now have a baby daughter."

The cable was from Eleanor. Their first baby, whom she named Ann Marion, had been born four days before, on March 10, in the Mitchell Methodist Hospital. Eleanor concluded the cable, "Child doing well. Love, Eleanor."

"I was just ecstatic," McGovern said. "Jubilant." But then he thought, Eleanor and I have brought a new child into the world today—at least I learned about it today—and I probably killed somebody else's kids right at lunchtime. Hell, why did that bomb have to hit there?

He went over to the officers club and had a drink—cheap red wine. He was toasted and cheered. But, he later said, "It really did make me feel different for the rest of the war. Now I was a father, I had not only a wife back home but a little girl, all the more reason why I wanted to get home and see that child." He returned to his tent and wrote Eleanor a long letter. He did not mention the farmhouse, but he couldn't get it out of his mind. "That thing stayed with me for years and years. If I thought about the war almost invariably I would think about that farm."[14]

Two days after the mission to Wiener Neustadt, the *Dakota Queen* flew again with the 455th, accompanied by the 454th. The primary target was weathered in so the Liberators dropped their bombs on the marshaling yards at Amstetten, Austria. The lead bomber, using its radar and flying out in front and a bit above the *Dakota Queen*, dropped its bombs. Cooper, acting as bombardier as well as navigator, tried to toggle his bombs so that they would strike in the same place. But the bombs were stuck. Cooper went to work and managed to free them, but by the time he toggled the eggs on the *Dakota Queen* it had flown over the river. The bombs landed on the other side. At the debriefing, Cooper told what had happened and why. He was informed that the bombs had dropped on a prisoner of war camp. Cooper and McGovern were devastated. There were American soldiers in the camp. For some months thereafter just thinking about it brought tears to Cooper's eyes. But in 1946, when Cooper was going to graduate school at Texas A&M, he met an Army Air Forces officer who had been a prisoner in the camp. They got to talking about the incident, and the former POW said, "I was there, and when you dropped those bombs one hit the fence, it opened it up and in all the confusion some of us got away and managed to join the Russians."[15]

Three days later McGovern and his crew flew again. The target was the marshaling yards at Mühldorf, Germany. The group dropped over 116 tons of bombs, with good results—over 55 percent fell within 1,000 feet of the aiming point. There was no flak. On March 21 it was back up into the sky—the third day in a row for the group, McGovern's second mission in three days. Some ninety-four tons of bombs were dropped, with outstanding accuracy—over 87 percent fell within 1,000 feet of the aiming point.

The following day, March 22, it was up again, target the oil refinery at Kralupy, Czechoslovakia—the group being escorted by P-51s. The formation got to within 125 miles of Berlin. The next day Cooper described what had happened in a note home. It had been a long mission, he said, altogether taking eight hours and twenty minutes after spending an hour forming up. "When we got back to the place we could come down from altitude," he wrote, "we had been on oxygen for four and a half hours and our supply was almost exhausted. There wasn't any real danger because any time Mac wants to come down from altitude, I know the area well enough I can bring him around all the flak. Funny—he doesn't worry when I'm navigating and I never worry when he's the pilot. Several times he's proved what a cool-headed and superior pilot he is."16

On March 25 the group took off for its seventh straight day of flying missions—the *Dakota Queen* was there, McGovern's fifth flight since March 16. It was his twenty-sixth mission, five ahead of the crew. The target was a tank factory in Prague, Czechoslovakia. Thirty-six Liberators dropped ninety-six tons of bombs, with good results. Flak was moderate but accurate—three aircraft were hit but managed to get back to Cerignola. Cooper wrote, "After yesterday's mission, Mac said he was lucky he got me and trusts me—doesn't worry when I'm with him. I feel the same way about him so we make a good team. I put him in for the DFC [Distinguished Flying Cross] for a couple of planes he's brought back safe." That didn't work, as McGovern already had a DFC.17

On March 31, Cooper was relaxing in the officers club, sitting in an easy chair, daydreaming. Another officer came in and told him, "Congratulations." He had just won a $500 war bond. He explained to his mother that it came as a result of an Easter drive drawing: "Each member of the squadron selected a number between 1 and 375 and paid a dollar. I selected the number of the plane that has been damaged a couple of times and brought Mac and Crew home safely." It was the last three numbers of the serial number of the bomber, 279. "I hope the luck holds as well in the air as it did on the ground."[18]

March was over. The group had flown twenty-six missions, putting 719 aircraft over the target areas, and dropped 1,376 tons of bombs. No enemy fighters had been seen, but two aircraft had been shot down by flak. In addition, six crew members had been severely wounded while three others had minor wounds. The group's history commented, "The concentration of flak around the major targets seemed to be increasing as the Germans appeared to be 'circling their wagons' for the final attacks."[19]

CHAPTER ELEVEN

Linz: The Last Mission

April 1945

ON APRIL 1, APRIL FOOL'S DAY, the *Dakota Queen* flew a mission to Kreglach, Austria, to bomb the railroad bridge there. Some twenty-seven B-24s dropped seventy-eight tons of bombs, but could not see the results because of smoke in the target area. It was a milk run—no flak, no jets, no other enemy fighters. All planes returned safely. McGovern and his crew stood down for the next ten days. On April 11 they flew again. The target was the railroad bridge at Ponte Gardena, Italy, but the 741st Squadron, plus two others, turned away because of cloud cover and instead went after the alternate target, the fuel depot at Goito, Italy. Flak was moderate, although one Liberator got hit badly enough that the controls were damaged to such an extent that the pilot took the plane to Switzerland. McGovern and the others got back to Cerignola.

The 455th flew eleven missions in the first twelve days of April, but none on April 13. McGovern was at the officers club that day. He recalled that the deputy squadron commander, Capt. Andrew Gramm, came into the club to announce, "Damn, you're not going to believe what just happened—the big guy died—Franklin Roosevelt, our commander in chief died. The war is over. The war is lost."

The other officers, although they were shocked, thought Gramm was overreacting in saying the war was lost. They consoled him and finally convinced him that the war was not lost. Gramm, who was a heavy drinker anyway, took a few good belts to ease the pain of Roosevelt's death.

After the liquor had begun to do its work, Gramm climbed up on the bar, which was about four feet high. He was a big man, weighed about 225 pounds. Standing on the bar, he said, "Now you guys catch me." He closed his eyes and fell forward. "He didn't know if the others were going to catch him or not but he didn't seem to care," McGovern said. "But they did—three or four guys did—practically broke their backs trying to. He repeated that four or five times. Finally a guy says, 'Look we're not going to do that again. We've had enough of this. You may not have to fly tomorrow but we do.'" McGovern added that he remembered the incident vividly "because it just struck me about how close we really were. Here we were 3,000 miles from home and yet the death of Roosevelt hit that group of men awfully hard. They weren't particularly political—it's just that they hadn't known any other president."[1]

McGovern flew again on April 15, then again on April 16, 17, and 18—four missions in four days. By this time the marshaling yards and oil refineries had been hit so often, and so effectively, that they were no longer the primary targets. Instead the Liberators participated in the drive up the Italian peninsula by engaging in tactical bombing, that is, giving direct and indirect support to the ground troops. The technique was to drop the bombs just ahead of the American troop lines, or to hit bridges to stop enemy ground transportation. Rather than the usual 500- or 1,000-pound bombs, the planes carried 250-pound general purpose bombs.

At the briefings, McGovern said, the officer in command would tell them that the campaign was being coordinated with the American ground forces. "We were told to fly until we were directly over the cutting edge of the American forces and were told that there would be smoke signals there, and there were. The Americans would set off the signals along the front of their line, and we were to drop right on that, so the forward motion of the bombs would carry them well ahead of the American forces." Another technique was to use white markers set along the front lines, 100 yards in length and 1,000 yards apart, to mark the location of the American troops. The bomber stream flew perpendicular to the line of troops. Dropping the bombs when they saw the smoke and/or the white lines, the Liberators put them down right on top of the Germans dug in on the other side.

At the briefing the following morning, the officer in charge would congratulate the crews. "Well, men, we did okay yesterday. We put those eggs right where we wanted them, and we're going to go back today and do it some more. The guys on the ground are indebted to us, and we want to be careful not to hit any of them. But we're going to try to make their way easier." They did. McGovern later talked to some of the infantry officers, who told him that the B-24s provided great assistance.

The Liberators came in perpendicular to avoid flak. Ground commanders wanted them to fly parallel to the lines, but the AAF refused, on the grounds that if they did every German gunner along the line would be firing at the bombers. By coming in perpendicular, the B-24s were over the line for just a second or two, depriving the Germans of a chance to fix their radar, aim, and fire.

Nevertheless, these were no milk runs. They were flying over the high Alps, near the Brenner Pass, and to ensure accuracy they were flying at 15,000 feet, low for the Liberators. The Germans had their 88s placed close to the mountaintops, at 12,000 or more feet. As this was so close to the front lines, the Germans had heavier artillery, 105 and 150 mms, firing at the planes. The German gunners, in McGovern's memory, "were shooting crossfire at us instead of shooting at us from ground zero to our usual altitude of 25,000 feet." When the planes were at 15,000 feet and the flak gunners were nearly that high, McGovern said, "that's a pretty good shot. They can really home in on you. And they did." He saw at least two planes get hit.[2]

From April 19 to April 22, McGovern stood down. On the twenty-third he flew the *Dakota Queen* again, against road bridges in the Alps. This time, there was no flak—a milk run. On the twenty-fourth, the 455th turned away from the primary target and went after the alternate, marshaling yards and an ammunition dump at Ossopo, Italy. Results were good, the flak was slight and inaccurate. All planes got home safely. It was McGovern's thirty-fourth mission.

––––––––––

"I hated Linz as a target," McGovern declared. To begin with, it was heavily defended because it was an important rail hub for the Germans. Through Linz, German troops moved back and forth from the eastern to the western front—boxcars, passenger cars, everything. Linz was Hitler's hometown. The 455th Group had hit it often. "I don't know how they could ever get a train in or out of that place," McGovern said, "but apparently they did, because we kept hitting it." He had been on the December 15, 1944, mission to Linz. It was his seventh mission, his second as pilot. "It was just deadly fear with me from that day on. I never talked about it much but I was scared to death with those shells going off. There was nothing you could do. Couldn't take evasive action, couldn't dodge them." It was on that mission that a piece of shrapnel had burst through the cockpit window and come within inches of killing him.

Now, on April 25, 1945, they were to go back. Before the men climbed into the *Dakota Queen,* McGovern spoke to them. He said it was usual to allow a pilot to go on a milk run for his last mission because the commanders did not want a pilot shot down on that one. But the target was Linz. Although he wanted to fly the mission, he said he did not want to endanger the crew just because he chose to fly it. He put it up to a vote. If the vote was negative, McGovern said no one would ever fault them, including him, and the commanders would excuse them. Ashlock remembered, "We voted to fly the mission." So they were off.[3]

All four squadrons of the 455th Group flew to Linz. Cooper recalled, "We had every plane that we could get airborne up there." Picture them at takeoff: one B-24 breaking ground, one halfway down the runway, picking up speed, a third releasing brakes after applying power. The men had been told at the briefing to expect heavy flak, as the Germans were bringing all their 88s back to protect their priority targets. The briefing officer said, "Our estimates are that there are 380 antiaircraft guns in Linz, and they're heavily concentrated." The weather was clear. After forming up, the group set off over the Alps to the target. To McGovern, "It was exciting going across the mountains. Those enormous snow-peaked mountains—and the endless meadows and fields, the trees and rivers and streams." Thinking back, he commented, "Europe is beautiful—except over the damn targets. It was our worst mission of the war."

According to the 455th's history, the flak over the target was "extremely intense." The Germans were using their box system—firing the 88s' shells into an area 2,000 feet on each of the four sides and 2,000 feet deep, just in front of the formation so that the planes would fly into it. "The sky just became solid black. Then in that solid black you'd see these huge, angry flashes of red, which was another shell exploding. How we avoided it, I'll never know." The *Dakota Queen* didn't avoid it all. McGovern said he could hear the shrapnel "smacking the side of the plane."

"It was terrible," McGovern said. "Linz was tougher on my last mission than it had been on my second as pilot. Hell can't be any worse than that. And remember, the people flying the plane or shooting the guns are children." Rounds and Higgins were twenty years old, and except for Cooper and engineer Valko the others were nineteen. Valko got into the cockpit and stood between McGovern and Rounds. "You could look at him and he seemed petrified," McGovern recalled. "Not just paralyzed, but petrified. Just sheer terror."[4]

"The first thing that I remember," said Cooper, "is this whomping. They had zeroed in on us. We were in their box right in the middle." A piece of shrapnel came through the nose. It passed through Cooper's map. On it he had made a "real tiny little pencil mark indicating our base at Cerignola, and I'm damned if those Germans didn't just put that piece of flak right through Cerignola."

Another piece of flak hit the hydraulic lines. The red fluid began spurting out. It looked like blood. Cooper took off his flak helmet to attempt to catch some of that fluid so they could use it after patching the line, but he was "slipping and sliding around in that stuff." The nose gunner saw him floundering around in what he thought was blood and cried, "Oh, no!" He tried to help, but Cooper shook him off. But the hydraulic lines were so mangled they were beyond repair, so the fluid Cooper had caught was useless.[5]

One piece of flak hit Ashlock. It traveled up his leg from the knee to lodge in his butt. Higgins went to apply first aid. Ashlock was hollering, Cooper was hollering, so too everyone else. McGovern got on the intercom. His voice was calm as he told everyone to be quiet. That quieted them down. Then he ordered Valko to check the airplane to try to see how much damage had been done. He did, and except for the loss of the hydraulic lines, Valko said the plane was more or less okay. McGovern then asked each crew member to check in. Except Ashlock, they said one by one that they were okay. As he turned away from the target, McGovern saw that the number three engine had been damaged and he feathered the prop.

Higgins ripped open Ashlock's pants. He examined the wound and told Ashlock it wasn't too bad. Because of the altitude and the cold, the blood had coagulated. Higgins poured powdered sulfa on the wound, then put a bandage around it. Higgins recalled that his patient "was making quite a racket on the intercom, so I finally just unplugged him." He gave Ashlock a shot of morphine and he lay down on the floor, where he stayed.

The *Dakota Queen* had slowed and lost altitude. It was now behind and below the formation. McGovern and Rounds got Cooper on the intercom and they discussed their alternatives. There were two: try to get back to Cerignola or turn east and try to land behind the Russian lines. With the hydraulic system a wreck, they had no brakes. The flaps were inoperative. An engine was missing. Nevertheless, they decided to head home.

As they got close, McGovern got on the radio with the tower, to describe his situation. The last squadron from the formation was landing—one plane at the far end of the runway turning off, another rolling halfway down the runway, and a third touching down. The officer in charge at the tower was glad to hear from the *Dakota Queen*, which had already been listed as missing in action. He told McGovern he had a number of choices: he could go out over the Adriatic shoreline and attempt a crash landing, or ditch in the sea, or bail out, or try to land on the runway. McGovern decided to accept the last alternative. On the intercom, he told the crew that if any one of them, or all of them, wanted to bail out they should feel perfectly free to do so. There would be no reflection on them: "If they felt safer bailing out it was fine with me."

What are you going to do, the men asked. "I'm going to land this airplane," he replied. So they all decided to stay. As they approached the field, Higgins fired a red flare to indicate an ambulance should be ready to receive a wounded man.

McGovern ordered Higgins and McAfee to attach a pair of parachutes by their harnesses to the yokes supporting the waist guns. They were to throw them out the windows when he told them to, then pull the rip cord. That would slow the plane, which had no brakes. It was a technique that McGovern had not previously used, but had heard about (and indeed another B-24 from the group used the parachute method of stopping that day).

The crew used the hand crank to lower the wheels—an exhausting process, but between them Valko, Higgins, and Cooper managed to get it done. A little yellow signal came on to tell McGovern that the wheels were locked.

The tower waved other planes off and told McGovern to come right on in. He was afraid to come in slow "because if we were short of the field I didn't think we could go around again. We were low on gas and I had one engine out." He came in too high "because of my fear of falling short of the field. I thought the worse thing that could happen was if I had to accelerate at the last minute. So I came in on a kind of flat landing, but considerably above the stalling speed."

When the *Dakota Queen* touched down, McGovern cut the throttles and ordered McAfee and Higgins to throw out the parachutes and pull the rip cords. When the chutes billowed open, McGovern could feel the plane slow down. Instinctively, he and Rounds were pushing as hard as they could on the brake pedals, even though they had no brakes. But the engines, without power, provided some drag.

McGovern had ordered the crew to go to the tail of the plane when it touched down, in order to bring the tail down so it would provide drag. Led by Cooper, they did. Seven of them, all but Ashlock and Rounds. McGovern thought the weight would bring the tail to the ground and stop the plane, but it didn't work. He later commented, "That B-24 was just too big and massive for even seven guys sitting in the tail to dump it back." The plane's nose at the end of the runway did a little plunge into a ditch. Then it started up on the other side of the ditch, and the tail went up, then crashed down. "It was quite a jar," Cooper recalled. But it stopped the plane.

"It wasn't one of my better landings," McGovern said. "It was too hot. I came in too fast. But I didn't want to take any chance on stalling out. I wanted to make sure that we got that plane on the ground without any screwup." Shaking his head at the thought, he added, "If I ever made that landing again, I would have made it slower."

The ambulance was there. The crew lifted Ashlock off the plane and put him on a stretcher. Cooper limped off—he had sprained his ankle at the jolt when the tail dropped down. Otherwise, everyone was okay, although Valko was so badly shaken that he was confined to a hospital with battle fatigue for some months thereafter.

The *Dakota Queen* had 110 holes in its fuselage and wings. Mc-Govern said, "I couldn't believe it. If you had looked at that airplane, you would not have known how it stayed in the air." But he had brought it in. Ken Higgins summed it up: "I always said George brought me home. He did that day."[6] The following day, Cooper wrote his fiancée. He had retrieved one of the parachutes, and told her, "Your worries about a wedding dress are over—that is, if you want one made of white silk." He described the mission, then said, "Actually I was too busy to be scared so it was all o.k."[7]

Another mission to Linz was scheduled for April 26. McGovern would not be going on it, as he had completed his thirty-five missions, but others would. They woke, went to the briefing, got into their Liberators, and hoped for a red flare from the tower signifying that the mission was canceled. Pilots started their engines. Then shouts of joy could be heard all over Cerignola—the red flare had been fired. As it turned out, the war was over for the combat crews.

It was over for every member of the Eighth and Fifteenth and Twelfth and Ninth Air Forces. No more missions. Less than two weeks later, on May 7, 1945, Germany surrendered unconditionally. It was a hot, sunny day in Cerignola. Very little celebrating was done. Most of the men just took it easy, getting a suntan and listening to all the notables on their radios. Somehow, the accolades sounded hollow, as praise often does. It was a poor replacement for the thoughts of those who had made the supreme sacrifice with their lives.[8]

The group had started 1945 with sixty Liberators. In the next four months it had flown 1,434 sorties. In that period it lost eight B-24s to flak and another thirty-four received flak damage. A total of seventy-four crewmen were missing in action, plus twenty wounded and sixteen killed. In its fifteen months in action, the group had flown enough miles on combat missions to circle the earth over ten times with a thirty-airplane formation. It had flown altogether a total of 252 combat missions, lost 118 Liberators. It had suffered nearly 1,000 casualties—men killed in action, wounded, missing, or taken prisoner.

The best news was, of course, that the Allies had won the war. A close second for the airmen was the release of the POWs. That was a joyous occasion. Lt. Col. Thomas Ramey of the 743rd Squadron, himself a POW, related: "We had 179 airmen lost from burning planes, ditching in icy cold water, crash-landing on rugged mountain terrain, often times wounded, only to become captured American POWs. [What they endured included] starvation diets, deprivation, abuse, humiliation, vermin-infested quarters, forced marches in sub-zero weather, considerable weight loss, inadequate or no medical attention, infamous German box car rides, and in many cases, torture." But then "the sounds of war came closer and closer until one day when armored tank columns overran the camps and the American flag flew once again." That was a joyous occasion.9

Fifty-four years after the end of the war in Europe, Ken Higgins—who was nineteen years old in 1945—spoke for many of his fellow airmen, and for many other veterans of all the armed services, when he said, "The war time was kind of unreal when I look back on it. It's hard to imagine that we went through all that."10

———

McGovern and his fellow men of the 741st Squadron had played a small role in one of mankind's greatest triumphs, the defeat of Nazi Germany. They had been a part of one of history's greatest undertakings, the Army Air Forces of World War II. After the war, there were disputes and arguments over which American service had done the most to bring about the victory. The ground forces, the Navy, and the AAF each asserted that "without us, it couldn't have been done. We were indispensable." The Army Air Forces claimed that they could have won the war alone. But then, so did the Navy. The Army ground forces replied that the AAF's power to destroy was not the power to control. To control, it is necessary to put a man on the spot with a gun in his hand.

General Eisenhower, who commanded all three services in the campaign in northwest Europe, knew that it took all three to win. His ground forces could not have gotten to the battle without the Navy. Nor could they have driven through France, Italy, Belgium, and Germany without the Army Air Forces. As the supreme commander of the Army, Navy, and AAF in the campaign, he became so concerned with the service rivalries that at one time—this was before the establishment of the Air Force Academy in Colorado—he wanted midshipmen and cadets to attend the other service's schools during their second class years. He talked about having them wear the same uniforms. He even proposed a single service academy. What he proposed never came to be, but it illuminates the answer to the question of which service was indispensable. They all were.

Critics of the AAF, while praising the tactical airplanes for their role in supporting the ground offensive, argued that the strategic bombing campaign was an unnecessary waste. All the production devoted to building the bombers, the enormous effort to train men to fly and maintain them, could have been better spent on fighters, ground troops, and the Navy. And it would have avoided the worst accusation of all, that in World War II the United States used a method of making war that killed hundreds of thousands of civilians and destroyed uncountable historic buildings, factories, and residences, without doing much of anything to win the war while creating the worst legacy of the war, made much more frightful with the development of the atomic bomb and the beginning of the Cold War—making civilians into targets. Perhaps 305,000 Germans were killed in the bombings, another 780,000 seriously injured. About 25 million Germans had been subjected to the terror of the bombings.

The bombs hit residences as well as factories, deliberately on the part of the RAF Bomber Command's night bombing, but also from the American precision bombing. The accuracy of free-falling bombs was far below the accuracy of artillery fire, not to mention rifle or machine gun fire. Most bombs fell considerably outside the target.

After the war, a Polish officer who had been captured in 1939 by the Germans and spent the war in a POW camp near Munich, then immigrated to the United States, was talking to B-24 tail gunner Sgt. Art Applin. The Polish officer said, "You know, when you guys would come over we would all run out of the barracks and start waving, screaming, and cheering and the German guards were trying to shut us up and get us back in the barracks." He then asked Applin, "Did you guys ever hit anything?" Applin's reply was, "Yeah, we always hit the ground."11

They did a lot better than that. In the last chapter, "Mission Accomplished," in the official history of the Army Air Forces in Europe, editors W. F. Craven and J. L. Cate give their assessment. Like all their work, it is judicious and authoritative. Much of the chapter is based on interviews conducted with German personnel after the unconditional surrender. The AAF wanted to know what they had done right, what was done wrong. The Germans were eager to talk, most of them. They knew there was little to be gained from withholding information. They were professionals in the art of war and wanted to discuss what had happened, and why. Some of them, no doubt, hoped to win better treatment for themselves by being cooperative. But whatever their motivations, they provided a unique glimpse of the other side of the hill.

The *Luftwaffe* commander, Hermann Göring, was voluble. His overall conclusion was that the Allied selection of targets had been excellent. He insisted that precision bombing was more effective than night raids. Still, he concluded that Germany could never have been defeated by airpower alone. But Nazi Germany's second and last führer, Grand Admiral Karl Dönitz, said that airpower was the decisive element. Field Marshal Gerd von Rundstedt believed that airpower was the first of several ingredients in the triumph of the Allies. Colonel General Alfred Jödl of Hitler's staff said the winning of air superiority altogether decided the war and that strategic bombing was the most decisive factor. Albert Speer, the minister of production, emphatically stated his opinion that the strategic bombing could have won the war without a land invasion.

The German leaders said that the Allies had underestimated Germany's industrial capacity. It was so huge that Germany had been able to mobilize at a leisurely pace. Her war production continued to increase until it reached its peak in mid-1944. But it was then that the strategic bombing campaign intensified. Of all the bombs that struck the Reich during the war, 72 percent fell after July 1, 1944. The official history notes, "In the following nine months the bombing campaign wrecked the enlarged German economy until it could not support military operations or supply the basic needs of the population. By January 1945, Germany had been almost paralyzed economically, and by April she was ruined."

In Craven and Cate's view, "Of all the accomplishments of the air forces, the attainment of air supremacy was the most significant, for it made possible the invasions of the continent and gave the heavy bombers their opportunity to wreck the industries of the Reich." And of all the multitudes of payoffs from winning air supremacy, the most significant was the strategic bombing campaign against oil refineries. This "deprived the German Air Force of aviation gasoline so that operations were possible only on rare occasions. German bombers practically disappeared from the air, and whenever fighters tried to interfere with Allied air fleets they invariably got the worst of the battle."[12]

In April 1944, Germany had adequate supplies of oil. Over the next year, the Eighth Air Force dropped 70,000 tons of bombs on the refineries, the Fifteenth Air Force some 60,000 tons. By April 1945, Germany's oil production was 5 percent that of the previous year. Toward the end, even the most senior Nazis in the hierarchy were unable to find gasoline for their limousines. German industries were badly crippled or gone. This despite an enormous amount of effort put into defending and rebuilding oil installations.

The second major effect of the strategic bombing campaign, in this case aided by the tactical air force, was transportation. The Allied planes attacked bridges, highways, trucks, tanks, or anything that moved, but most of all the bombers went after railroad marshaling yards. By the spring of 1945 the German transport system was so badly wrecked that only the highest-priority military movements could be started with any prospect of getting to their destination. In Craven and Cate's words, "The bombings of rail centers leading to the Russian front, attacks on marshalling yards in all parts of Germany, the Fifteenth Air Force missions against southern European railways piled up calamity for the Germans. If they produced they could not haul. Their dispersal programs strangled, and the country became helpless."[13]

The price of the transportation victory had been huge. The Eighth Air Force had dropped one third of its bombs, 235,312 tons, on marshaling yards. The Fifteenth Air Force put almost one half its total bombs, 149,476 tons, on them.

Along with their acknowledgment of the effectiveness of the strategic bombing campaign, the German leaders being interrogated had criticisms. For example, they thought the Army Air Forces' conviction was wrong that there had to be one critical German industry that, if destroyed, would bring the country to ruin. The great raids on Schweinfurt, for example, designed to deprive German vehicles of ball bearings and thus bring their army to a standstill, caused some destruction and problems, but they were carried out at great risk and high cost and still hardly slowed Germany down. The Germans were able to use ball bearings already in the plants, or on their way there. They dispersed the industry. In the end, the German leaders declared, German armaments production suffered no serious effects from a shortage of ball bearings.

Göring and Speer believed that going after electric power stations, which were highly vulnerable to air attack, would have benefited the Allies more. Or the Allies could have weakened Germany, perhaps brought her to surrender, by going after powder and explosive plants—in fact, the Germans said they would have rated such plants second only to oil. Another possibility, generally ignored, was the chemical plants that produced nitrogen and methanol. But whatever their criticisms, and there were many more, the German leaders knew that the tremendous requirements of air raid defense had absorbed much German manpower, scientific energies, and guns and ammunition—an effort that, if applied to the ground forces, might have been decisive for them.

We will never know because it was not done that way. We do know that what the Allies did won the war. What McGovern did, what the 741st Squadron did, along with the rest of the 455th Bomb Group and all the Fifteenth Air Force, and the Eighth Air Force, most especially in their attacks against oil refineries and marshaling yards, was critical to the victory. McGovern, his crew, and all the airmen had spent the war years not in vain but in doing good work. Along with all the peoples of the Allied nations, they saved Western civilization.

Bernard Baruch quoted Clemenceau, who wrote, "They were kittens in play but tigers in battle."

EPILOGUE

IN JANUARY 2000, my son Hugh and I spent two weeks in Rome, with a two-day trip to Cerignola, interviewing George McGovern, who was then the U.S. ambassador to the United Nations Food and Agriculture Organization. Six hours a day, sometimes seven, occasionally eight, and on the drive to Cerignola and back to Rome, constantly. Hugh and I have worked together on many books. We have done many interviews, alone or together. Earlier in my life I spent hours, days, weeks interviewing Dwight Eisenhower about the war and his presidency. That was different from interviewing McGovern, and obviously hearing Eisenhower's accounts of his activities was memorable, a highlight of my life. So too my interviews with thousands of veterans of World War II. But for me and Hugh, listening to McGovern's account of his youth, his training, and his missions in Italy was especially noteworthy.

What follows is my account of our last interview, filled in with other interview information. The subject was: What happened after your last mission and the end of the war?

Promotions were frozen, which McGovern thought cost him a certain captain's promotion. Everyone was just waiting for orders to return to the States. For those who had completed their required thirty-five missions, like McGovern, that would mean discharge. For those who had thirty missions, like the men of McGovern's crew, the victory in Europe meant they would be going off to the Pacific to engage in the war against Japan.

Except Tex Ashlock, who was in the hospital. McGovern had

promised him that he would pay a visit, and one day he "borrowed" an Army truck and drove into Cerignola to visit him. When McGovern came into the ward, Ashlock began to cry. Soon he was sobbing. "Here he was, this great big guy, just sobbing like a child," McGovern recalled. McGovern said, "Well, Tex, you're going to be okay. They've got good doctors here and we will see you back in the States."

"If I get back," Ashlock replied.

"You're going to get back," McGovern said. "I wouldn't leave here if I thought there was any doubt at all about you coming home. You'll be back there soon."

The other crew members also visited Ashlock, who did get back.

Almost immediately when the war ended, the AAF started to close down the air base in Cerignola and those across southern Italy. What to do with the food supplies was a problem. The mess sergeant in Cerignola had hundreds of boxes of powdered eggs, powdered milk, potatoes that could be reconstituted, thousands of cans of Spam and cheese, orange marmalade, raisins, peanut butter, flour, cornmeal. Tons of food, and that was true of every airfield. The AAF wasn't going to let the men they had spent so much time, money, and effort training go hungry.

The high command decided, in McGovern's words, that "there are hungry people all over Europe and we don't need this stuff back in the States. There's no market for powdered eggs in Brooklyn. So we'll give it away, to the Europeans." McGovern was asked if he would participate. He said yes. "So that's what we did. We started flying a few days after the end of the war, taking this food up there." They flew from Cerignola to a field about forty miles north of Trieste. McGovern's crew loaded the *Dakota Queen* with wooden and cardboard boxes of rations and on landing would hand the food out of the bomb bay to GIs, who would put it into trucks and drive it to villages, towns, cities. Soon the AAF began trucking unneeded rations from other bases to Cerignola for the airlift.

"We gave away everything we had," McGovern said. To the people of Europe, including the surrendered troops: "It didn't make any difference whether they were German troops."

"This was the first Berlin airlift," I said. "In a way the beginning of the Marshall Plan." "On a small scale, yes," McGovern replied. He was glad to be doing it and took satisfaction in showing that the B-24s "could so something other than bomb people. All those people that we were feeding, we'd hit with bombs. Now we're giving them food. There was real pride on the part of the crew." Besides, he added, it gave the men something to do while waiting for orders.[1]

After the wartime missions, flying was a bit dull. McGovern lightened it up a bit. C. W. Cooper related one incident. "We were over Yugoslavia when we saw a B-17 below. McGovern says, 'Hey, let's have some fun.' He put the plane in a steep dive and, just before we went sailing past the '17, he cut the number four engine (the one closest to the '17) as if to say, 'We're that much faster on three engines than you in that flying glider are on four.'"[2]

On the second or third flight to Trieste, McGovern had an unexpected encounter. After completing his landing, he did a U-turn and came back to the unloading area, where he pulled up, parked, and cut his engine. As the *Dakota Queen* was unloading, another B-24 came in. "He went to pull around me. I thought he was doing it kind of fast, a little too much of a hot rod technique. And I'll be damned if he didn't hit the leading edge of my wing with his wing. He just turned too sharp."

The pilot leaned out his window. He looked at McGovern, sitting in the pilot's seat, and said, "God, I'm awfully sorry about that. I hope I haven't damaged your wing."

"No, I don't think so," McGovern replied. Then he looked at the pilot again and exclaimed, "Jim Peterson, from Mitchell, South Dakota!"

McGovern had gone to high school in Mitchell with him, but did not know that Peterson was in the AAF. They chatted, reminisced, renewed their acquaintanceship. Peterson went on to become an architect and lived in Mitchell. On every trip back to South Dakota, Mc-Govern would get together with him.[3]

When he was not flying, McGovern thought about the future. On May 30 he wrote his friend Bob Pennington (who had gotten engaged via the mails to Eleanor's twin sister, Ila; they later married), who had told McGovern that he was intent on getting his Ph.D. when he returned to the States. McGovern said he too would go after a Ph.D. "As soon as possible if finances will permit it. I'm quite sure I can swing it. For a while I was pretty shaky about my interest in teaching. The lack of material reward just about had me in the dark for quite a while last winter. That coupled with my seeming intellectual decline had me guessing." Bill Rounds's father had offered him "a very attractive job with his company," and that was tempting. "Now though I've discovered that old driving interest to learn rather than make money is still there. I'm afraid I'm 'doomed' to the life of a student and teacher. But as you say it has a multitude of advantages to offset its more tangible disadvantages."[4]

———————

From May until mid-June, McGovern continued to fly to Trieste to deliver food, or, sometimes, he would fly over Vienna, Munich, and other former targets, with the ground crew members as passengers. The AAF wanted the mechanics to see what the planes they had worked on had done to the Germans. Ken Higgins went along, to operate the radio, but he never liked it. "I just didn't want to be in that darned old airplane," he explained, fearing an accident might happen.[5]

Cooper wanted no more, either. Like everyone else, he wanted to go home. On May 12, he wrote his fiancée that "Mac left for Naples yesterday. He'll be sweating out a boat there for several weeks probably." He thought he would be stuck in Italy for some time. "There's nothing but rumors yet but when they decide to move us it will be sudden and homeward bound." Two weeks later, he wrote again:

"Who should be here to greet me when I got back yesterday but Mac, our pilot! I thought he caught a fast liner in Naples and was in the States but they sent him back so I guess his 35 missions don't mean any more than my 32."[6]

Pilot Ed Soderstrom related what happened. Four pilots of the 741st, Charles Painter, McGovern, Howard Surbeck, and Soderstrom, had finished their tours and headed for Naples to catch a boat home. But when they tried to board the troopship, their names were not on the orders. Instead they had orders to return to the squadron, where they were told they were to fly their airplanes back to the States, and meanwhile they would continue to fly food to Trieste.[7]

On June 16, Cooper wrote, "As Mac and I were starting home from the club last night, we had a surprise. We met a man in black slacks and a black shirt. He was half Cherokee Indian from Oklahoma and was just wandering around seeing the world. How he ever got here we don't know." He was, possibly, one of the "code-talkers," Indians who served as radiomen with the ground troops—the Army figured, rightly, that there was no need to use coded messages when the Indians could speak to each other in their own language and the Germans would never understand them.

The following day, Cooper wrote his fiancée that while McGovern and Rounds were going to fly a B-24 back to the States the next day, he didn't expect to be on the plane. "It makes me sad to see my old skipper, Mac, leaving and me not going with him. I hate to trust him with any other navigator and he doesn't particularly relish a long hop without me along, so it's mutual."[8]

Bill Rounds had flown several of the supply missions to Trieste. In his diary on May 20, he wrote, "I flew cargo in a B-24. I buzzed Venice. It was beautiful." He did other things, such as collecting a hoard of German Luger pistols. Once he talked a friend, who was a fighter pilot, into taking him to Florence in his P-47. Somehow he squeezed into the cockpit, riding piggy-back. In Florence, the two men got drunk, went to the opera, got seats in a box, and found the music to be dull. So they began to blow up condoms, tie them at the end, and throw them down on the audience. They laughed uproariously at the sight of those "balloons" coming down.[9]

McGovern, Surbeck, Soderstrom, and Painter were first on the list of pilots to fly home. On June 17, they decided that before doing so they would fly one last "mission." They took off in their planes, formed up, and buzzed the squadron area. Painter flew the lead ship, McGovern was in the number two spot, Surbeck was number three, and Soderstrom number four. They came in so close to the ground that they just missed a power line running along the road, then buzzed the headquarters of the 456th Bomb Group. They were so low their prop wash ripped the flag off the headquarters building. The 456th commanding officer was furious. He decided that Painter, McGovern, Surbeck, and Soderstrom would be the last, not the first, to leave Italy, but by the time the orders were cut it was too late.[10]

On June 18, McGovern took off for North Africa. Cooper, it turned out, was the navigator. Indeed all the crew, except Ashlock, were on the plane, along with a half-dozen sergeants, AAF meteorologists going to the States from Europe, then on to the Pacific. These men tossed in their duffel bags, arranging them as well as they could, and sat or lay down. They had some sandwiches and soft drinks aboard. The crew and passengers began laughing. They were leaving Italy. The war in Europe war over.

McGovern took off. They would be flying alone. First stop, Marrakesh, North Africa. "I hadn't had any flying like that during the war," McGovern said. "I was always used to having formations around, and scores of airplanes dotting the sky, and somebody shooting at us." This time no one was shooting, it was quiet, the plane was all alone, all the engines were working without any problems. Coming into Marrakesh, McGovern said to Rounds that perhaps they could pick up some food as well as gasoline. "George," Rounds replied, "those people haven't got any food. They're eating each other." It was a brief stop, fortunately, as in late July it was fearfully hot.

Next stop, the Azores. But about a hundred miles from the islands, Cooper called McGovern on the intercom to say that he was lost. "I think it's just temporary," he remarked, "and I'll get a fix." But when they got to where the islands were presumed to be, there was nothing except blue water.

McGovern was "just furious." He thought, God, we've gone through thirty-five missions and my navigator can't find the air base? How can we possibly be this unlucky. We're going into the drink out here in the Atlantic because Cooper can't find the Azores. He turned on his radio and, thankfully, raised the tower at the field. He asked what heading he should fly on, based on his present position, to get to the base.

The tower told him to turn to such-and-such a heading. He did and brought the islands into view. "Here's this eleven-thousand-foot runway. We hadn't seen a runway like that since we left the States." He brought the plane down, got his tanks refilled, and took off for the next stop, Gander, Newfoundland. McGovern got her aloft, climbed to a few thousand feet, and people began falling asleep. All the meteorologists. Indeed everyone but McGovern, the navigator, and Higgins. "Bill Rounds conked off, just sound asleep. You could hear this heavy breathing all over the plane."

It was a beautiful night, the air clear, a huge round moon making it almost as light as daylight. McGovern put the plane on autopilot, something he never did even once during the war, and he too fell sound asleep. Higgins put his head down on his table and fell asleep. So did Cooper.

After some time, McGovern shook himself awake. The moon was beautiful, the stars shining, he was the only one awake. "I was almost overwhelmed with a sense of peace. Sheer joy. We were going home. I finally realized the war was over, and I'm going to see Eleanor, and my mother, and my little girl, then four or five months old. Everything now is going to be all right."

At Gander, as the plane was refueling, McGovern called Eleanor on the telephone. "It was wonderful, to hear that voice again." He didn't want to exceed three minutes on the long-distance call—too expensive—so he merely said he would be back in Mitchell in two or three days.

"Well, I want to meet you," Eleanor replied. "I want us just to be the two of us when you first come in."

He said he expected to be discharged at Fort Snelling, near Minneapolis. She said she would meet him there.

Off again, this time to Camp Miles Standish outside Boston. "I regret to say that was the last landing of the war for me and one of the worst landings I ever made. I couldn't believe it. I leveled off and that B-24 dropped about six feet. Just *bang*, we hit the ground. I got on the intercom and I said, 'Well fellas, we've just *hit* the United States.'" No one minded the bump. There were cheers, laughter, tears.

Within two days, McGovern was at Fort Snelling. Eleanor met him. They spent the first night in a hotel in Minneapolis. Then off by train to Mitchell, where he immediately enrolled for the fall semester.

We asked if he had brought any souvenirs home from his year in Italy. He replied that he had with him that piece of flak that had been only inches away from taking his head off, but has since misplaced or lost it. He had his uniform—which he had paid for out of his own pocket—but he gave his flight jacket to the Air Force museum in Pueblo, Colorado. He did keep his wings, dog tags, and the bracelet with his name and serial number.

———

As were nearly all the veterans of the war, McGovern was a good, hardworking student, eager to make up for lost time, earn his undergraduate degree and get off to graduate school to pursue his Ph.D. in history. But one night, needing a break from his studies, he took Eleanor to a movie at the Paramount Theater in Mitchell. On the newsreel, the announcer was saying, "American bombers that were flying a few short weeks or months ago in England and Italy and the

Pacific are now being collected in Arizona, Nevada, New Mexico, and other Western states to be salvaged."

The newsreel showed bulldozers coming along and shoving hundreds of B-24s into a heap. One of them had a name on it, *Yo-Yo.* The cameraman zoomed in on it so people could see the name.

"God, I just couldn't believe it." He had flown that plane, although he and his crew called it the *Dakota Queen.* But it was *Yo-Yo* he had flown. "I felt like just getting right up out of my seat. We nursed those bombers back as carefully as we could, and conserved the gas, and protected the oil, and watched the oil pressure and the other gauges, and tried to land them as well as we could, and we brought back the precious airplane. Now it was being turned into junk. I couldn't believe it. I reacted almost violently. I wanted to get up and tell the audience what we had just seen was sheer waste and extravagance. Made no sense at all. It really stirred my Scotch-Irish soul to see it taking place."

Within less than a year after the war, virtually all the B-24s had been salvaged. Fifty-five years after the war, there are three B-24s in museums, only one still flying. And except for those who flew them, or serviced them, they are today virtually forgotten.

At the end of our last interview, McGovern said that for more than half a century he had not thought much about his war experiences. As a politician, especially in 1972, running for president, he had done interviews with reporters on the subject, but usually for five minutes or so and never for more than a half-hour or in any depth. He said our two-week-long interview "has forced me to dig deeply into my memory and my psyche." And what he especially recalled was Eleanor's life with him, what traveling to all those airfields during his training had meant to her and to him, "and what it was like having that baby when I'm 3,000 miles away and not even knowing whether Eleanor would ever see me again."

He paused, then said, "It's made me realize how much I love that woman. I have known for years I was in love with her, but being asked to probe into my life during the war has really brought that home to me in a different way. Shared history is a big part of being in love."

We asked McGovern to sum up his war experience. With his answer, he spoke for every airman, every GI, every sailor, Marine, every Coast Guard man of World War II. "Piloting a B-24 in combat with eight other guys, sometimes nine other guys, took every ounce of physical energy I had, every bit of mental abilities I had, and literally every shred of spiritual resource that I had. I can't recall any other stage of my life, unless it was the closing days of the '72 presidential campaign, that so demanded everything I had. I gave that World War II effort everything except my life itself, and I was ready to give my life. It literally exhausted every resource of mind and body and spirit that I had."

For Hugh and myself, I replied, "Thanks for what you did to help win the victory, and thus save the world." We always say something like that at the end of every interview with a veteran of the war, because it is the truth. Where did America find such men?

In 1985, McGovern was lecturing at the University of Innsbruck. A director of Austrian television's state-owned station contacted him to ask if he would do an interview for a documentary he was producing on Austria in World War II. He wanted McGovern to talk about what it was like bombing Austrian targets. McGovern was not inclined but finally let himself be talked into doing it. A woman reporter did the interview. She said that Senator McGovern was known around the world for his opposition to the war in Vietnam, and especially the bombing of South and North Vietnam. Yet he had been a bomber pilot in World War II. The reporter asked, "Senator, did you ever regret bombing beautiful cities like Vienna, Salzburg, Innsbruck, and others?"

McGovern answered, "Well, nobody thinks that war is a lovely affair. It is humanity at its worst, it's a breakdown of normal communication, and it is a very savage enterprise. But on the other hand there are issues that sometimes must be decided by warfare after all else fails. . . . I thought Adolf Hitler was a madman who had to be stopped.

"So, my answer to your question is no. I don't regret bombing strategic targets in Austria. I do regret the damage that was done to innocent people. And there was one bomb I've regretted all these years."

The reporter snapped that up. "Tell us about it."

McGovern told her about the bomb that had stuck in the bomb bay door and had to be jettisoned, on March 14, 1945. "To my sorrow it hit a peaceful little Austrian farmyard at high noon and maybe led to the death of some people in that family. I regret that all the more because it was the day I learned my wife had given birth to our first child and the thought went through my mind then and on many, many days since then, that we brought a young baby into the world and probably killed someone else's baby or children."

When the documentary appeared on Austrian TV, the station received a call from an Austrian farmer. He said he had seen and heard McGovern. He knew it was his farm that was hit, because it was high noon on a clear day and exactly as McGovern described the incident.

"I want you to tell him," the man went on, "that no matter what other Austrians think, I despised Adolf Hitler. We did see the bomber coming. I got my wife and children out of the house and we hid in a ditch and no one was hurt. And because of our attitude about Hitler, I thought at the time that if bombing our farm reduced the length of that war by one hour or one minute, it was well worth it."

The television station called McGovern and told him what the farmer had said. For McGovern, it was "an enormous release and gratification. It seemed to just wipe clean a slate."

NOTES

PROLOGUE

1. Marguerite Madison Aronowitz, *Maternity Ward: Final Flight of a World War II Liberator*, 11–12; Larry Davis, *B-24 Liberator in Action*, 6.

2. William Carigan, *Ad Lib: Flying the B-24 Liberator in World War II*, 73.

CHAPTER ONE. WHERE THEY CAME FROM

1. Michael Takiff interview with McGovern, Eisenhower Center.

2. George McGovern, *Grassroots: The Autobiography of George McGovern*, 10. Other information on McGovern's youth comes from interviews with McGovern by Stephen and Hugh Ambrose, from interviews with McGovern by Michael Takiff, and from Robert Sam Anson, *McGovern*, 17–21.

3. Ambrose interview with McGovern.

4. Ibid.; McGovern, *Grassroots*, 19.

5. Robert S. Capps, *Flying Colt: Liberator Pilot in Italy*.

6. Anson, *McGovern*, 40.

7. R. J. Hammer, *Small Tales: Tall Tales: Poetry: Fiction*, 1–7.

8. Roland Pepin's memoirs, written and typed for his grandchildren, copy in the Eisenhower Center.

9. William Barnes to Ambrose letter, June 5, 2000. Barnes wrote a book, *Disaster at Bari: Top Secret!*.

10. Shostack to Ambrose letter, March 31, 2000.

11. Eugene Hudson interview with Hugh Ambrose, Eisenhower Center.

12. C. W. Cooper interview with Stephen and Hugh Ambrose, Eisenhower Center.

13. Barnes interview, Eisenhower Center.

14. Hammer, *Small Tales*, 6.

15. Pepin memoirs, Eisenhower Center.

16. Cooper interview with Stephen and Hugh Ambrose, Eisenhower Center.

17. McGovern to Pennington, January 31, 1943, Dakota Wesleyan Library.

18. McGovern interview, Eisenhower Center.

CHAPTER TWO. TRAINING

1. Wesley Frank Craven and James Lea Cate, eds., *The Army Air Forces in World War II*, Vol. 6, *Men and Planes*, xi.

2. McGovern interview, Eisenhower Center.

3. Ibid.

4. Craven and Cate, *Men and Planes*, xxv.

5. Dwight Eisenhower interview with Ambrose, Eisenhower Center.

6. Charles A. Watry, *Washout! The Aviation Cadet Story*, 7–8; Craven and Cate, *Men and Planes*, xxviii.

7. Watry, *Washout!*, 10.

8. Kenneth Higgins interview with Hugh Ambrose, Eisenhower Center.

9. Ibid., 69.

10. McGovern interview, Eisenhower Center.

11. Ibid.

12. Daryl Lembke, "McGovern's War Years," *The Daily Democrat,* Woodland, California, Oct. 10, 1972.

13. Watry, *Washout!*, 83.

14. Thomas P. Reynolds, *Belle of the Brawl: A Biographical Memoir of Walter Malone Baskin,* 11.

15. Ibid., 21–22.

16. John G. Smith, *Wouldn't Change a Thing: A Memoir,* 66–71.

17. C. W. Cooper interview with Hugh and Stephen Ambrose, Eisenhower Center.

18. Pepin memoirs, Eisenhower Center.

19. Watry, *Washout!*, 157.

20. Cooper interview; Pepin memoirs, Eisenhower Center.

21. Donald Kay to Ambrose, April 21, 2000, Eisenhower Center.

22. Ibid.

23. Homer Socolofsky, *The Honorable Richard Dean Rogers, Senior United States District Judge*, 38.

24. Robert "Ken" Barmore memoirs, Eisenhower Center.

25. Hammer, *Small Tales*, 8–9.

26. Thomas Childers, *Wings of Morning: The Story of the Last American Bomber Shot Down over Germany in World War II*, 8–14. The figure on those graduating from gunnery school is from Craven and Cate, *Men and Planes*, 590.

27. McGovern to Pennington, August 2, 1943, Dakota Wesleyan Library.

28. McGovern interview, Eisenhower Center.

29. Reynolds, *Belle of the Brawl*, 18.

30. McGovern interview, Eisenhower Center.

31. Lembke, "McGovern's War Years," Oct. 10, 1972.

32. McGovern interview, Eisenhower Center.

33. Watry, *Washout!*, 96–97.

34. McGovern interview, Eisenhower Center.

35. Barmore interview, Eisenhower Center.

36. Watry, *Washout!*, 111–12.

37. McGovern to Pennington, February 8, 1944, Dakota Wesleyan Library.

38. McGovern interview, Eisenhower Center.

39. Smith, *Wouldn't Change a Thing*, 73–74.

40. Watry, *Washout!*, 117–19.

41. Barmore interview, Eisenhower Center.

42. Watry, *Washout!*, 15.

43. McGovern interview, Eisenhower Center.

44. Anson, *McGovern*, 38.

45. Watry, *Washout!*, 142–43.

46. Reynolds, *Belle of the Brawl*, 18.

47. Smith, *Wouldn't Change a Thing*, 77.

48. Craven and Cate, *Men and Planes*, xxxiv.

49. Ibid.

CHAPTER THREE. LEARNING TO FLY THE B-24

1. McGovern interview, Eisenhower Center.

2. *Briefing: Journal of the International B-24 Liberator Club* 63, Winter 1997, p. 15.

3. Anson, *McGovern*, 39.

4. Craven and Cate, *Men and Planes*, xx, xxix, xxxvii.

5. These figures are for model B-24D and are taken from Davis, *B-24 Liberator in Action*, 4–6, 17. See also Frederick A. Johnsen, *B-24 Liberator*.

6. Craven and Cate, *Men and Planes*, 207.

7. McGovern interview, Eisenhower Center.

8. Craven and Cate, *Men and Planes*, 566–78.

9. Walter Hughes, *A Bomber Pilot in World War II: From Farm Boy to Pilot.*

10. Donald R. Currier, *50 Mission Crush*, 5.

11. McGovern interview, Eisenhower Center.

12. Smith, *Wouldn't Change a Thing*, 77–78.

13. McGovern to Pennington, November 8 and 15, 1943, Dakota Wesleyan Library.

14. McGovern to Pennington, December 28, 1943, Dakota Wesleyan Library.

15. McGovern to Pennington, August 25, 1944, Dakota Wesleyan Library.

16. Shostack interview with Hugh Ambrose, Eisenhower Center.

17. Pepin memoirs, Eisenhower Center.

18. Kay memoirs, Eisenhower Center.

19. Reynolds, *Belle of the Brawl*, 24–33.

20. Barmore memoir, Eisenhower Center.

21. Hammer, *Small Tales*, 11.

22. Childers, *Wings of Morning*, 15–20.

23. Ibid., 21–27.

24. McGovern, *Grassroots*, 23.

25. Anson, *McGovern*, 40.

26. McGovern, *Grassroots*, 24.

27. Lembke, "McGovern's War Years," Oct. 10, 1972.

28. Ibid.

29. McGovern interview, Eisenhower Center.

30. Lembke, "McGovern's War Years," Oct. 10, 1972; Michael S. Sherry, *The Rise of American Air Power: The Creation of Armageddon,* 205.

31. Lembke, "McGovern's War Years," Oct. 10, 1972; Tom Zito, "George McGovern and His Flight Crew," *The Washington Post,* Nov. 23, 1970; McGovern interview, Eisenhower Center; Anson, *McGovern,* 40–41.

32. Sherry, *The Rise of American Air Power,* 215–16.

33. McGovern to Pennington, July 29, 1944, Dakota Wesleyan Library.

34. McGovern interview, Eisenhower Center.

35. Shostack interview, Eisenhower Center.

CHAPTER FOUR. THE FIFTEENTH AIR FORCE

1. Both quotations are from Sherry, *The Rise of American Air Power,* 8–10.

2. Ibid., 24.

3. Ibid., 23–24.

4. Ibid., 15.

5. Ibid., 40–41.

6. Ibid., 124.

7. Ibid., 135.

8. Wesley Frank Craven and James Lea Cate, eds., *The Army Air Forces in World War II,* Vol. 2, *Europe: Torch to Pointblank, August 1942 to December 1943,* ix.

9. Ibid., xii.

10. Sherry, *The Rise of American Air Power,* 206.

11. Ibid., 207.

12. Ibid., 212.

13. Craven and Cate, *Europe: Torch to Pointblank,* 477.

14. Ibid., 440.

15. Ibid., 477–84; McGovern interview, Eisenhower Center.

16. Craven and Cate, *Europe: Torch to Pointblank,* Chapters 16 and 21.

17. Peter J. Unitt, "Fifteenth Air Force in World War II," *Friends Journal* 17, No. 4 (Winter 1994), p. 4.

18. Wesley Frank Craven and James Lea Cate, eds., *The Army Air Forces in World War II*, Vol. 3, *Europe: Argument to V-E Day, January 1944 to May 1945*, 280–87.

19. Ibid., 298; Alfred Asch, Hugh Graff, and Thomas Ramey, *The Story of the Four Hundred and Fifty-fifth Bombardment Group (H) World War II: Flight of the Vulgar Vultures*, 109–10.

20. Craven and Cate, *Europe: Argument to V-E Day*, 303.

21. Ibid., 305.

22. Ibid., 304–5.

23. Ibid., 303.

24. Aronowitz, *Maternity Ward*, 90.

25. Ibid., 307.

26. Asch et al., *Flight of the Vulgar Vultures*, 48.

27. Ibid., 56.

28. Ibid., 96–97.

29. Currier, *50 Mission Crush*, xii.

CHAPTER FIVE. CERIGNOLA, ITALY

1. McGovern interview, Eisenhower Center.

2. Pepin memoirs, Eisenhower Center.

3. Asch et al., *Flight of the Vulgar Vultures*, 31.

4. McGovern interview, Eisenhower Center.

5. Capps, *Flying Colt*, 42.

6. Ibid., 19–20.

7. Horace Lanford interview with Hugh Ambrose, Eisenhower Center.

8. Ibid.

9. Hammer, *Small Tales*, 14–15.

10. Capps, *Flying Colt*, 47.

11. Daryl Lembke, "McGovern's War Years," *The Daily Democrat*, Woodland, Calif., Oct. 11, 1972.

12. McGovern, *Grassroots*, 24–25.

13. Donald Kay memoirs, Eisenhower Center.

14. Pepin memoirs, Eisenhower Center.

15. Eisenhower interview, Eisenhower Center; Asch et al., *Flight of the Vulgar Vultures,* 40.

16. Smith, *Wouldn't Change a Thing,* 86.

17. Shostack interview, Eisenhower Center.

18. Higgins interview, Eisenhower Center.

19. Currier, *50 Mission Crush,* 84.

20. Ibid., 82.

21. Pepin memoirs, Eisenhower Center.

22. Sgarro Ruggiero interview, Eisenhower Center.

23. Ray Zinck, *The Final Flight of Maggie's Drawers,* 10.

24. Anthony Picardi memoirs, Eisenhower Center.

25. Francesco Musto interview with Hugh and Stephen Ambrose; Michele Bancole interview with Hugh and Stephen Ambrose, Eisenhower Center.

26. Gionanna Pistachio Colucci interview, Eisenhower Center.

27. Bancole interview, Eisenhower Center.

28. Mario Carpocefala interview with Hugh and Stephen Ambrose, Eisenhower Center. Mario continued to work at the air base through the war. Later he corresponded with some of the officers and made a trip to the United States to visit with them. A half century after the war he became the mayor of Cerignola.

29. Musto interview, Eisenhower Center.

30. McGovern interview, Eisenhower Center.

31. Capps, *Flying Colt,* 22, 46.

32. Asch et al., *Flight of the Vulgar Vultures,* 188–89.

33. Higgins interview, Eisenhower Center.

34. Phillips letter, *Briefing: Journal of the International B-24 Liberator Club* 63, Winter 1997.

35. Walter Shostack memoirs, Eisenhower Center.

36. Mel TenHaken, *Bail-Out! POW, 1944–1945,* 29.

37. Ibid., 30–31.

38. Shostack memoirs, Eisenhower Center.

39. McGovern interview, Eisenhower Center.

CHAPTER SIX. LEARNING TO FLY IN COMBAT

1. This description is based on all the interviews with the men of the AAF, now in the Eisenhower Center, most of all the McGovern interview. Other sources include Smith, *Wouldn't Change a Thing*, 90–91; TenHaken, *Bail-Out!*, 31; Currier, *50 Mission Crush*, 63; Zinck, *The Final Flight of Maggie's Drawers*, 50–51; Asch et al., *Flight of the Vulgar Vultures*, 4.

2. Smith, *Wouldn't Change a Thing*, 91–92.

3. John Lindquist interview, Eisenhower Center.

4. McGovern interview, Eisenhower Center. Some pilots insisted that the members of their crew did at least some flying so that in the event of an emergency they could bring the plane home.

5. Ibid.

6. Vincent F. Fagan, *Liberator Pilot: The Cottontails' Battle for Oil*, 33.

7. Smith, *Wouldn't Change a Thing*, 93.

8. Asch et al., *Flight of the Vulgar Vultures*, 143–44.

9. Ibid., 94.

10. Aronowitz, *Maternity Ward*, 59.

11. McGovern interview, Eisenhower Center.

12. Robert Reichard memoirs, online at the 456th Bomb Group website, http://www.456thbombgroup.Org/reichard/flak.html.

13. Fagan, *Liberator Pilot*, 95.

14. J. I. Merritt, *Goodbye, Liberty Belle: A Son's Search for His Father's War*, 32–35; Art Johnson memoirs, Eisenhower Center.

15. Asch et al., *Flight of the Vulgar Vultures*, 129–30; McGovern interview, Eisenhower Center; Glenn Rendahl memoirs, Eisenhower Center.

16. Pepin memoirs, Eisenhower Center.

17. Hammer, *Small Tales*, 17–18.

18. Childers, *Wings of Morning*, 82–91.

19. Asch et al., *Flight of the Vulgar Vultures*, 129–30.

20. Daryl Lembke, "McGovern's War Years," *The Daily Democrat*, Woodland, Calif., Oct. 13, 1972.

21. TenHaken, *Bail-Out!*, 33–37.

22. The Eisenhower Center has different versions of this poem.

23. Currier, *50 Mission Crush*, 65.

24. Kay memoirs, Eisenhower Center.

25. Picardi memoirs, Eisenhower Center.

26. McGovern interview, Eisenhower Center.

CHAPTER SEVEN. DECEMBER 1944

1. McGovern interview, Eisenhower Center.

2. Ibid.

3. Henry Burkle interview with Hugh Ambrose, Eisenhower Center.

4. Fagan, *Liberator Pilot*, 12.

5. McGovern interview, Eisenhower Center.

6. Fagan, *Liberator Pilot*, 13.

7. McGovern interview, Eisenhower Center.

8. Hughes, *A Bomber Pilot in World War*, 65.

9. Eddie Picardo, *Tales of a Tail Gunner: A Memoir*, 155.

10. Hughes, *A Bomber Pilot in World War II*, 59.

11. McGovern interview, Eisenhower Center.

12. Ibid.

13. Currier, *50 Mission Crush*, 69–70.

14. William McAfee interview with Hugh Ambrose, Eisenhower Center.

15. McGovern interview, Eisenhower Center.

16. Ibid.

17. Henry Paris memoirs, Eisenhower Center.

18. Daryl Lembke, "McGovern's War Years," *The Daily Democrat*, Woodland, Calif., Oct. 12, 1972.

19. McGovern interview, Eisenhower Center.

20. Asch et al., *Flight of the Vulgar Vultures,* 132.

21. McGovern interview, Eisenhower Center.

22. Lembke, "McGovern's War Years," Oct. 12, 1972.

23. Anson, *McGovern,* 44.

24. Edi Selhaus, *Evasion and Repatriation: Slovine Partisans and the Rescued American Airmen in World War II,* 187.

25. Ibid.

26. McGovern interview, Eisenhower Center; Lembke, "McGovern's War Years," Oct. 12, 1972.

27. McGovern interview, Eisenhower Center.

28. Asch et al., *Flight of the Vulgar Vultures,* 132.

CHAPTER EIGHT. THE ISLE OF CAPRI

1. Daryl Lembke, "McGovern War Years," *The Daily Democrat,* Woodland, Calif., Oct. 1, 1972.

2. Ashlock interview with Hugh Ambrose, Eisenhower Center.

3. McGovern, *Grassroots,* 25.

4. Anson, *McGovern,* 46.

5. Victor McWilliams interview with Hugh Ambrose, Eisenhower Center.

6. Francis G. Hosimer memoirs, Eisenhower Center.

7. Stephen E. Ambrose, *Eisenhower: Soldier, General of the Army, President-Elect,* 267.

8. Pepin interview, Eisenhower Center.

9. Higgins interview, Eisenhower Center.

10. Ted Withington, *Flight to Black Hammer: The Letters of a World War II Pilot,* 87.

11. Hammer, *Small Tales,* 15.

12. Daryl Lembke, "McGovern's War Years," Oct. 1, 1972.

13. McGovern interview, Eisenhower Center.

14. Ibid.

15. Pepin interview, Eisenhower Center.

16. Anson, *McGovern,* 43.

17. Ibid., 47–48.

18. Asch et al., *Flight of the Vulgar Vultures*, 134.

CHAPTER NINE. THE TUSKEGEE AIRMEN FLY COVER: FEBRUARY 1945

1. Asch et al., *Flight of the Vulgar Vultures*, 135.

2. Ibid., 140–41.

3. Craven and Cate, *Europe: Argument to V-E Day*, 783.

4. Rendahl memoirs, Eisenhower Center.

5. Ibid.

6. Pepin memoirs, Eisenhower Center.

7. John B. Holway, *Red Tails, Black Wings: The Men of America's Black Air Force*, 186–87, 197.

8. Lembke, "McGovern's War Years," Oct. 1, 1972.

9. Higgins interview, Eisenhower Center.

10. Asch et al., *Flight of the Vulgar Vultures*, 141–42.

11. Cooper interview, Eisenhower Center.

12. Cooper to Prendergast, Feb. 19, 1945, Eisenhower Center.

13. Cooper interview, Eisenhower Center.

14. Hammer, *Small Tales*, 18.

15. Asch et al., *Flight of the Vulgar Vultures*, 137.

16. Hammer, *Small Tales*, 18–19.

17. Asch et al., *Flight of the Vulgar Vultures*, 145–48.

18. Reprinted in Horace Lanford, *741st Bomb Sq. History*, privately printed, Vol. 1, 25–26.

19. Asch et al., *Flight of the Vulgar Vultures*, 138.

CHAPTER TEN. MISSIONS OVER AUSTRIA: MARCH 1945

1. McGovern interview, Eisenhower Center.

2. McAfee interview, Eisenhower Center.

3. McGovern, *Grassroots*, 28.

4. Cooper's letter is in the Eisenhower Center.

5. McGovern interview, Eisenhower Center.

6. Edgar D. Hoagland, *The Sea Hawks: With the PT Boats at War,* 3–4.

7. McGovern interview, Eisenhower Center.

8. Art Applin memoirs, Eisenhower Center.

9. McGovern interview, Eisenhower Center.

10. Higgins interview, Eisenhower Center.

11. McGovern interview, Eisenhower Center.

12. Pepin memoirs, Eisenhower Center.

13. Cooper interview, Eisenhower Center.

14. McGovern interview, Eisenhower Center.

15. Cooper interview, Eisenhower Center.

16. Cooper's letters are in the Eisenhower Center.

17. Ibid.

18. Ibid.

19. Asch et al., *Flight of the Vulgar Vultures,* 153.

CHAPTER ELEVEN. LINZ: THE LAST MISSION: APRIL 1945

1. McGovern interview, Eisenhower Center.

2. Ibid.; Asch et al., *Flight of the Vulgar Vultures,* 158.

3. Ashlock interview, Eisenhower Center.

4. McGovern interview, Eisenhower Center.

5. Cooper interview, Eisenhower Center.

6. McGovern, Cooper, Higgins, and McAfee interviews, Eisenhower Center.

7. Cooper's letter is in the Eisenhower Center.

8. Asch et al., *Flight of the Vulgar Vultures,* 160.

9. Ibid., 159.

10. Higgins interview, Eisenhower Center.

11. Applin memoirs, Eisenhower Center.

12. Craven and Cate, *Europe: Argument to V-E Day,* 792.

13. Ibid., 796–97.

EPILOGUE

1. McGovern interview, Eisenhower Center.

2. Cooper interview, Eisenhower Center.

3. McGovern interview, Eisenhower Center.

4. McGovern to Pennington, May 30, 1945, Dakota Wesleyan Library.

5. Higgins interview, Eisenhower Center.

6. Cooper's letters are in the Eisenhower Center.

7. Ed Soderstrom interview with Hugh Ambrose, Eisenhower Center.

8. Cooper letter, Eisenhower Center.

9. Cooper interview, Eisenhower Center.

10. Soderstrom interview, Eisenhower Center.

BIBLIOGRAPHY

BOOKS

Ambrose, Stephen E. *Eisenhower: Soldier, General of the Army, President-Elect.* New York: Simon and Schuster, 1983.

Anson, Robert Sam. *McGovern.* New York: Holt, Rinehart and Winston, 1972.

Aronowitz, Marguerite Madison. *Maternity Ward: Final Flight of a World War II Liberator.* Prescott, Ariz.: Pine Castle Books, 1998.

Asch, Alfred, Hugh Graff, and Thomas Ramey. *The Story of the Four Hundred and Fifty-fifth Bombardment Group (H) World War II: Flight of the Vulgar Vultures.* Appleton, Wis.: Graphic Communications Center, 1991; reprinted 1999.

Barnes, William. *Disaster at Bari: Top Secret!* New York: Ace, 1973.

Birdsall, Steve. *Log of the Liberators.* New York: Doubleday, 1973.

Bowman, Martin W. *B-24 Liberator, 1939–45.* Privately printed; copy in Eisenhower Center, New Orleans.

Capps, Robert S. *Flying Colt: Liberator Pilot in Italy.* Privately printed; copy in Eisenhower Center, New Orleans.

Carigan, William. *Ad Lib: Flying the B-24 Liberator in World War II.* Manhattan, Kans.: Sunflower University Press, 1988.

Childers, Thomas. *Wings of Morning: The Story of the Last American Bomber Shot Down over Germany in World War II.* Reading, Mass.: Addison-Wesley, 1995.

Copp, DeWitt S. *Forged in Fire: Strategy and Decisions in the Airwar over Europe, 1940–1945.* New York: Doubleday, 1982.

Craven, Wesley Frank, and James Lea Cate, eds. *The Army Air Forces in World War II,* Vol. 2, *Europe: Torch to Pointblank, August 1942 to December 1943.* Chicago: University of Chicago Press, 1949.

————. *The Army Air Forces in World War II,* Vol. 3, *Europe: Argument to V-E Day, January 1944 to May 1945.* Chicago: University of Chicago Press, 1951.

————. *The Army Air Forces in World War II,* Vol. 6, *Men and Planes.* Chicago: University of Chicago Press, 1955.

Currier, Donald R. *50 Mission Crush.* Shippensburg, Penn.: Burd Street Press, 1992.

Davis, Larry. *B-24 Liberator in Action.* Carrollton, Tex.: Signal Publications, 1987.

Fagan, Vincent F. *Liberator Pilot: The Cottontails' Battle for Oil.* Carlsbad, Calif.: California Aero Press, 1991.

Francis, Devon. *Flak Bait.* Washington, D.C.: Zenger Publishing, 1948.

Hammer, R. J. *Small Tales: Tall Tales: Poetry: Fiction.* Privately printed, Sidney, Mont., 1990.

Hastings, Max. *Bomber Command: The Myths and Realities of the Strategic Bombing Offensive, 1939–45.* New York: Dial Press, 1979.

Hoagland, Edgar D. *The Sea Hawks: With the PT Boats at War.* Novato, Calif.: Presidio Press, 1999.

Holway, John B. *Red Tails, Black Wings: The Men of America's Black Air Force.* Las Cruces, N.M.: Yucca Tree Press, 1997.

Hughes, Walter. *A Bomber Pilot in World War II: From Farm Boy to Pilot.* Privately printed, 1994.

Jablonski, Edward. *Airwar.* New York: Doubleday, 1971.

Johnsen, Frederick A. *B-24 Liberator: Combat and Development of the Liberator and Privateer.* Privately printed, 1993.

Lanford, Horace. *741st Bomb Sq. History.* Privately printed, Vols. 1–4, 1991.

Lloyd, Alwin T. *Liberator: America's Global Bomber.* Missoula, Mont.: Pictorial Histories, 1993.

McGovern, George. *Grassroots: The Autobiography of George McGovern.* New York: Random House, 1977.

Merritt, J. I. *Goodbye, Liberty Belle: A Son's Search for His Father's War.* Dayton, Ohio: Wright State University Press, 1993.

Picardo, Eddie. *Tales of a Tail Gunner: A Memoir.* Seattle: Hara Publishing, 1996.

Piekalkiewicz, Januse. *The Air War, 1939–1945.* Poole, Dorset: Blandford Press, 1985.

Reynolds, Thomas P. *Belle of the Brawl: A Biographical Memoir of Walter Malone Baskin.* Paducah, Ky.: Turner Publishing Company, 1996.

Rochlin, Fred. *Old Man in a Baseball Cap.* New York: HarperCollins, 1999.

Rust, Kenn C. *Fifteenth Air Force Story.* Temple City, Calif.: Historical Aviation Album, 1976.

Selhaus, Edi. *Evasion and Repatriation: Slovene Partisans and the Rescued American Airmen in World War II.* Manhattan, Kans.: Sunflower University Press, 1993.

Sherry, Michael S. *The Rise of American Air Power: The Creation of Armageddon.* New Haven: Yale University Press, 1987.

Smith, John G. *Wouldn't Change a Thing: A Memoir.* Chicago: Adams Press, 1996.

Socolofsky, Homer. *The Honorable Richard Dean Rogers, Senior United States District Judge.* The United States District Court, Kansas. Newton, Kans.: Mennonite Press, 1995.

Stevens, Bob. *"There I Was . . .": 25 Years.* Bonsall, Calif.: Village Press, 1990.

TenHaken, Mel. *Bail-Out! POW, 1944–1945.* Manhattan, Kans.: Sunflower University Press, 1990.

Ulanoff, Stanley M., ed. *Bombs Away!* New York: Doubleday, 1971.

Watry, Charles A. *Washout! The Aviation Cadet Story.* Carlsbad, Calif.: California Aero Press, 1983.

Watry, Charles A., and Duane L. Hall. *Aerial Gunners: The Unknown Aces of World War II.* Carlsbad, Calif.: California Aero Press, 1985.

Whitehouse, Arch. *The Years of the Warbirds.* New York: Doubleday, 1960.

Withington, Ted. *Flight to Black Hammer: The Letters of a World War II Pilot.* Brunswick, Maine: Biddle Publishing Company, 1993.

Zinck, Ray. *The Final Flight of Maggie's Drawers.* Paducah, Ky.: Turner Publishing Company, 1998.

JOURNALS

Briefing: Journal of the International B-24 Liberator Club

The Daily Democrat. Woodland, California.

Friends Journal

INDEX

Photo Credits

**POCKET
BOOKS**

BAND OF BROTHERS

Stephen E. Ambrose

The *Sunday Times* #1 bestseller and a major BBC series
produced by Tom Hanks and Steven Spielberg.

In BAND OF BROTHERS, Stephen E.
Ambrose pays tribute to the men of Easy
Company, a crack rifle company in the US
Army. From their rigorous training in
Georgia in 1942 to the dangerous parachute
landings on D-Day and their triumphant
capture of Hitler's 'Eagle's Nest' in
Berchtesgarden, Ambrose tells the story of
this remarkable company. Repeatedly sent
on the toughest missions, these brave men
fought, went hungry, froze and died in the
service of their country.

'Superb . . . his scholarly writing style seems
to know that heroism needs no cheap embel-
lishment. Gripping and humbling'
GLASGOW HERALD

PRICE £6.99
ISBN 0 7434 2990 7

**POCKET
BOOKS**

D-DAY

JUNE 6, 1944

Stephen E. Ambrose

D-DAY is the brilliant telling of the battles of
Omaha and Utah beaches. Hailed as the premier
American narrative and military historian, Ambrose
relives the epic victory of democracy on the most
important day of the twentieth century.

'Definitive . . . His evidence is overwhelming'
Wall Street Journal

'*D-Day* is mostly about people, but goes even
further in evoking the horror, the endurance,
the daring and, indeed, the human failings in
Omaha Beach . . . Outstanding'
The New York Times Book Review

'Reading this history, you can understand why for
so many of its participants, despite all the death
surrounding them, life revealed itself in that
moment at that place'
The New York Times

PRICE £7.99
ISBN 0 7434 4974 6

**POCKET
BOOKS**

CITIZEN SOLDIERS
THE US ARMY FROM THE NORMANDY BEACHES TO THE SURRENDER OF GERMANY
Stephen E. Ambrose

The *Sunday Times* #1 bestselling author.

This sequel to D-DAY opens at 00:01 hours, June 7, 1944 on the Normandy Beaches and ends at 02:45 hours, May 7, 1945 with the overrunning of Germany. From the enlisted men and junior officers, Ambrose draws on hundreds of interviews from those on both sides of the war. The experience of these citizen soldiers reveals the ordinary sufferings and hardships of war.

'History boldly told and elegantly written . . .
Gripping' *Wall Street Journal*

'*Citizen Soldiers* is about the most gripping account of the Second World War that I have ever read'
Joseph Heller

'*Citizen Soldiers* is an unforgettable testament to the World War II generation' *The New York Times*.

**PRICE £7.99
ISBN 0 7434 5015 9**

**SIMON &
SCHUSTER**

This book and other **Simon & Schuster UK Ltd** titles are available from your book shop or can be ordered direct from the publisher.

☐ 0 684 86615 3	**The Brigade**	Howard Blum	£16.99
☐ 0 684 86621 8	**Silent Night**	Stanley Weintraub	£12.99
☐ 0 671 02213 X	**To See You Again**	Betty Schimmel	£5.99
☐ 0 7434 5015 9	**Citizen Soldiers**	Stephen Ambrose	£7.99
☐ 0 7434 4974 6	**D-Day**	Stephen Ambrose	£7.99
☐ 0 671 67156 1	**Pegasus Bridge**	Stephen Ambrose	£6.99
☐ 0 684 85629 8	**The Victory**	Stephen Ambrose	£12.99
☐ 0 684 84609 8	**Nothing Like It In The World**	Stephen Ambrose	£20.00
☐ 0 7432 0074 8	**Comrades**	Stephen Ambrose	£7.99

Please send cheque or postal order for the value of the book, and add packing within the UK inc. BFPO 75p per book; OVERSEAS inc. EIRE £1 per book.

OR: Please debit this amount from my:

VISA/ACCESS/MASTERCARD ....

CARD NO ....

EXPIRY DATE ....

AMOUNT £ ....

NAME ....

ADDRESS ....

....

SIGNATURE ....

Send orders to: SIMON & SCHUSTER CASH SALES
PO Box 29, Douglas, Isle of Man, IM99 1BQ
Tel: 01624 675137, Fax 01624 670923
www.bookpost.co.uk   email: bookshop@enterprise.net
Please allow 28 days for delivery.
Prices and availability subject to change without notice.